THE CULTURAL POLITICS OF NATIONALISM AND NATION-BUILDING

Rituals and performances are a key theme in the study of nations and nationalism. With the aim of stimulating further research in this area, this book explores, debates and evaluates the role of rituals and performances in the emergence, persistence and transformation of nations, nationalisms and national identity.

The chapters comprising this book investigate a diverse array of contemporary and historical phenomena relating to the symbolic life of nations, from the Yasukuni Shrine in Japan to the Louvre in France, written by an interdisciplinary cast of world-renowned and up-and-coming scholars. Each of the contributors has been encouraged to think about how his or her particular approach and methods relate to the others. This has given rise to several recurring debates and themes running through the book over how researchers ought to approach rituals and performances and how they might best be studied.

The Cultural Politics of Nationalism and Nation-Building will appeal to students and scholars of ethnicity and nationalism, sociology, political science, anthropology, cultural studies, performance studies, art history and architecture.

Rachel Tsang is an analyst for the UK Government. She received her PhD in Government from the London School of Economics, UK.

Eric Taylor Woods is Lecturer in Sociology at the University of East London, UK, and Faculty Fellow of the Centre for Cultural Sociology at Yale University, USA.

THE CULTURAL POLITICS OF NATIONALISM AND NATION-BUILDING

Ritual and performance in the forging of nations

Edited by Rachel Tsang and Eric Taylor Woods

Routledge
Taylor & Francis Group

LONDON AND NEW YORK

First published 2014
by Routledge
2 Park Square, Milton Park, Abingdon, Oxon OX14 4RN

and by Routledge
711 Third Avenue, New York, NY 10017

Routledge is an imprint of the Taylor & Francis Group, an informa business

British Library Cataloguing in Publication Data
A catalogue record for this book is available from the British Library

Library of Congress Cataloging in Publication Data
The cultural politics of nationalism and nation-building: ritual and
performance in the forging of nations/edited by Rachel Tsang,
Eric Taylor Woods.
pages cm
Includes bibliographical references and index.
1. Politics and culture. 2. Ethnology. 3. Ethnic relations – Political
aspects. 4. Nationalism. 5. Nation-building. I. Tsang, Rachel.
GN357.C8436 2013
306.2 – dc23
2013011450

ISBN: 978-0-415-87064-1 (hbk)
ISBN: 978-0-415-87065-8 (pbk)
ISBN: 978-1-315-88691-6 (ebk)

Typeset in Bembo and Stone Sans
by Florence Production Ltd, Stoodleigh, Devon, UK

CONTENTS

PART II
Applications 85

FIGURES

CONTRIBUTORS

John Breen is Professor of Japanese Studies at the International Research Centre for Japanese Studies (Nichibunken), Japan. His recent publications include *A New History of Shinto* (2010, Wiley-Blackwell) and the chapter 'Voices of rage: six paths to the problem of Yasukuni' in *Politics and Religion in Modern Japan: Red Sun, White Lotus* (2011, Palgrave). Breen is currently writing a history of Ise shrines in modern Japan.

Randall Collins is Dorothy Swaine Professor of Sociology at the University of Pennsylvania. His recent books include *Violence: A Micro-Sociological Theory* (2008, Princeton University Press), *Interaction Ritual Chains* (2004, Princeton University Press), *Macro-History: Essays in the Sociology of the Long-Run* (1999, Stanford University Press) and *The Sociology of Philosophies: A Global Theory of Intellectual Change* (1998, Belknap Press of Harvard). Collins is currently completing a book on the time dynamics of conflict.

Carol Duncan is Professor Emerita of Art History at Ramapo College of New Jersey. She holds an interdisciplinary master's degree from the University of Chicago and a PhD in Art History from Columbia University. She has written on European and American art from the eighteenth century to the present, exploring such topics as the representation of the family and patriarchal authority in eighteenth-century art, class and sexual politics in nineteenth- and twentieth-century art, and art institutions of the past and the present. A collection of her essays on these subjects, *The Aesthetics of Power* (1993), was published by Cambridge University Press. For the past three decades, art museums have been the main focus of her research. *Civilizing Rituals: Inside Public Art Museums* (1995, Routledge) and *A Matter of Class: John Cotton Dana, Progressive Reform, and the Newark Museum* (2010, Periscope Publishing) represent her major published work in that field.

Jon E. Fox is Senior Lecturer in the School of Sociology, Politics and International Studies and Assistant Director of the Centre for the Study of Ethnicity and Citizenship at the University of Bristol. His research interests include nationalism, ethnicity, racism and migration. Fox's recent articles include 'The racialization of the new European migration to the UK' (with L. Moroşanu and E. Szilassy) in *Sociology* (2013), 'Backdoor nationalism' (with P. Vermeersch) in *Archives Européennes de Sociologie* (2010) and 'Everyday nationhood' (with Cynthia Miller-Idriss) in *Ethnicities* (2008).

Jonathan Hearn is Senior Lecturer in Sociology at the University of Edinburgh. His recent publications include *Theorizing Power* (2010, Palgrave), *Rethinking Nationalism: A Critical Introduction* (2006, Palgrave) and *Claiming Scotland: National Identity and Liberal Culture* (2000, Edinburgh University Press). Hearn is currently interested in the impact of the financial crisis on nationalism and the legitimacy of the financial sector, as well as the emergence of reflexive competition as an organizing idea/ritual of modern liberal society.

Rachel D. Hutchins is Associate Professor at the University of Lorraine, France. Recent publications include 'Traditional heroes and the renegotiation of national identity in United States history textbooks: representations of George Washington and Abraham Lincoln, 1982–2003' in *Nations and Nationalism* (2011). She is currently writing a book on national identity in history education in France and the United States.

Athena S. Leoussi is a founding member and former chair of the Association for the Study of Ethnicity and Nationalism (ASEN), and a founding editor and currently one of the editors of ASEN's journal, *Nations and Nationalism*. She is Co-Director of European Studies at the University of Reading, UK, and a member of the Committee of the British Association of Centres of European Studies (BACES). Recent publications include *Nationalism and Classicism: The Classical Body as National Symbol in Nineteenth-Century England and France* (1998, Palgrave Macmillan), *Encyclopaedia of Nationalism* (2001, Transaction Publishers) and *The Call of the Homeland: Diaspora Nationalisms, Past and Present* (2010, Brill, co-edited with Allon Gal and Anthony D. Smith). She is currently working on a manuscript on parliamentary architecture in the age of nationalism.

Christopher McDonald is Senior Lecturer in Architecture at the Victoria University of Wellington. His current research interests are in nineteenth-century colonial town planning in New Zealand and Australia, and street patterns in New Zealand cities. McDonald has published numerous governmental reports and research articles on a variety of aspects of urban design.

Anthony D. Smith is Emeritus Professor of Nationalism and Ethnicity at the London School of Economics, President of the Association for the Study of Ethnicity and

Nationalism (ASEN) and Chief Editor of the journal *Nations and Nationalism*. He is the author of numerous books and articles on nations, nationalism and ethnicity, and his books have been translated into 21 languages. His most recent book is entitled *The Nation Made Real: Art and National Identity in Western Europe, 1600–1850* (2013, Oxford University Press).

Rachel Tsang is an analyst on the UK Civil Service Fast Stream. Currently working in strategy at the Department for Work and Pensions, Tsang is the research manager for the department's forthcoming evaluations of changes to housing benefit in the private rented sector and the local authority insight survey. Tsang is also a deputy managing editor at *Studies in Ethnicity and Nationalism*. She received her PhD in Government from the London School of Economics and Political Science in 2012 and co-chaired the Association for the Study of Ethnicity and Nationalism's 2011 conference, Forging the Nation.

Eric Taylor Woods is Lecturer in Sociology and Politics at the University of East London, Advisor to the Association for the Study of Ethnicity and Nationalism (ASEN), Junior Editor of the journal *Nations and Nationalism*, and Faculty Fellow at the Centre for Cultural Sociology at Yale University. Recent publications include 'A cultural approach to a Canadian tragedy: the Indian residential schools as a sacred enterprise' in *International Journal of Politics, Culture, and Society* (2013), 'A cultural sociology of nations and nationalism' in *Nations and Nationalism* (2013, co-edited with Mira Debs), 'Beyond multination federalism: reflections on nations and nationalism in Canada' in *Ethnicities* (2012) and *Nationalism and Conflict Management* (2012, Routledge, co-edited with Robert Schertzer and Eric Kaufmann). Woods is currently completing a book for Palgrave on the acknowledgement of injustice.

ACKNOWLEDGEMENTS

The editors would like to express their gratitude to the contributors of this volume for their insightful comments, patience and enthusiasm with this project. In addition to the three anonymous reviewers, Anthony Smith, Jon Fox, John Hutchinson, Eric Kaufmann and Athena Leoussi were also particularly generous with their feedback.

The editors would also like to acknowledge the crucial role played by the Association for the Study of Ethnicity and Nationalism (ASEN). ASEN's 21st annual conference, on the theme of this book, provided a forum in which many of the issues and questions contained within this volume were discussed, debated and developed. The conference also received funding from the Department of Government at the London School of Economics. In particular, the editors also benefited from the input of several key members of the ASEN Executive Committee, including Vivian Ibrahim, Jennifer Jackson, Jakob Lehne, Barak Levy, Chris Moffat, Robert Schertzer and Margit Wunsch.

The editors also acknowledge the generosity of the Alexander Turnbull Library, New Zealand, for the use of several images.

Finally, the editors wish to thank Heidi Bagtazo, Alexander Quayle and the rest of the editorial team at Routledge for their advice and support.

1

RITUAL AND PERFORMANCE IN THE STUDY OF NATIONS AND NATIONALISM

Eric Taylor Woods and Rachel Tsang

Introduction

In the aftermath of the terrorist attacks of 11 September 2001, millions of Americans expressed their solidarity and mourning by interacting with the symbols of their nation. This was perhaps most visible in the manifold ways that the national flag was employed and presented in response to the tragedy. The flag was raised, lowered and waved; flown from buildings, porches and balconies; pasted on to windows, walls and doors; pinned to suits, shirts and sweaters; stitched on to T-shirts and school bags; and even draped over the columns of the New York Stock Exchange. In addition to such spontaneous performances of national sentiment, the collective need to perform the nation in response to the tragedy also gave rise to new national rituals of commemoration, such as the moment of silence that the president formally asks American citizens to observe annually on 11 September – now officially designated as Patriot Day and National Day of Service and Remembrance.

On a less sombre note, just over a decade later, in the United Kingdom, amid a summer of celebrations that included the Queen's Diamond Jubilee and the London Olympics, many British citizens similarly felt compelled to express national sentiment through ritual and performance. Whether this was by participating in the flotilla of a thousand ships that sailed down the River Thames to celebrate the jubilee, or by tuning in to watch the nightly broadcast of British athletes at the Olympic Games, the summer of 2012 was characterized by an array of parades, concerts and street parties all geared towards celebrating the British nation.

The events of 2001 and 2012 represent two extremes: the former marking a time of trauma, of intense pain and sorrow; the latter marking a time of great celebration, joy and excitement. Yet, despite such contrasts, both events prompted great surges in expressions of nationalism, which manifested themselves through new and old rituals and performances. These national rituals and performances encompassed actions that originated among elites and masses, that were scripted and spontaneous, and self-aware at times but also unconscious at others. What prompted so many individuals to channel their emotions by collectively wearing, waving or flying symbols of their nations, to participate in elaborate national rituals and to openly 'perform their nation'? And what is the significance of this behaviour for the salience of national identity and the enduring appeal of nations and nationalism in the modern era? Is it in some way constitutive of national sentiment or is it but an epiphenomenal expression of other political, economic and social forces? Furthermore, if we are to undertake to resolve these questions, what is the best approach and methodology?

The aim of this volume is to explore, debate and evaluate the role of rituals and performances in the emergence, persistence and transformation of nations, nationalisms and national identity. To put this more succinctly, our focus is on how national sentiment is *experienced*. To address these aims, the chapters comprising this book investigate a diverse array of contemporary and historical phenomena, from the Yasukuni Shrine in Japan to the Louvre in France, written by leading experts on nationalism as well as performance and ritual. It is our hope that this interdisciplinary approach will bear fruit in the form of new insights. Moreover, by exploring the significance of national rituals and performances, this book also seeks to address fundamental questions about how to study nations and nationalism, considering whether a renewed focus on rituals and performances demands new or revised approaches and methodologies.

We should also be clear at the outset that we do not claim that the investigation of rituals and performances alone can explain why nationalism remains so integral to the modern world. Clearly, any such investigation cannot lose sight of power, materiality, interests and discourse. However, if we are properly to understand the persistence of nationalism, and why it is more important in certain periods and less important in others, then we need to pay more attention to the way that it is enacted. Thus, in our view, while rituals and performances do not themselves provide sufficient explanation, they are nevertheless necessary.

In this introductory chapter, we address the concepts of ritual and performance and how they have been heretofore treated in the literature on nationalism, before providing a conceptual and structural framework for the chapters that follow.

Ritual and performance: a conceptual overview

Rituals and performances are central to modern life. Indeed, it sometimes seems as though their significance is increasing, with new forms of rituals and performances emerging everywhere. At an everyday level, we can see this in a diverse range of phenomena, from the rise of roadside shrines commemorating the victims of car and cycle accidents, to the spread of new kinds of life-cycle rituals celebrating pregnancy, birth, marriage, divorce and death. In the realm of politics, the trend towards ritual and performance seems even more pronounced. Democratic contests for power unfold as mediated social dramas, citizens-to-be undergo elaborate rituals to join prospective nations and political apologies have become commonplace. All of this has caught the attention of the social sciences and humanities. From political science to film studies, rituals and performances have risen in the scholarly agenda. This section touches on several key aspects of how these concepts are defined and operationalized in this diverse body of literature. Towards the end of this section, we also discuss the differences *between* rituals and performances.

Rituals and performances have long been objects of study, producing numerous important works: from Émile Durkheim's (1995 [1912]) classic discussion of the intense feelings of solidarity that can arise from collectively performed rituals to Victor Turner's (2008 [1969]) insights on their transformational potential, and from Erving Goffman's (1959) work on the dramaturgical aspects of everyday interactions to Judith Butler's (1988) elucidation of the performative aspects of identity – to name but a few key texts. Notwithstanding this sustained history of research, there has recently been an upsurge of scholarly interest in the ways that the social and political life is performed and ritualized. This burgeoning body of research is highly varied, encompassing the macro and micro, the scripted and unscripted, the habitual and the spontaneous, the historical and the contemporary. Even the view that rituals and performances are somehow tied to bodily practices has been loosened: the analysis of 'media rituals' is now commonplace (e.g. Dayan and Katz, 1992), and non-human objects are now said to be 'performative' (e.g. Barad, 2003).

The growing diversity of ways in which the concepts of ritual and performance are employed in social research has resulted in their definitions becoming unmoored and even increasingly entwined. For this reason, we have deliberately avoided the potential morass of attempting to provide specific definitions of these concepts. Indeed, in light of the diversity of approaches in this book, such an endeavour would be counterproductive. That being said, we do think it is useful to shed light on how these concepts have been employed in a general sense, even if such an endeavour can only be partial at best.

From a broad, ecumenical perspective, ritual and performance generally refer to expressive behaviour, which can be highly stylized and follow certain conscious or unconscious behavioural patterns. The stylized and patterned aspects of rituals and performances are what distinguish them from instrumental behaviour and suggest that they involve meanings beyond that of the action itself. Robert Wuthnow (1989: 107) supplies a useful contrast here between eating a snack and taking part in the Christian tradition of the Eucharist. Whereas eating a snack might be seen as a purely instrumental act aimed at alleviating hunger, sipping the wine and eating the bread during the ritual of receiving the Eucharist is laden with more meaning than the mere act of eating.

In the structural functional literature of the post-war period, the meanings and norms associated with rituals and performances – referred to as 'an ordered system of meaning' (Parsons and Shils, 2001 [1951]) – are seen as structuring the ways in which rituals and performances are carried out. Hence, it is the sacred meanings associated with the Eucharist that ensures that it is performed in a particular way. However, that being said, just as rituals and performances might be seen as expressions of underlying meaning systems, there is also a growing trend in the social sciences and in performance studies to see rituals and performances as having the capacity to transform meaning systems – as Jeffrey Alexander (2004) has discussed in depth. In this regard, demonstrations by the People for the Ethical Treatment of Animals might be seen as performances aimed at attaching new meanings to animals.

While, at their core, all rituals and performances can be seen as a form of expressive behaviour, as the various examples used in this chapter suggest, they encompass a wide range of activities. Some are highly stylized and tightly regulated, such as the moment of silence observed annually on 11 September at the Manhattan site of the terrorist attacks. Others can appear more spontaneous, such as suddenly erupting into a cheer at witnessing a point scored by one's favourite sports team. Rituals and performances can also be more, or less, rigorously formal. They encompass a spectrum ranging from highly ceremonial occasions set off from the rhythms of daily life, such as the moment of silence mentioned above, to everyday mundane activities, such as shaking hands during a greeting ritual. Rituals and performances can also be carried out with their meanings more, or less, consciously expressed. Thus, the participants in the moment of silence might be quite conscious about the meanings associated with the ritual. In contrast, the meanings associated with a handshake might be more unconscious.

Because of their association with meaning, rituals and performances are seen as a central aspect of communication. Thus, Mary Douglas (2002 [1966]: 62) writes: 'it is not too much to say that ritual is more to society than words are to thought . . . it is impossible to have social relations without symbolic [read: expressive] acts'. From this perspective, the stylized and patterned aspects of rituals and performances can be seen as signalling devices used to facilitate the communication of meaning. Thus, to return to the example of the Eucharist, the various patterns of behaviour associated with this ritual help to convey its meaning. Notably, the kind of communication that rituals and performances facilitate is not necessarily ratiocinative. Rather, by drawing on underlying meaning systems, rituals and performances are often argued to communicate via emotion. Thus, as we will discuss in more depth in the following section, according to Durkheim (1995 [1912]), the intense emotions that can be generated among the participants in a collective ritual play a critical role in conveying meaning.

Although rituals and performances are seen as a form of communication, it is important to note that they do not necessitate face-to-face interaction, as is apparent in the large body of research, as mentioned above, on the performative and ritualistic aspects of the media. In contemporary societies, meaning is communicated via numerous forms of media, including television, internet, radio and newsprint. Furthermore, it is also worth mentioning that some analysts have suggested that rituals and performances can even be carried out privately, in the absence of communication. For example, as Wuthnow (1989: 103) observes, privately performed acts such as meditations and prayers might be conceived as expressive behaviour. Wuthnow (ibid.: 104) conjectures that such private rituals might be expressions of the 'disciplining' of an individual's interests and thus convey meaning in the sense that they express the relationship of the individual to society.

To conclude this section, a few words are in order as to what, then, distinguishes rituals from performances. The study of ritual, on the one hand, and performance, on the other, initially proceeded along separate tracks. In general, whereas ritual referred to symbolic action, performance referred to theatre. If the concept of performance was used outside of the confines of the theatre, it was as a metaphor. To be sure, the dramaturgical metaphor remains an important heuristic device, yet it is also true that the very meaning of what is a 'performance' has begun to migrate beyond the stage. Richard Schechner, in collaboration with Victor Turner, played no small part in this development. Schechner suggests that all activities associated with ritual or theatre should be seen as performances. In his view, whether or not a particular performance is closer to theatre or ritual depends on its function. A performance that is aimed more at entertainment is closer to theatre, whereas a performance that is aimed more at effecting social transformations is closer to ritual (Schechner, 1988: 130). Thus, although previously two distinct lines of enquiry, recently these topics have converged. In keeping with this development, in this volume we have adopted an inclusive definition of expressive behaviour that encompasses rituals and performances.

Ritual and performance in the study of nations and nationalism

Having discussed the concepts of ritual and performance, in this section we provide a brief review of their treatment in the study of nations and nationalism. Our intent here is to situate the current volume within the literature and to highlight its potential contributions. In sum, our review suggests that, after a period of sustained interest in rituals and performances within the field following the Second World War, such interest declined in the face of widespread criticism of the prevailing approaches. Recently, however, the study of nations and nationalism has seen renewed interest in rituals and performances, reflecting wider trends in social research, as mentioned above. The intent of this book is to add to, and shape, this fast-growing body of research.

Research on the significance of rituals and performances for nations and nationalism in the decades following the Second World War was driven mainly by anthropologists. This was a result of the resurgence of interest in ritual in this period within anthropology. Durkheim's (1995 [1912]) masterwork, *Elementary Forms of the Religious Life*, played a particularly influential role in the literature of this period. As such, we will briefly explicate this work before addressing its influence.

Through an analysis of ethnographic data of Australian corroboree rites, Durkheim argues that the object of collective rituals is to communicate a group's meaning systems to the members of the group, thereby periodically enhancing and sustaining group solidarity. As Catherine Bell (1992: 20) neatly summarizes:

'[Durkheim] reintroduces ritual as the means by which collective beliefs and ideals are simultaneously generated, experienced, and affirmed as real by the community. Hence, ritual is the means by which individual perception and behaviour are socially appropriated and conditioned.' As we noted above, in Durkheim's view the intense emotions generated among ritual participants – which he refers to as collective effervescence – enables this process to occur. As Durkheim (1995 [1912]: 216) writes in relation to the corroboree rites: 'once the individuals are gathered together a sort of electricity is generated from their closeness and quickly launches them into an extraordinary height of exaltation'.

Although Durkheim's analysis of ritual is based on religious rites of small pre-industrial societies, he frequently alludes to the applicability of his argument to secular modern societies. This insight proved fertile ground for research in the decades following the Second World War. In such research, nationalism is seen as a secular religion premised on the worship of the nation, with attendant rituals and beliefs. In a much-discussed study, Edward Shils and Michael Young (1953) draw on Durkheim in an analysis of Queen Elizabeth II's coronation, suggesting that it was an integrative ritual reaffirming the shared values of British society and the centrality of the monarchy as its national symbol. In turn, the legacy of this essay can be seen in a number of important related studies published in subsequent years, including William Lloyd Warner's (1959) analysis of Memorial Day in the US and Robert Bellah's (1970) characterization of John F. Kennedy's inauguration.

The tradition of Durkheimian analysis in the post-war era did much to shed light on the underlying 'religious' character of ostensibly secular nations and the importance of collective rituals in their endurance. Indeed, it continues to produce important insights, notably the recent analysis of American nationalism by Carolyn Marvin and David Ingle (1999), who argue that it is a civil religion organized around a 'sacred' flag, whose followers engage in ritualized self-sacrifice through warfare to maintain solidarity. However, despite its important contributions, Durkheimian analysis of this kind is limited by its tendency to downplay the differences between small pre-modern societies and their modern corollaries, with their high degree of internal segmentation and reflexivity. This tendency began to attract much criticism in the 1970s.

In a particularly strident and much-cited critique, Steven Lukes (1975) rebukes what he refers to as 'neo-Durkheimian' scholarship for three linked reasons: (1) ignoring social segmentation within modern societies and the concomitant possibility that rituals may actually be as divisive as they are integrative; (2) not addressing the possibility that rituals and, by extension, 'value consensus' may not be a necessary condition for cohesion in a society; and (3) focusing too much on top-down, society-encompassing rituals, thereby ignoring how rituals among subordinate groups can potentially harden, rather than dissolve, intra-societal segmentation. This kind of criticism has continued into the present day and can be found, for example, in Gordana Uzelac's (2010) essay on the impact of national ceremonies on the formation of national identity. Lukes's critique also finds echoes in Jon Fox's contribution to this book. However, as we will discuss shortly, such criticism has begun to be incorporated into the analyses of the new generation of Durkheimians.

Before moving beyond the post-war era of literature, it is important to note the study by George Mosse (1975), published on the cusp of the decline of anthropological interest in national rituals and performances. While drawing on Durkheim, Mosse nevertheless also sought to account for the differences associated with modern social life. Concerned particularly with explaining Nazism's success in interwar Germany (and also mass movements in the nineteenth century), Mosse suggests that the terror and propaganda associated with it cannot sufficiently explain its popularity. It is here that Mosse turns to Nazism's use of large-scale collective rituals, suggesting that it was a 'civic religion' whose success lay in the ways that it drew upon myths, symbols, music and practices that had deep historical roots in the German national consciousness. According to Mosse, the result was that these ritual performances generated a kind of Durkheimian collective effervescence, thereby unifying large numbers of ordinary Germans under the banner of Nazism.

Mosse's analysis provides an important development on the Durkheimian tradition of his predecessors for several reasons. First, in many ways, he treats modern rituals as analogous to theatrical performance. This allows Mosse to account for the possibility of the 'failure' of some collective rituals, in the sense that they risk being deemed 'artificial' by their participants if they are not effectively performed (Mosse, 1975: 90). Second, Mosse also takes care in his analysis to distinguish the producers of the ritual, the liturgy (i.e. the particular ritual form being enacted) and the ritual participants. Bracketing out these different elements allows for a better accounting of social hierarchies and segmentation and, in this way, presages Jeffrey Alexander's (2004) call to integrate all the elements of a social performance into its analysis.

Although Mosse's insights represent an important development, he did not dwell on them at length, nor did he seek to develop them further. The result is that, for at least one critic, Mosse does not go far enough in accounting for challenges associated with successfully enacting rituals and performances in modern society (Uzelac, 2010). Nor were Mosse's insights taken up by his contemporaries: much of the scholarly interest in Mosse did not emerge until fairly recently. This may be due, in part, to the fact that research on national rituals and performances began to wane around the time of the publication of his book.

Going into the 1980s, if anthropologists had turned their attention elsewhere, historians of nations and nationalism were just beginning to become increasingly interested in rituals and performance. The impetus was, in large part, provided by the publication of Eric Hobsbawm and Terence Ranger's (1983) edited volume on the 'invention of traditions'. Although not solely focused on the phenomena of nations and nationalism, it quickly became associated with their study – probably, in no small part, because of Hobsbawm's own deepening interest in nations and nationalism in subsequent years.

The historians brought with them the kinds of concerns associated with their discipline. Whereas the 'neo-Durkheim' scholarship of the post-war era is interested more in function, the 'invention of tradition' literature is more concerned with origins. In what might be seen as a critique of Mosse's contention that rituals 'succeed' when they draw on aspects of culture that have deep historical roots, the research agenda triggered by Hobsbawm and Ranger has demonstrated in countless instances that many of the most successful rituals are actually fairly recent inventions (e.g. Guss, 1994; Handler and Linnekin, 1984; Linnekin, 1991). However, although the 'invention tradition' literature has done much to stimulate the study of rituals and their relationship to nations and nationalism, it has not been without criticism. For example, Anthony Smith (2004, especially Chapter 3) criticizes the research agenda for overemphasizing the degree to which national rituals and traditions can be wholly invented, suggesting that they might be better seen as attempts at reinvention or renewal. In her fascinating chapter in this volume, Athena Leoussi similarly questions Hobsbawm's arguments via an analysis of the ethno-classical revival in France at the turn of the nineteenth century.

Moving forward into the 1980s, aside from the then rapidly emerging literature on the 'invention of traditions', the most prominent debates in nationalism studies had become oriented towards large-scale historical comparative research on the rise of nations of nationalism and its relationship to processes of modernization (e.g. Anderson, 1991 [1983]; Breuilly, 1993 [1982]; Gellner, 2006 [1983]; Giddens, 1985; Smith 1986; Tilly, 1975). Indeed, these debates continue to dominate the field in the present day. Generally, although rituals and performances do feature in such analyses, they are treated as epiphenomenal of wider political, economic and cultural processes. While rituals and performances may feature tangentially in recent major works, their significance has been largely inferred, and the processes related to how and why they contribute to the construction and endurance of nationhood have been largely neglected. Certainly, Smith (e.g. Smith, 2003) has frequently pointed in his works to the significance of rituals and performance for the endurance of nations and nationalism, however his concerns are much broader, and he does not go into depth into the dynamics of the function or impact of such rituals. By contrast, in his contribution to this volume, Smith places ritual and performance firmly at the centre of his analysis, arguing compellingly that their significance lies not in whether or not they may be popular at any given time, but in their regularity and their historicity.

A notable exception to the tendency of macro-historical comparative literature to downplay the significance of ritual and performance is Benedict Anderson's highly influential *Imagined Communities* (Anderson, 1991 [1983]), wherein ritual is accorded a central role in the instantiation of a shared national imagination. Anderson's approach to ritual marks a significant departure from the 'neo-Durkheimian' and 'invention of tradition' literatures. Rather than focus on large ritual events marked by intense passion, Anderson focuses on the habitual. In Anderson's view, it is the mass performance of everyday rituals that contributes to the construction of a shared national imagination. Anderson pays particular attention to the significance of the daily ritual of reading a newspaper as a result of the spread of print capitalism in the nineteenth century. In this regard, Anderson writes:

> The significance of this mass ceremony – Hegel observed that newspapers serve modern man as a substitute for morning prayers – is paradoxical. It is performed in silent privacy, in the lair of the skull. Yet each communicant is well aware that the ceremony he performs is being replicated simultaneously by thousands (or millions) of others of whose existence he is confident, yet of whose identity he has not the slightest notion. Furthermore, this ceremony is incessantly repeated at daily or half-daily intervals throughout the calendar. What more vivid figure for the secular, historically clocked, imagined community can be envisioned?
>
> (Anderson, 1991 [1983]: 35)

Imagined Communities is perhaps the single most influential text in the study of nationalism. Its impact can be seen in the explosion of research on how nations and national identities are constructed via written texts such as newspapers and textbooks. However, Anderson's insights on the role of the habitual and everyday rituals in the construction of the imagined national community remain a largely untapped vein of potential research. Such research might also draw on important work by Randall Collins (2004), who, by combining Goffman and Durkheim, suggests that underlying social structures are maintained by way of countless everyday 'interaction ritual chains' among individuals. Such a research agenda might also bolster the burgeoning body of research on the significance of nationalism in everyday life (e.g. Billig, 1995; Brubaker *et al.*, 2006; Edensor, 2002; Fox and Miller-Idriss, 2008; Palmer, 1998), which has heretofore focused more on discourse than on enactment.

Although the debates of the 1980s and 1990s continue to loom large in the study of nations and nationalism, recent years have seen a renewed interest in ritual and performance. In the following paragraphs, we will briefly address these developments, before discussing where we think this book can contribute. Because there is not space to go over all the new lines of research, we will focus on two areas that have been particularly fruitful. These include the ongoing revival of diverse strands of Durkheimiam analysis, albeit in a much more nuanced form, as well as the emergence of interest in the phenomena of nations and nationalism from the interdisciplinary field of performances studies.

Perhaps unsurprisingly, Durkheim's stature has grown again in the recent spate of research on national rituals and performances. His influence can be seen in several recent works covering a wide variety of phenomena, including (but not limited to) commemorations (e.g. Gillis, 1996; Spillman, 1997), sporting events (e.g. Bairner, 2001), national days (e.g. Elgenius, 2011; McCrone and McPherson, 2009), truth and reconciliation commissions (e.g. Goodman, 2006), and official apologies (e.g. Barkan and Karn, 2006). However, while Durkheim is a significant influence in this new body of work, it is important to note that it is generally much more nuanced than the post-war generation of Durkheimians we discussed above.

Where current work differs from the earlier generation of Durkheimians is that the function and impact of rituals and performances are not assumed. In other words, not all national rituals and performances are assumed to provoke a uniform response among the participants. Instead, the fact that national rituals and performances often provoke differing meanings and responses among participants and can even be hotly contested is generally foregrounded. Importantly, the role of the mass media in conveying and potentially fuelling such contestation is now also widely acknowledged (e.g. Burney, 2002; Marvin and Ingle, 1999; Mihelj, 2008; Wardle and West, 2004). In this volume, Rachel Hutchins focuses on the contentious role played by the media in analysis of the ongoing struggles over the American national identity.

In the hands of many of the new Durkheimians, the analysis of ritual events therefore has the potential to become a powerful heuristic for uncovering mediated conflicts over the meaning and definition of the nation. This has been taken up by a group of new Durkheimians building on the approach developed by Jeffrey Alexander (Eyerman, 2008; Goodman, 2006; Kane, 2012; Spillman, 1997; Woods and Debs, 2013a). Drawing on Durkheimian distinctions between the sacred, profane and mundane, the general thrust of this work is to uncover how particular meanings and cultural forms are contested, replaced and established in the national 'collective consciousness'. Given its emphasis on the relative independence of culture, this research agenda has the potential to strongly complement the culturalist approaches to nations and nationalism put forward by Anthony Smith (2009) and John Hutchinson (2005), which tends towards the historical, by adding a strongly processual component (see Woods and Debs, 2013b).

In addition to the resurfacing of Durkheim, there has been a small but growing area of research germane to the study of nationalism, which also draws on the burgeoning field of performance studies literature (e.g. Cole, 2001; Kear and Steinberg, 1999; Mason and Gainor, 2001; Taylor, 1997). This new area of research tends to be strongly interdisciplinary, reflecting the research agenda put forward by Turner (1982) and Schechner (1988). Instead of merely analysing rituals or analogizing them as a form of theatre, this literature also analyses 'real' theatrical performances. In a study of Argentina during the 'dirty war', Diana Taylor (1997) brings to light a struggle over Argentina's national identity through analysis of a wide array of ritualized *and* theatrical performances, including military parades, football matches, theatre festivals and the famous marches by the Mothers of the Plaza de Mayo.

In the preceding paragraphs, we briefly traced some of the key developments in the research on national rituals and performances. In the following chapters that comprise this book, we hope to build upon the diverse areas of research touched on in this section in order to stimulate new debates and new lines of inquiry. By demonstrating the vitality of one area of research that we believe has much potential to generate new insights, our overarching aim with this volume is to reinvigorate the study of nations and nationalism. In the light of the increasing heterogeneity of research on rituals and performances within nationalism studies, we particularly hope that this volume will provoke further conversation and debate not only on the significance of rituals and performances for nations and nationalism, but also on questions related to approach and methodology. Thus, while we intentionally assembled a diverse body of contributors employing a wide variety of approaches and methods, we have also encouraged the contributors to think about how their particular approaches and methods relate to the others. This has given rise to several recurring debates and themes running through the book over how we ought to approach rituals and performances and how they might best be studied. It is our hope that these debates will find their way into future research.

Approach and methodology

As noted above, a key theme of this book concerns approach and methodology. In light of the growing diversity of approaches and methods in the study of ritual and performance, we feel that it is time to initiate further discussion of their relative strengths and weaknesses in relation to the study of nationalism. For instance, should we focus primarily on extraordinary events, such as the royal wedding or 11 September and its aftermath, or can we learn more about nations by observing everyday interactions, such as regularly drinking at the pub after work or pledging allegiance to the flag before class? Is there greater value in observing the construction of high culture by elites, such as the opera and national museums, or should there be greater emphasis on popular culture, such as the widely watched television programmes *America's Got Talent* or *Eurovision Song Contest*? Such methodological questions are discussed and, indeed, at times hotly debated across the various chapters comprising this book.

It is worth noting, however, that many of the questions concerning how to study ritual and performance are related to wider debates within the field of nationalism studies. For instance, scholars such as Rogers Brubaker (Brubaker, 2004; Brubaker *et al.*, 2006) have advocated investigating how 'ordinary' people respond to, and enact, elite-level representations of nations and nationalism. Similarly, others, such as Michael Billig (1995), have highlighted the importance of exploring the informal, everyday processes that produce and reproduce nationhood. By contrast, other scholars, such as Anthony Smith (2010), while acknowledging the importance of these new approaches, have argued that a proper understanding of the persistence of particular nations and nationalism requires a continued focus on their historical genealogy and the role of elites (on this debate, see Fox *et al.*, 2008). The reader will find this debate, in particular, taken up in the context of rituals and performances in the contributions by Smith and Fox.

As Smith highlights in his contribution to the volume, a greater focus on rituals and performances may also help push the field of nationalism studies towards uncovering and analysing new sources of information beyond literary texts and survey data. When seeking to explain questions related to nations and nationalism, the tendency has been to focus on data gleaned from government reports, textbooks, censuses, surveys, newspapers, speeches, diaries, and so on. While these texts have been, and continue to be, extremely useful, if we are to properly understand the meaning of national rituals and performances, there may also be scope for paying more attention to other sources of data, including art, archaeology, architecture, music, drama, film and sport. This, in turn, suggests that there is greater scope for ethnographic and other forms of participatory and observational research in nationalism studies than has heretofore been the case.

Structure and outline

The book is divided into two parts: approaches and applications. The chapters in the first part are concerned primarily with how to study rituals and performances, with each of them presenting what are often conflicting analytic frameworks. The chapters in the second part are concerned more with understanding and explaining specific empirical phenomena. Yet, it is important to note that this is a very broad distinction, as all of the contributors to the volume are concerned with approach and all engage with a variety of specific case studies. Indeed, providing the structure for this volume was a daunting task because, although we are keen to highlight a number of important themes and issues, we do not wish to create or sustain dichotomies. The rationale behind the structure of the book is therefore primarily to serve as a guide for how to develop an understanding of this fascinating and complex topic. Thus, although each chapter provides an independent argument, for scholars who are new to this topic we suggest reading the chapters in the order in which they are situated in the book – this applies particularly to the chapters in the first part.

Part I: approaches

In Chapter 2, Anthony Smith provides a thorough introduction to the significance and key themes of performance and ritual for the study of nations by undertaking a broad comparative historical analysis of celebratory and commemorative rituals, as well as non-textual sources of the nation. Smith argues that ritual and performance play a central role in the forging and reforging of national communities. However, against those who argue that analysis should proceed primarily from the perspective of ordinary citizens, Smith seeks to demonstrate that attention must also be paid to the elites who design and represent collective rituals, as well as the genealogy of such rituals, if their role in the persistence of nations is to be fully understood.

By observing national holiday commemorations, in Chapter 3, Jon Fox highlights a crucial issue for ritual and performance in the study of nations; namely, how to identify and measure the success of a ritual or performance. While the scholarship on nationalism has generally assumed the success of such commemorations, scholarship on ritual and performance has generally assumed the opposite.

Nevertheless, Fox argues that both views are united by a 'top-down' logic and, thus, against the position taken by Smith, Fox argues for a study of national rituals and performances that focuses primarily on the perspective of ordinary citizens. Observing that there is often a disjuncture between the officially intended meaning of a particular national ritual and the way that it is perceived and received by ordinary citizens, Fox suggests an emphasis on the latter will help researchers to focus on the particular rituals and performances that are of national significance.

In Chapter 4, Randall Collins explores the significance of rituals by theorizing nationalism as a process of surges in time. Like Fox, Collins acknowledges the fact that nationalism and national identity remain, for the most part, latent. Collins thus attempts to explain the ebb and flow of national sentiment through social movements. At their peak, Collins argues that these movements manifest themselves as huge interaction rituals, which are time-bubbles, lasting for a few weeks or months before fading, and are subject to a refractory period during which they cannot be mobilized at that same intensity. In this view, rituals thus possess great explanatory power in theorizing the rise and fall of nationalist sentiment. Collins draws upon evidence from the aftermath of 11 September 2001 and the Arab Spring of 2011 to illustrate his case.

In Chapter 5, Jonathan Hearn argues that, rather than simply examining their content, greater emphasis should be placed on exploring the *form* of rituals. Hearn's contribution also provides an excellent discussion on the definition of ritual. Unlike Smith and Fox, Hearn is not concerned with questions about the design and reception of rituals; rather, by drawing on the ritual of competition in liberal national states to illustrate his case, Hearn emphasizes the significance of underlying ritual processes. For Hearn, formalized competition is the defining ritual for core liberal political and economic institutions (e.g. elections and markets), as well as a cultural trope that permeates society as a whole, in education, sports, entertainment and the arts. Hearn's underlying argument, therefore, is that we need to look beyond the more overt civic rituals that affirm national identity and social solidarity (e.g. national days, funerals of public figures, pilgrimages to historic sites, etc.) and look for those rituals that, in their very form, affirm and dramatize the constitution of society.

Part II: applications

The first two chapters in the second half of the book discuss efforts by elites to construct or embody the 'authentic' nation. By focusing on elite design and adopting a historical perspective, we see echoes of Anthony Smith's contribution to the volume in both of these chapters.

Of all the means through which elites have sought to capture the spirit of the nation, perhaps none have been applied as universally as the national art museum. In Chapter 6, art historian Carol Duncan theorizes the experience of a national art museum as 'civilizing ritual' that transforms individuals into national citizens. Describing the genesis of the national art museum in eighteenth-century France and beyond, Duncan argues that art museums' combination of architectural features and art installations constitute a ritual scenario, a kind of score or script that structures the visitor's experience (even if visitors are not equally prepared to enact it).

In Chapter 7, Athena Leoussi explores the engagement of avant-garde French artists in the movement for national physical regeneration that followed the Franco-Prussian War of 1870–1871. Leoussi demonstrates how the French tried to revive the ancient Greek cult of the body. This body-centred, ethno-classical revival became associated with a Catholic revival that reaffirmed chastity and motherhood and celebrated another 'golden age', that of the Gothic cathedrals, an age of moral virtue. She explores how these two ideals of the two French 'national' traditions, the classical and Catholic, were appropriated by elites and enacted or performed in French art, and especially in the art of the Impressionist artists Paul Cézanne and Pierre-Auguste Renoir. In their paintings, the two artists showed the new French ideal: France regenerated, physically and morally, by a return to the Mediterranean homeland and way of life.

In Chapter 8, Japan specialist John Breen draws on a similar theme to that of Randall Collins by exploring the rise and fall in the significance of a national ritual. By focusing on Yasukuni, a contentious shrine to the Japanese war dead in Tokyo, Breen also raises issues about how national memory and mourning become manifest in ritual. Breen sheds light on Yasukuni's rise to prominence as a national ritual site before and during the Second World War, arguing that it played a vital role during the Second World War by which the imperial nation could be experienced. However, in democratic post-war Japan, Breen suggests that the strict constitutional separation between church and state has led to the decline of the Yasukuni as the 'nation's shrine'.

The final two chapters of the volume both focus on attempts to redefine or re-appropriate national identity through ritual and performance. The focus of Rachel Hutchin's Chapter 9 is the Rally to Restore Sanity, which was held on 30 October 2010 in Washington DC and was organized by Jon Stewart, the host of cable television's *The Daily Show*. Initially billed as a counter-protest against the Tea Party movement (including the Restoring Honor Rally of August 2010, which featured Fox News's Glenn Beck), the rally led various media outlets and commentators to struggle to define its meaning. Hutchins draws upon themes set out by Fox and Collins on the success of rituals and performances, demonstrating how the rally, media coverage of it, and participants' perceptions and objectives often included discourse relating to national identity – from the hosts' abundant, somewhat ironic use of American flags and flag motifs, to explicit proclamations of national greatness and calls for national unity. The rally is an example of extraordinary collective action that provides an opportunity to examine both the salience and conceptions of national sentiment and national identity.

By examining Maori imagery in ephemera produced for the 1901 visit of the Duke and Duchess of Cornwall, Chris McDonald's Chapter 10 demonstrates how 'pakeha' New Zealanders fashioned identities not just for Maori, but also for themselves as a distinctive group of British colonists. McDonald argues that the

colonists were aware of their own difference and sought to define this positively, often as an extrapolation from recognized 'British' characteristics or ideals.
By creating the appearance of a bicultural state, '*pakeha*' New Zealanders were
able to situate themselves in the vanguard of a new breed of empire builders,
differentiating New Zealand from the newly federated Australia where 'the race
issue' was more problematic. In making this distinction, '*pakeha*' New Zealanders
avoided direct comparison with their cousins 'at home' and defined unique aspects
of their identity as a series of contrasts with colonists elsewhere.

Concluding remarks and suggestions for further research

Although ritual and performance have largely remained peripheral subjects of enquiry
within the discipline over the past two decades, an explosion of recent scholarship
reflects a rapidly growing interest in the area. As we have sought to demonstrate
above, this scholarship encompasses both a resurgence of established issues and
debates, as well as the emergence of novel questions and modes of enquiry. This
volume seeks to draw together many of these diverse topics, questions and
approaches, and attempts to highlight key theoretical and methodological issues
with the aim of developing understanding of this topic and stimulating further
research.

The study of ritual and performance forces us to reconsider the role of elites
and masses, of societal structures and micro-processes, of different approaches and
methodologies, of unconsidered behaviour and scripted practices, of the everyday
nation and extraordinary national moments. We hope that the reader will find echoes
of all of these issues and debates in the chapters that follow, and be prompted to
take up further enquiry. Yet we are also aware that there are many other significant
topics that are not covered here. Constricted by both space and time, for instance,
this book has a predominantly Western focus. The history of nationalism demonstrates the diversity of its origins, forms and functions across the globe. There is
much that can be said about the role of ritual and performance for emerging nations
and transnational identities, and for nationalisms outside the West. It is our
hope that this volume can provide the foundation for further discussion of these
complex and fascinating issues.

References

Alexander, J. C. (2004) 'Cultural pragmatics: social performance between ritual and strategy',
    Sociological Theory, 22(4): 527–73.
Anderson, B. (1991 [1983]) *Imagined Communities: Reflections on the Origins and Spread of
    Nationalism*, London: Verso.
Bairner, A. (2001) *Sport, Nationalism and Globalization: European and North American
    Perspectives*, New York: SUNY Press.
Barad, K. (2003) 'Posthumanist performativity: toward and understanding of how matter
    comes to matter', *Signs*, 28(3): 801–31.

Barkan, E. and Karn, A. (eds) (2006) *Taking Wrongs Seriously: Apologies and Reconciliation*, Palo Alto, CA: Stanford University Press.

Bell, C. (1992) *Ritual Theory, Ritual Practice*, Oxford: Oxford University Press.

Bellah, R. N. (1970) *Beyond Belief: Essays on Religion in a Post-Traditional World*, New York: Harper & Row.

Billig, M. (1995) *Banal Nationalism*, London: Sage.

Breuilly, J. (1993 [1982]) *Nationalism and the State*, 2nd edn, Manchester: Manchester University Press.

Brubaker, R. (2004) *Ethnicity Without Groups*, Cambridge, MA: Harvard University Press.

Brubaker, R., Feischmidt, M., Fox, J. and Grancea, L. (2006) *Nationalist Politics and Everyday Ethnicity in a Transylvanian Town*, Princeton, NJ: Princeton University Press.

Burney, S. (2002) 'Manufacturing nationalism: post-September 11 discourse in United States media', *SIMILE: Studies in Media and Information Literacy Education*, 2(2): 1–9.

Butler, J. (1988) 'Performative acts and gender constitution: an essay in phenomenology and feminist theory', *Theatre Journal*, 40(4): 519–31.

Cole, C. M. (2001) *Ghana's Concert Party Theatre*, Bloomington, IN: Indiana University Press.

Collins, R. (2004) *Interaction Ritual Chains*, Princeton, NJ: Princeton University Press.

Dayan, D. and Katz, E. (1992) *Media Events: The Live Broadcasting of History*, Cambridge, MA: Harvard University Press.

Douglas, M. (2002 [1966]) *Purity and Danger: An Analysis of Concept of Pollution and Taboo*, London: Routledge.

Durkheim, É. (1995 [1912]) *Elementary Forms of the Religious Life*, trans. K. E. Fields, London: Simon & Schuster.

Edensor, T. (2002) *National Identity, Popular Culture and Everyday Life*, Oxford: Berg.

Elgenius, G. (2011) *Symbols of Nations and Nationalism: Celebrating Nationhood*, Basingstoke: Palgrave Macmillan.

Eyerman, R. (2008) *The Assassination of Theo Van Gogh: From Social Drama to Cultural Trauma*, Durham, NC: Duke University Press.

Fox, J. E. and Miller-Idriss, C. (2008) 'Everyday nationhood', *Ethnicities*, 8(4): 536–62.

Fox, J. E., Miller-Idriss, C. and Smith, A. D. (2008) 'Debate', *Ethnicities*, 8(4): 563–76.

Gellner, E. (2006 [1983]) *Nations and Nationalism*, 2nd edn, Oxford: Blackwell.

Giddens, A. (1985) *The Nation-State and Violence: Volume 2 of a Contemporary Critique of Historical Materialism*, Berkeley, CA: University of California Press.

Gillis, J. (ed.) (1996) *Commemorations: The Politics of National Identity*, Princeton, NJ: Princeton University Press.

Goffman, E. (1959) *The Presentation of Self in Everyday Life*, Garden City, NY: Doubleday.

Goodman, T. (2006) *Staging Solidarity: Truth and Reconciliation in a New South Africa*, Boulder, CO: Paradigm.

Guss, D. M. (1994) 'Syncretic inventions: "Indianness" of the day of the monkey', in C. Stewart (ed.) *Syncretism/Anti-Syncretism: The Politics of Religious Synthesis*, London: Routledge, pp. 145–60.

Handler, R. and Linnekin, J. (1984) 'Tradition, genuine or spurious', *Journal of American Folklore*, 97(385): 273–90.

Hobsbawm, E. and Ranger, T. (1983) *The Invention of Tradition*, Cambridge: Cambridge University Press.

Hutchinson, J. (2005) *Nations and Zones of Conflict*, London: Sage.

Kane, A. (2012) *Constructing Irish National Identity: Discourse and Ritual During the Land War, 1879–1882*, Basingstoke: Palgrave Macmillan.

Kear, A. and Steinberg, D. L. (eds) (1999) *Mourning Diana: Nation, Culture and the Performance of Grief*, London: Routledge.

Linnekin, J. (1991) 'Cultural invention and the dilemma of authenticity', *American Anthropologist*, 93(2): 446–9.

Lukes, S. (1975) 'Political ritual and social integration', *Sociology*, 9(2): 289–308.

McCrone, D. and McPherson, G. (eds) (2009) *National Days: Constructing and Mobilising National Identity*, Basingstoke: Palgrave Macmillan.

Marvin, C. and Ingle, D. W. (1999) *Blood Sacrifice and the Nation: Totem Rituals and the American Flag*, Cambridge: Cambridge University Press.

Mason, D. J. and Gainor, J. E. (2001) *Performing America: Cultural Nationalism in American Theater*, Ann Arbor, MI: University of Michigan Press.

Mihelj, S. (2008) 'National media events: from displays of unity to enactments of division', *European Journal of Cultural Studies*, 11(4): 471–88.

Mosse, G. (1975) *The Nationalisation of the Masses*, New York: Howard Fertig.

Palmer, C. (1998) 'From theory to practice: experiencing the nation in everyday life', *Journal of Material Culture*, 3(2): 175–99.

Parsons, T. and Shils, E. (2001 [1951]) *Toward a General Theory of Action: Theoretical Foundations for the Social Sciences*, Piscataway, NJ: Transaction.

Schechner, R. (1988) *Performance Theory*, 2nd edn, London: Routledge.

Shils, E. and Young, M. (1953) 'The meaning of the coronation', *The Sociological Review*, 1(2): 63–81.

Smith, A. D. (1986) *The Ethnic Origins of Nations*, Oxford: Blackwell.

Smith, A. D. (2003) *Chosen Peoples: Sacred Sources of National Identity*, Oxford: Oxford University Press.

Smith, A. D. (2004) *The Antiquity of Nations*, Cambridge: Polity Press.

Smith, A. D. (2009) *Ethnosymbolism and Nationalism: A Cultural Approach*, London: Routledge.

Smith, A. D. (2010) *Nationalism*, 2nd edn, London: Polity Press.

Spillman, L. (1997) *Nation and Commemoration: Creating National Identities in the United States and Australia*, Cambridge: Cambridge University Press.

Taylor, D. (1997) *Disappearing Acts: Spectacles of Gender and Nationalism in Argentina's 'Dirty War'*, Durham, NC: Duke University Press.

Tilly, C. (1975) *The Formation of National States in Europe*, Princeton, NJ: Princeton University Press.

Turner, V. W. (1982) *From Ritual to Theatre: The Human Seriousness of Play*, New York: Performing Arts Journal Publications.

Turner, V. W (2008 [1969]) *The Ritual Process: Structure and Anti-Structure*, Piscataway, NJ: AldineTransaction.

Uzelac, G. (2010) 'National ceremonies: the pursuit of authenticity', *Ethnic and Racial Studies*, 33(10): 1718–36.

Wardle, C. and West, E. (2004) 'The press as agents of nationalism in the Queen's Golden Jubilee: how British newspapers celebrated a media event', *European Journal of Communication*, 19(2): 195–214.

Warner, W. L. (1959) *The Living and the Dead: A Study of the Symbolic Life of Americans*, New Haven, CT: Yale University Press.

Woods, E. T. and Debs, M. (2013a) 'A cultural sociology of nationalism', special section on cultural sociology and nationalism, *Nations and Nationalism*, 19(4).

Woods, E. T. and Debs, M. (2013b) 'Towards a cultural sociology of nations and nationalism', *Nations and Nationalism*, 19(4).

Wuthnow, R. (1989) *Meaning and Moral Order: Explorations in Cultural Analysis*. Berkeley, CA: University of California Press.

PART I

Approaches

2

THE RITES OF NATIONS

Elites, masses and the re-enactment of the 'national past'

Anthony D. Smith

When we seek to study and explain the rise of nations and the role of nationalisms, we normally have recourse to texts of various kinds: chronological narratives, descriptions of political regimes, economic and demographic statistics, the speeches and diaries of nationalist leaders and the programmes of nationalist organizations. But this exclusive concern with the 'literature of nationalism', as we may call it, obscures a range of other kinds of consideration and evidence. I have in mind such extra-literary genres as musical performances, works of art, architecture and urban planning, and the artefacts of archaeological excavations. In this regard, the rituals and performances associated with large-scale 'mass' nationalisms are of particular significance. Without them, I shall argue, it is doubtful whether national sentiments and ideals in the modern world could be embedded in wider populations and could reproduce themselves across the generations. While I would not want to claim that national rituals and performances constitute either a necessary or a sufficient condition of the persistence of nations and nationalisms, their ubiquity and regularity gives them a special role and significance in the forging and the reproduction of nations.

My approach in this chapter will focus on the ways in which celebratory and commemorative rituals have often taken on a 'life of their own', appealing to generations distant from the events that engendered them. For though rituals, or more precisely rites and ceremonies, may undergo addition or amendment over time, there remains a remarkable degree of formal consistency in their design and, even to a large extent, in their performance. This was very much the focus of Émile Durkheim's (1915 [1912]: book II, especially chapters 2 and 4) classic treatment in his *The Elementary Forms of the Religious Life* of the various types of rite found among aboriginal tribes in Australia, and, more importantly, of his insistence on the centrality of ritual in religion and society.

Closely allied to this theoretical concern is an emphasis on non-textual sources of data, particularly paintings, sculpture and photography that depict past national rituals and performances, but also remain as witnesses to ongoing national rites and ceremonies. Visual art, unlike music or literature, summarizes the appearance of rituals and records specific moments of their performance in single memorable, and sometimes iconic, images, thereby rendering the abstract concept of the nation palpable, tangible and widely accessible (through prints and engravings). Through such historical and contemporary recreations, visual images endow 'the nation' with 'body', a seeming physical presence and a symbolic and territorial location in the vivid record of mass performances.[1]

A third element in the approach adopted here is the need to balance elite organization and popular participation in the analysis of national rites and ceremonies. Typically, the latter involve the choreographed movements of large numbers of ordinary members of the national community in their public performances – the physical embodiment of a mass civic cult of the nation, of the kind that George Mosse (1975, especially chapter 3) analysed in his survey of rites and monuments in Germany from the Napoleonic Wars to the Third Reich. This has given rise to a debate about whether we should be focusing our attention on the sentiments and activities of the 'masses' (i.e. the ordinary members of the community) rather than the intentions and organizations of the elites – an issue to which I shall return later.

A final strand in my approach is the need to ground the analysis of national rites and ceremonies in their historical context, and avoid undue emphasis on the immediate present. After all, the actions of the majority of individuals are undertaken within communities, national or other, which have been forged over several generations. This means that any analysis of the rites and ceremonies of nations must consider the impact of 'historic nationhood' (i.e. the traditions, memories, myths and symbols of the national community, which are shared to a greater or lesser extent by most of the members), and nowhere is this more the case than in the vital domain of the various kinds of ritual activity in which their members participate.[2]

Nature and types of national rituals

We can start by distinguishing ritual activities in traditional communities from those occurring in more modern contexts. In the former, rituals form an intrinsic component of the religious tradition, where the meaning of the term 'religion' itself may be understood as 'rehearsing rites'. I should add that what we might consider to be theatrical 'performances' may, in such societies, constitute rituals of the communal religion, as with the rites and ceremonies of Dionysus that formed the context of the ancient Greek tragedies put on at the Great Dionysia festival in Athens and that, for Aristotle at least, constituted not entertainment, but a cleansing of the soul through pity and terror. To this day, there are communities whose life is centred on a religious tradition in which the rehearsal of ritual activity remains paramount, for example among many Catholics and Orthodox Jews, even when in other respects their members participate in modern secular society. It is not so much their meaningfulness or their effectiveness, much less their authenticity, that are at stake in such activities; rather, it is respect for tradition per se and what it embodies, and the desire to continue it in the future. When Moses (Exodus 12:14) commanded the children of Israel to observe the Passover in all their generations, he did not commend it because it was rich in meaning or effective as performance or as 'truly authentic', but simply to be an everlasting statute and memorial.[3]

On the other hand, even in traditional societies popular participation was often integral to ritual. In principle, such activity involved every member of the community and all who adhered to it. Again, in his final speech on the plains of Moab, Moses (Deuteronomy 29:14-15) told the assembled Israelites that the covenant and oath he is making is 'with him that standeth here with us this day before the Lord our God, and also with him that is not here with us this day', thereby uniting the forebears, the members and the unborn – a claim often echoed by modern nationalists, though with rather more limited success. Perhaps the Israelite case was somewhat unusual. More often, ritual activity was confined to processions of monarchs, priests and exclusive orders, before a largely passive audience, popular participation being only one element, albeit a vital one, in these rites.

This is also true of more modern societies. Despite the democratic rhetoric of their polities, national ritual activity is never simply a question of the participation of ordinary citizens. Enacting the nation symbolically is not on a par with popular national discourse or national preferences (i.e. with 'talking' about or 'consuming' the nation). It is at once more elaborate, more collective, more impersonal and abstract, with prescribed forms, liturgies and choreographies that are iterated at regular intervals and handed down the generations, in these respects not unlike those that are familiar from earlier religious traditions.

There are many kinds of ritual activity. But, as far as national rites are concerned, two are especially significant: celebratory and commemorative rites. The first type includes celebrations by members of the foundation of the nation, the giving of its constitution, conversion to its state religion, and the renewal of the nation through social and political revolution. Typically, flags will be flown, anthems sung, parades and processions held, with holidays given for all citizens and schools closed. Flags, anthems and processions also mark the second type, in which members commemorate the sacrifice of those who fell in battles fought on behalf of the national community. But, given the difference in purpose, the rituals of commemoration take place only at specified places – tombs, cenotaphs, monuments and cemeteries – and the music, liturgy and choreography reflect the solemnity and pathos of a rite of national mourning. Of course, the number of those who actually participate in national rituals, including the involved and supporting onlookers, can only constitute a fraction of the total population of any national community, though to these we need to add the many thousands, sometimes even millions, who follow the rituals on radio or television, or who read about them in the press.[4]

The immediate question is: what is the relationship between these participants (actual and supporting), the tradition (with its liturgy and choreography), and the organizers of these national rites and ceremonies? For there are always organizers, and to forget or exclude them would be an error as serious as the opposite one of focusing only on their role. This is the case even with what Erica Fischer-Lichte (2005: chapters 4–6) in her brilliant analysis of twentieth-century ritual and drama, describes as 'self-organised and organising' ritualized performances that spring from immediate social and political concerns; her examples include the workers' dramas in Russia immediately after the October Revolution, the popular German Thingspiel dramas of the early 1930s, which Goebbels absorbed and coordinated, and the Zionist political dramas in America in the 1930s and 1940s. In these cases, there were no official leaders or scripts, yet even here the popular actions required stage directions, some sequential notes for action and considerable choreographed expressive movement; and hence some kind of self-proclaimed producers. The result was a combination of ritual with dramatic performance that aimed not to entertain, but to involve everyone present in the reproduction and rehearsal of immediate political situations.

The relevance, even similarity, of these ritualized dramas to the celebratory rites of nations should be clear. But there are also some important differences. In the case of national rites, the role of ideologues is crucial. Not only do they often supply the liturgies, but they may also provide the decor, accessories and choreography of the ritualized drama. A second difference is the role of institutions, especially the church and the state. Already in the ancient world, priesthoods and temples played a major role in such ritual festivities as the great New Year celebrations in Mesopotamia and Persia, just as the college of priests supervised Roman festivals and secular state authorities such as the senate organized Roman triumphs. The same holds for the Middle Ages, where the Catholic and Orthodox Churches staged public festivals, and their leaders anointed and crowned kings in often elaborate ceremonies. Equally important were such secular rituals as the Royal Entry of the French kings into Paris and the installation of new members into chivalric orders or communal associations. As we saw from the latter, ordinary members of the community were excluded; in the other examples I have cited, the 'populace' was an indispensable, if often passive, part of the ritual.[5]

The French model

The rites of nations simply take this popular involvement further by assigning 'the people' a specific ideological role as 'the nation'. We see this first in the Dutch commemorations of the seige of Leiden by the Spanish forces in 1574, where the city folk were eulogized as heroes of Leiden, but also as patriots of a putative Dutch nation, God's chosen people, in righteous revolt against the Spanish oppressors. As the Spanish armies ravaged the country, such examples of dual urban and national patriotism multiplied, and were increasingly undergirded by the Calvinist equation of the Netherlands with the children of Israel in their exodus from the Egyptian oppressor. In these Dutch rituals of civic and national commemoration, ideologues in the form of predikants and rhetoricians played a significant role; but equally important were the activities of civic authorities and the urban populace, as we can see from the coinage with its biblical parallels, the prayer days and bible-themed floats that they organized (see Gorski, 2000; Schama, 1987: chapter 2).

A similar combination can be discerned in the great *fêtes* of the French Revolution. Here, we encounter both kinds of ritual. The first, the Fête de la Fédération of July 1790, though it commemorated the fall of the Bastille a year earlier, was mainly celebratory. On the Champs de Mars, before a crowd of 400,000, some 50,000 National Guards, along with representatives of the Paris Commune, delegates of the departments and members of the National Assembly participated in the ceremony of Mass and the Benediction at the 'Altar of the Fatherland' presided over by Talleyrand, who intoned: 'Sing and weep tears of joy, for on this day France has been made anew'. Then Lafayette, on a white charger, asked the king's permission to administer the oath to the assembled *fédérés*, and was answered by a thunderous chorus of '*je le jure*', followed by a volley of cannon (Schama, 1989: 507–11).

The next great ceremony, a year later, was a private initiative by a citizen of Sellières where Voltaire's remains lay, requesting that they be transported to Paris to be reinterred in Soufflot's church of St Geneviève, which had been recently converted into the Panthéon, the new mausoleum for France's illustrious dead. A watercolour by Francois Lagrenée the Younger, *The Transportation of Voltaire's Last Remains to the Panthéon* (1791), shows the funeral procession of 11 July 1791 approaching the Panthéon, flanked by mounted guardsmen. The gilded chariot bearing the sarcophagus over which a winged victory stands guard, all in antique Roman style, was designed by Jacques Celerier, who also supplied the Roman tunics and togas of those who accompanied it. Ideologically, the *mise en scène* underlined two propositions: that the Revolution was the fulfilment of the Enlightenment, with its promise of liberty, reason and a better future, and that the cult of the great man who embodied these ideals was the Revolution's answer to absolute monarchy, with its cult of a Royal Entry.[6]

On that occasion, the private initiative had been taken over by the state authorities. The funeral of Marat in 1793, on the other hand, was left in the hands of the Cordeliers Club (see Schama, 1989: 741–6). They commissioned Jacques-Louis David to organize the funeral and arrange for Marat's body to be embalmed; but due to its decomposition in the July heat, it could only be displayed briefly in the church of the Cordeliers. Thereafter, a procession followed his bier through the streets to the garden of the club, where it was buried in a rocky grotto, while his separately embalmed heart was placed in an agate urn and suspended from the ceiling of their meeting hall, an immortal witness and invisible critic of all their debates. The parallel with the slain and risen Jesus was plain, the Cordelier Morel intoning: 'O heart of Jesus, heart of Marat. O heart of Marat, sacré coeur'. The point was made even more clearly in David's famous painting, *The Death of Marat* (1793), which combined the shocking reportage of a contemporary murder with a secularized pietà, though one fit for a revolutionary hero and friend of the people, with the body of the latter-day saint surrounded by his sacred accessories set against a vast dark void.[7]

Perhaps because of the speed of events, this ritual could not be organized or supervised by the state authorities; it was left to the club and the Paris sections. The Festival of the Supreme Being, in contrast, celebrated on 8 June 1794, was from start to finish the product of the highest state authorities, the Committee of Public Safety and, in particular, of Robespierre himself, whose brainchild it was. Two thousand four hundred delegates from the Paris sections, divided into old men, mothers, young girls, boys and small children, sang antiphonal choruses with the mass audience, and thereafter in unison for the Hymn of the Supreme Being. Robespierre then appeared to burn the effigy of atheism and reveal the statue of wisdom. In the afternoon, a grand parade headed for the Champs de Mars, with a triumphal car drawn by eight oxen, their horns painted gold, and bearing a printing press and a plough, examples of officially approved labour. In the Champs de Mars, David had built a huge plaster-and-cardboard mountain topped by a colossal statue of Hercules, representing the French people, on a 50-foot column. To Gossec's music, the deputies of the convention, garlanded in flowers, ascended to the top of the mountain, and at the climax Robespierre himself descended from the mountain like a latter-day Jacobin Moses. Not seven weeks later, he was guillotined (see Herbert, 1972; Schama, 1989: 831–6).

These revolutionary French examples illuminate some more general points. The first is historical. Whether as a result of French military power, especially under Napoleon, or her cultural hegemony, the French models profoundly influenced subsequent European rites of national celebration. In Germany, the celebrations at the Wartburg castle in 1817 and at Hambach in 1832 drew on French models, both in their general spirit of national renewal and in the specifics of choreography, with processions, oaths, speeches, hymns, etc. Similarly, the sescentennial Swiss celebrations of 1 August 1891, which commemorated the foundational Oath of the Rütli in 1291, and were initially the project of Bernese citizens, displayed massed choirs, banners, orations and anthems at Schwyz and on the Rütli meadow organized by the state in the service of a quest for national renewal.[8]

Second, as these examples indicate, the conduct of the ritual was just as important as any literary text, if not more so. For it was in and through the well-rehearsed choreography that both participants and onlookers were enabled to 'feel the nation'. This is not just a matter of numbers, important as that is. It is even more a result of the physical involvement and the excitement of the atmosphere generated by the contrasting and interlocking movements of members and citizens – the self-same atmosphere that Max Reinhardt sought to generate in his great people's dramas in early twentieth-century Germany (see Fischer-Lichte, 2005: chapter 2). This is true even in the case of the more sombre commemorative rites, which combine mourning with dedication and hope. I will return to these shortly.

Third, in none of these cases can we speak simply of symbolic enactment of the nation by ordinary people. To begin with, most of these national rituals were state-sponsored; or, if not, they were organized by particular cities, clubs or associations. Moreover, they were initiated, for the most part, by groups with particular interests in the ideals that they enacted, whether these be politicians, ideologues or leaders of veterans' associations. As to the role of ordinary citizens, it was one of participation, active or passive, as organized groups in a ritual drama prescribed by state or other elites. There was no role for the individual citizen, ordinary or not, but only for the leaders and the organized or self-organizing 'masses'. This is quite different from their other everyday roles as consumers or voters or commentators of the nation.

There is a further issue. National rites presuppose some kind of national history, be it feudal and monarchical or imperial and colonial, if the community is to be celebrated and renewed as a 'nation'. Even recent 'independence days' and 'constitution days' presuppose their opposites, the days of oppression, subjection and dictatorship. In other words, as Benedict Anderson (1991) points out, the nation has a specific trajectory, which the rituals presuppose. This is true even of the revolutionary French case: Robespierre and his associates were continually inveighing against the long history of tyranny in France and the threat, real or imaginary, that it continued to pose. Hence, it is not just the role of elites that we must consider, but we must also take into account the pre-existing freight of national history, its memories, traditions, symbols and values, if we want to assess how far national rites can help to forge, or at least refashion, the nation.[9]

Commemorative rites

The French model, choreographic participation, the importance of institutions (notably the state), a presupposed national history: all these are even more prominent and pervasive in national rites of commemoration. Commemorative rituals have a long history; we have only to recall the memorial services for the dead or for ancestors in many religions, as well as secular rites of commemoration in ancient Greece and in imperial Rome, the best-known example being Pericles' oration to his fellow Athenians on the first anniversary of the Peloponnesian War. Specifically, *national* commemorations are first found in the Netherlands in the early 1600s, especially in relation to William of Orange, the *Pater Patriae*. His tomb in the Nieuwe Kerk in Delft was designed by Hendrik de Keyser and erected in 1614–20 by the States General to accommodate the great throng of pilgrims to William's grave since his assassination in 1584. The marble figure of the prince is shown calm and recumbent, with a bronze figure of fame at his feet, and it is enclosed by a decorated Renaissance pavilion with bronze statues of the cardinal virtues at each corner.[10]

Subsequent rituals focused on military leaders and geniuses, who, over the next two centuries, were increasingly identified by their participants and spectators with the nation and its fortunes. In Britain, in a long line of generals commemorated in Westminster Abbey, Wolfe and Nelson stand out, the first because his victory at Quebec caught the public imagination and spawned a number of paintings, along with the tomb by Wilton, notably Benjamin West's *Death of Wolfe* (1770), itself a carefully staged record of a national sacrifice with strong overtones of a pietà (see Abrams, 1986: chapter 8; Bonehill and Quilley, 2005). The funeral of Admiral Nelson in St Paul's in 1806 was a colossal act of triumphant mourning, and it also inspired several paintings of Nelson's last moments on HMS *Victory* (see Hoock, 2010: 184–7).

Not to be outdone, the French, as we saw, interred their great men and martyrs with all the requisite pomp and ceremony. They even dedicated a temple, Aux Grand Hommes La Patrie Reconnaissante, which is the inscription on the pediment of the Panthéon, where Voltaire's remains had been reburied, and was to become the last resting place for many of France's heroes and geniuses. But, if St Paul's crypt housed the grand tombs of Nelson and Wellington, it was to an enormous circular hall at the base of the Invalides that Napoleon's remains were transferred and interred. Though it was not the only, let alone universally approved, cult in France – that of Joan of Arc was to become equally popular, especially in Orléans – in many ways, it marked the apotheosis of the cult of the charismatic hero who had ostensibly fought and died for France.[11]

But, by then, the era of the great man, and the cult of the hero, was waning. With the middle and the working classes enrolled in their masses into the armies of the nations and subsequently enfranchised as citizens, the nature of war changed forever. The Great War unleashed the full destructive power of modern military technology and put to the test the newly forged national ideal of solidarity. With the dissolution of states in the East, and fear of class conflict in the West, the ruling classes were rapidly persuaded to recognize the massive sacrifices of 'the people' in the war and sanction popular demands for local and national monuments and rituals of national commemoration.[12]

What, exactly, did these popular national rituals commemorate? In France, from 1919, the remembrance ceremony for the fallen in the Great War, and subsequently the Second World War and other wars, was conjoined to the festivities of Bastille Day. 14 July, therefore, saw both a commemorative rite for the war dead, the fallen soldiery of the nation, held first at the Tomb of the Unknown Warrior beneath the Arc de Triomphe, where a flame was lit in their memory, followed by a military parade down the Champs-Élysées to the Place de la Concorde, where the President of the Republic took the salute at the march past of the army. Outside Paris, similar remembrance ceremonies are held, followed by celebrations and festivities under the ubiquitous *tricolor*, with the singing of the Marseillaise and with dancing and fireworks in many town and village squares. The French case, therefore, combines both kinds of ritual activity, the commemorative and the celebratory, the sacrificial and the regenerative. If, in Paris, the national rites are organized by the full panoply of the state, across France it is the *mairie* and its officials that lay on the locally based national rites, but the local populace participates fully and takes possession of the celebrations. Moreover, unlike the pilgrimages to the tombs of heroes that, like those to saints in the Middle Ages, are optional, fluid and a matter for the individual alone, the national rites for the war dead and the celebrations thereafter are forever calendrically fixed and annually iterated collective rituals, which take place irrespective of the wishes and sentiments of individual citizens. For it is the continued existence of the 'nation' that the rites rehearse, its ceaseless death and rebirth, its unmatched capacity for suffering and regeneration.[13]

We find rather more sombre versions of these commemorative rites in Australia and Britain. ANZAC Day (25 April), the day when the Australian and New Zealand Army Corps landed at Gallipoli in the Dardanelles in 1915, is commemorated in services at the various war memorials in towns and cities, and especially at the main war memorial in Canberra, constructed from 1928 to 1941, which Bruce Kapferer (1988: part II) describes as Mesopotamian in inspiration, reflecting the originary, primordial quality of ANZAC symbolism. In the lancet windows of the central Hall of Memory, we can see the main egalitarian qualities of self-reliant 'mateship' that formed the national ideal of Australian manhood: coolness (in action), control (of self), audacity, endurance and decision. The landings themselves proved to be a ghastly failure: 10,000 soldiers were killed and 20,000 wounded before the inevitable withdrawal the following December. Horror at the waste of life in war, coupled with pride in the comradeship, endurance and perseverance of the soldiers, are reflected in the simple, egalitarian and participatory rites: the dawn services organized by the Returned Services League, followed by silences and wreath-laying, and thereafter social gatherings with much drinking in clubs and hotels.

In a society that combines hierarchy with democracy, British commemorative rites are characterized by a duality of the official and the popular. Interestingly, there were no British popular celebratory or commemorative national rites before the twentieth century; they tended to be subsumed under the coronation and funerary ceremonies of the monarchy. Attempts to celebrate St George's Day have met with little success. It was the trauma of the Great War that called forth a commensurate response in the form of the Remembrance Day ceremonies fixed on the Sunday in November nearest to Armistice Day and organized by the British Legion. Stemming from a victory parade in 1919 at a hastily erected catafalque in Whitehall, in response to popular pressure, the rites consist of three parts. The first was the selection and reburial, with trench helmet and khakhi belt, and a Crusader sword, of the Unknown Warrior in Westminster Abbey, in the presence of the king and dignitaries of the land, on the same day in 1920 as his French counterpart. The second was the monument and its setting. As George Mosse (1975: chapter 3; 1991) emphasized in his study of German commemorative monuments, the choreography of the citizen masses required large spaces; hence, the positioning of Lutyens' Cenotaph in the middle of the broad thoroughfare of Whitehall. Unveiled in 1920, partly to channel public discontent, by popular acclaim it was made permanent, as were the rites that were conducted beneath it.

The Cenotaph is in Lutyens' 'elemental mode', an austere, strictly geometrical, ecumenical and abstract 'empty tomb', a tomb for no one and for everyone; on it is inscribed simply 'The Glorious Dead'. While neither Christian nor overtly patriotic (Lutyens himself was a pantheist), the Cenotaph is able to convey the timeless presence and all-encompassing nature of death in war. Of its minimalist simplicity, Jay Winter writes:

> It says so much because it says so little. It is a form on which anyone could inscribe his or her own thoughts, reveries, sadnesses. It became a place of pilgrimage, and managed to transform the commemorative landscape by making all of 'official' London into an imagined cemetery.
>
> (Winter, 1995: 104)

The ceremony over which the Cenotaph presides and which is watched by the array of spectators in Whitehall but also by millions on television, is suffused with Christian symbolism, especially in its first 'official' part. As the populace assembles, massed bands play stirring and solemn marches and classical excerpts such as Elgar's *Nimrod*, Purcell's *Dido's Lament* and Beethoven's *Funeral March*. This is followed by a two-minute silence at the eleventh hour; gun salutes; wreath-laying by the monarch, royal family and politicians on behalf of the nation; a solemn Christian service; and finally reveille, in a carefully choreographed sequence of movements. Thereafter, the mood changes. As the official parties leave, solemnity gives way to proud, even joyful, camaraderie. The band plays popular songs and marches, and regiments of ex-servicemen and -women march briskly past the Cenotaph, saluting as they pass, as they recall the bravery and equality in death of their dead comrades. Clearly, this is a more personal part of the ceremony, as grief at the loss of so many friends and family and horror at the senseless waste of human life are mingled with devotion to their memory and pride in their courage and self-sacrifice.[14]

Elite design and popular participation

It must be apparent from the above descriptions of national rituals that the participation of ordinary citizens was often crucial to their significance and performance, at least until the Second World War. But, in view of more recent changes in the 'mass' reception of elite-organized national performances and rituals, debate has recently centred on whether we should be focusing on the attitudes and sentiments of ordinary citizens, and the ways in which they engage every day in national issues, including national rites and ceremonies, rather than the national projects and designs of the elites. This was, in fact, the subject of an earlier exchange between Jon Fox and Cynthia Miller-Idriss and myself (Fox and Miller-Idriss, 2008; Smith, 2008).

In his contribution to this book, Fox continues that discussion by focusing on the different kinds of response of ordinary citizens, in particular the indifference to organized rituals that is so often found in contemporary Western societies. This is not, he contends, a question of bad design by the elites, the organizers of the rituals, or a failure of audience resonance or 'reception', but a more fundamental problem of apathy and cynicism among the majority of the nation's members, the 'people' who are the ostensible object of national rituals. Whereas previous scholarship had, for the most part, adopted an elite perspective, a 'view from above', the alternative 'view from below' espoused by the study of 'everyday nationhood' reveals a very different, even contrasting, picture of the lack of popular participation or interest in national rituals, insofar as we can establish this.[15]

Part of the disjunction in findings on popular participation between the two approaches may be put down to the impact of the Second World War. Unlike the First World War, the Second World War produced a widespread physical and psychological exhaustion, which, for a time, restrained earlier strong national sentiments and nationalist movements, and produced a world-weary cynicism among many people in Western states, coupled with anxiety over the new threat of Soviet communism. In this context, economic survival and liberal democracy trumped nationalism, encouraging greater individualism and scepticism towards state-inspired national rituals.

But there has been one important exception to this trend. There has been no noticeable decline in popular respect and participation in national *commemorative* rites. Wherever large numbers of nationals have been killed defending their countries, from America and Russia to Australia and Israel, annual commemorative rites have flourished and, with them, an often solemn and sorrowful respect on the part of many co-nationals (Winter and Sivan, 2000). The spate of national memorials and monuments, and the recurrent ceremonies performed in their presence, bear ample testimony to this phenomenon. Hence, the findings of theorists of 'everyday nationhood' about considerable popular indifference to national *holidays* must be treated with caution when applied to national *remembrance days*. For we are dealing here not simply with acts of national celebration, but with the impact of often large-scale national *sacrifice*, and, as Ernest Renan observed:

> The nation, like the individual, is the culmination of a long past of endeav-ours, sacrifice, and devotion . . . Where national memories are concerned, griefs are of more value than triumphs, for they impose duties, and require a common effort. A nation is therefore a large-scale solidarity, constituted by the feeling of the sacrifices one has made in the past and of those one is prepared to make in the future.
>
> (cited in Bhabha, 1990: 19)

Without subscribing to Renan's definition of the concept of the nation, we may nevertheless agree with his emphasis not only on national sacrifices, but on their cumulation over generations, and hence with the vital role of history and historical context in shaping the nation and its rituals. This suggests that the study of 'everyday nationhood' – the cultural practices of ordinary citizens in talking about, consuming, voting and symbolically enacting the nation – must be complemented by that of 'historic nationhood' – the historical developments in culture, politics and society that have shaped particular national communities across generations, and in particular the shared memories, myths, symbols and traditions of those communities. In this way, the view 'from above' and that 'from below' can be brought together to form a richer and more nuanced understanding of nations and their sacrificial rituals.

The functions of national rituals

But key questions remain: rituals of sacrifice for whom, or for what? For family and friends? For the succeeding generations? For the 'nation'? Whatever the motivations of the participants, does not the 'nation' recurrently demand the ultimate sacrifice of a proportion of its members, as some authors claim? Given their lack of choice in both world wars, there is considerable plausibility in this view. But to what end? Do the members of the nation imagine that they can only survive as a national community on the basis of periodic self-sacrifice of some of their own? And, therefore, that war is not only the great test of national survival, but actually its ultimate guarantor? And would this, in turn, help to explain the strength and persistence of national rites of commemoration? If so, what of the other, more celebratory kinds of ritual? Have they lost their function, or must they be conjoined to commemorative rites, as the French have seen fit, in order to survive?[16]

I have no doubt that, in the past, war played a major role in forging, and reforging, nations, and that the war experience, as I said, has inspired the many monuments to the fallen in numerous countries from Russia (Merridale, 2001) to Israel (Sivan, 2000), with the most intense and widely respected, as well as the most poignant, national rituals being those that commemorate the sacrifice of fallen soldiers in a national context (see Hutchinson, 2007). But this can only be a partial explanation. In today's world, though violence and warfare remain endemic, wars are neither so vast in scale nor so widespread in extent as previously, and, among democracies at least, war has become highly unlikely, if not altogether unthinkable. But what of ritual activities? Why have they persisted? Part of the answer must lie with the role of an ever more intrusive state. Whatever may happen locally, the great central rites and ceremonies are calendrically established and willed into being by state elites, often with and through the agency of veterans' associations. As a result, in today's large-scale societies, we can never divorce the ritual activity of individual citizens from state supervision and the agency of elites.

But there are other reasons for the persistence and role of national rites of celebration and commemoration. Let me conclude by suggesting three of them. The first is iteration. Unlike coronations or funerals of great individuals, which bring the members of a national community together for a brief period, and never again, national rites of celebration and commemoration are repeated at regular intervals, usually annually, and they become a fixture in the national calendar, overriding, at least in theory, other diurnal activities, much like the sacred festivals of the great religions. Moreover, they tend to preserve, at least in outline, their original form. There may, of course, be additions and amendments to the ceremonies as national circumstances dictate. But, essentially, their liturgies and choreographies remain the same; and this perennial sameness, this regularity of form, this consistent repetition is, once it is popularly approved, part of their continuing appeal. So, unlike a secular mass performance, which may unite an audience and create solidarity through a kind of emotional and physical involvement, but which is always dissipated at the end of the performance (Fischer-Lichte, 2005: chapter 1), fixed ritual activity remains part of the national landscape of expectations and serves as a taken-for-granted anchor for sacred national values and traditions.

A second reason lies in the narrative drama rehearsed by the ritual activity. I say 'rehearsed' rather than 'performed' not only because of the theatrical connotations of the term 'performance' as entertainment, but to stress the abstract, impersonal, even sacred nature of this kind of ritual drama. It is one that is conducted largely through choreography, symbolism and atmosphere. The French may not storm the Bastille or defend Verdun again, nor do the British re-enact Paesschendale or Dunkirk. But the ritual dramas bring to mind once again the memories and values of grief and sacrifice, comradeship and freedom, that were so much in evidence in these moments of crisis, and through them the narrative of the events that inspired them. Like Lutyens's monument, the impersonal and abstract nature of the ritual drama, and its symbolic, allusive quality, encourages individual memories to resurface and attach themselves to the larger sacred narrative of the national community as rehearsed by the rites and ceremonies. From this standpoint, it matters little that their forms were initiated by state or other elites, but only that they provide through the narrative drama they rehearse a receptacle, a vessel, for the private memories, the grief and the pride of families and individuals, the citizens of the national communion.

Finally, there is the twofold role of art. The first is its ability to make the abstract national ideals rehearsed by the rituals appear accessible and 'real'. The second is its capacity for preserving the memory of national sacrifice through iconic images. For, unlike music and literature, which must be played or read over a period of time, the visual arts can provide once-for-all, memorable images that encapsulate seemingly authentic narratives of events and personages, such as Benjamin West's depiction of the dying Wolfe or David's of the slain Marat. As far as the translation of abstract ideals into palpable images is concerned, artists have been employed in designing and staging celebratory or commemorative rites and ceremonies even before the French Revolution, including the processions, banners, triumphal arches, floats, etc. that make up a large part of national rituals. They have also designed the monumental sacred buildings for heroes and organized the spaces in which to 'realize' the nation in set pieces of mass physical movement. In these ways, they bring home to the massed individuals the 'actuality of the nation' and its vibrant physical presence, thereby helping to forge it in their minds and in their hearts each time anew.[17]

As to their role in the preservation of memories, artists have been able to create images that teach morality by embodying the hero or heroine and their *exempla virtutis*, and to evoke a distinctive atmosphere though 'authentic' locations and settings. The embodied memories of the sacrifice of a Leonidas, a Regulus, a Joan of Arc or a Wolfe can thus be made to stand for the whole community as precursors and models of the self-sacrifice its members must make as much as of the perennial renewal and national regeneration they can expect. Such was the message of literally physical regeneration that Stanley Spencer, who served as a voluntary orderly on the Macedonian Front in 1917, conjured in his great *Crucifixion* (1928–32) in Sandham Chapel, Burghclere (see Bell, 1980: 96–113). Here, it is not the resurrection of Christ, an important but diminutive figure in the background, that is at stake, but of all the soldiers who perished in the Great War who are shown bringing their crosses with them as they rise up from the dead in a vision of hope of immortality. It is in ways such as these that artists preserve the narrative drama of the national rites long after the processions have ceased and the flags are taken down.[18]

Conclusion

In a brief review such as this, I have only been able to touch on some aspects of the role of national rites and ceremonies in the forging, or better reforging, of nations. From such a review, I hope that I have clarified why it is necessary to combine the roles of elites with those of ordinary citizens, and relate the study of everyday nationhood to that of historic nationhood, at least in the investigation of the role of national rites and ceremonies in the forging of nations. If I have stressed the latter's quasi-autonomous role, and their sacred, abstract and impersonal regularity, it is not to deny the indispensable role of the citizens who rehearse them, but rather to highlight their intergenerational persistence and their capacity for inspiring, if not national solidarity, then at least a measure of national continuity and consciousness, even in periods of rapid change. How far such continuity and consciousness are likely to characterize nations well into the twenty-first century as future generations are farther removed from the events that gave rise to the rituals in the first place, it is impossible to tell. All we can say is that if the decline of nations will spell the demise of national rites, so equally the withering of national rites will announce the decay of nations. But, as of now, neither is in sight, and we are likely instead to witness the continued power of national rites to reforge the communion of the nation and rehearse and inspire the national drama of its 'timeless' trajectory.

Notes

1 On historical recreations, see Smith (2011); see also Hobsbawm and Ranger (1983: introduction and chapter 7).
2 See Peel (1989) on 'blocking presentism'. On myths, memories and symbols of ethnic communities, see Smith (1986).
3 On the Great Dionysia in ancient Athens, see Easterling and Muir (1985: 115–27).
4 On flags, waved and unwaved, see Billig (1995) and Elgenius (2011).
5 On ancient Mesopotamian rituals, see Frankfort (1948). For the royal rituals of medieval France, see Beaune (1991) and Le Goff (1998).

6 For details of the procession and chariot of Voltaire, see Reichardt and Kohle (2008: chapter 1).
7 On David's painting, see the essays in Vaughan and Weston (2000).
8 For the German celebrations, see Mosse (1975: chapter 3); the Swiss anniversary and its background are described by Kreis (1991).
9 For Robespierre, see the biography by Scurr (2006).
10 On William's Tomb, see Slive (1995: 268–9, with the painting of it in 1650 by Gerard Houckgeest).
11 On the Panthéon, see Ozouf (1998). For the cults of Napoleon Bonaparte, see Gildea (1994: 89–111). For the cult of Joan of Arc, see Nora (1996–8, vol. 3: 433–80).
12 For the circumstances surrounding the first commemorations of the Great War, see Mosse (1991); also Winter (1995, especially chapter 4).
13 For the Bastille Day celebrations, see Elgenius (2011: 104–12).
14 See the fuller description in Smith (2003: Chapter 9).
15 See also the questions raised by Elgenius (2011: 25–6) and by Uzelac (2010). For an extended set of studies of everyday nationhood from the 'view from below', see Edensor (2002).
16 For this thesis, see Marvin and Ingle (1999).
17 For the nation as a sacred communion, see Smith (2003; 2013: chapter 6). On national commemorations, see Gillis (1994).
18 For Stanley Spencer's *Crucifixion* (1928–32) at Burghclere chapel, see Bell (1980).

References

Abrams, A. U. (1986) *The Valiant Hero: Benjamin West and Grand-Style History Painting*, Washington, DC: Smithsonian Institution Press.
Anderson, B. (1991) *Imagined Communities: Reflections on The Origin and Spread of Nationalism*, 2nd edn, London: Verso.
Beaune, C. (1991) *The Birth of an Ideology: Myths and Symbols of the Nation in Late Medieval France*, trans. S. Huston, Berkeley, CA: University of California Press.
Bell, K. (ed.) (1980) *Stanley Spencer, R.A.*, London: Weidenfeld & Nicolson.
Bhabha, H. (ed.) (1990) *Nation and Narration*, London and New York: Routledge.
Billig, M. (1995) *Banal Nationalism*, London: Sage.
Bonehill, J. and Quilley, G. (eds) (2005) *Conflicting Visions: War and Visual Culture in Britain and France, c. 1700–1830*, Aldershot: Ashgate.
Durkheim, É. (1915 [1912]) *The Elementary Forms of the Religious Life*, trans. J. W. Swain, London: George Allen & Unwin.
Easterling, P. E. and Muir, J. V. (1985) *Greek Religion and Society*, Cambridge: Cambridge University Press.
Edensor, T. (2002) *National Identity, Popular Culture and Everyday Life*, Oxford and New York: Berg.
Elgenius, G. (2011) *Symbols of Nations and Nationalism: Celebrating Nationhood*, Basingstoke: Palgrave Macmillan.
Fischer-Lichte, E. (2005) *Theatre, Sacrifice, Ritual: Exploring Forms of Political Theatre*, London and New York: Routledge.
Fox, J. and Miller-Idriss, C. (2008) 'Everyday nationhood', *Ethnicities*, 8(4): 536–63, 573–6.
Frankfort, H. (1948) *Kingship and the Gods*, Chicago, IL: University of Chicago Press.
Gildea, R. (1994) *The Past in French History*, New Haven, CT: Yale University Press.
Gillis, J. (ed.) (1994) *Commemorations: The Politics of Identity*, Princeton, NJ: Princeton University Press.
Gorski, P. (2000) 'The mosaic moment: an early modernist critique of modernist theories of nationalism', *American Journal of Sociology*, 105(5): 1428–68.

Herbert, R. (1972) *David, Voltaire, Brutus and the French Revolution*, London: Allen Lane.

Hobsbawm, E. and Ranger, T. (eds) (1983) *The Invention of Tradition*, Cambridge: Cambridge University Press.

Hoock, H. (2010) *Empires of the Imagination: Politics, War and the Arts in the British World, 1750–1850*, London: Profile Books.

Hutchinson, J. (2007) 'Warfare, remembrance and national identity', in A. Leoussi and S. Grosby (eds) *Nationalism and Ethnosymbolism: History, Culture and Ethnicity in the Formation of Nations*, Edinburgh: University of Edinburgh Press, pp. 42–52.

Kapferer, B. (1988) *Legends of People, Myths of State: Violence, Intolerance and Political Culture in Sri Lanka and Australia*, Washington, DC: Smithsonian Institution Press.

Kreis, J. (1991) *Der Mythos von 1291: Zur Enstehung des Schweizerischen Nationalfeiertags*, Basle: Friedrich Reinhardt Verlag.

Le Goff, J. (1998) 'Reims, city of coronation', in P. Nora (ed.) *Realms of Memory: The Construction of the French Past, Vol. 3: Symbols*, New York: Columbia University Press, pp. 193–251.

Marvin, C. and Ingle, D. (1999) *Blood Sacrifice and the Nation: Totem Rituals and the American Flag*, Cambridge: Cambridge University Press.

Merridale, C. (2001) *Night of Stone: Death and Memory in Russia*, London: Granta Books.

Mosse, G. (1975) *The Nationalisation of the Masses: Political Symbolism and Mass Movements in Germany from the Napoleonic Wars through the Third Reich*, Ithaca, NY: Cornell University Press.

Mosse, G. (1991) *Fallen Soldiers*, Oxford: Oxford University Press.

Nora, P. (ed.) (1996–8) *Realms of Memory: The Construction of The French Past*, ed. L. Kritzman, 3 vols, New York: Columbia University Press. [Originally *Les Lieux de Mémoire*, 7 vols, Paris: Gallimard, 1984–92.]

Ozouf, M. (1998) 'The pantheon, the ecole normale of the dead', in P. Nora (ed.) *Realms of Memory: The Construction of the French Past, Vol. 3: Symbols*, New York: Columbia University Press, pp. 325–46.

Peel, J. (1989) 'The cultural work of Yoruba ethno-genesis', in E. Tonkin, M. McDonald and M. Chapman (eds) *History and Ethnicity*, London: Routledge, pp. 198–215.

Reichardt, R. and Kohle, H. (2008) *Visualising the Revolution: Politics and the Pictorial Arts in Late Eighteenth-Century France*, London: Reaktion Books.

Schama, S. (1987) *The Embarrassment of Riches: An Interpretation of Dutch Culture in the Golden Age*, London: William Collins.

Schama, S. (1989) *Citizens: A Chronicle of the French Revolution*, New York: Knopf.

Scurr, R. (2006) *Fatal Purity: Robespierre and the French Revolution*, London: Chatto & Windus.

Sivan, E. (2000) 'Private pain and public remembrance in Israel', in J. Winter and E. Sivan (eds) *War and Remembrance in the Twentieth Century*, Cambridge: Cambridge University Press, pp. 177–204.

Slive, S. (1995) *Dutch Painting, 1600–1800*, New Haven, CT: Yale University Press.

Smith, A. D. (1986) *The Ethnic Origins of Nations*, Oxford: Blackwell.

Smith, A. D. (2003) *Chosen Peoples: Sacred Sources of National Identity*, Oxford: Oxford University Press.

Smith, A. D. (2008) 'The limits of everyday nationhood', *Ethnicities*, 8(4): 563–73.

Smith, A. D. (2011) 'National identity and vernacular mobilisation in Europe', *Nations and Nationalism*, 17(2): 223–56.

Smith, A. D. (2013) *The Nation Made Real: Art and National Identity in Western Europe, 1600–1850*, Oxford: Oxford University Press.

Uzelac, G. (2010) 'National ceremonies: the pursuit of authenticity', *Ethnic and Racial Studies*, 33(10): 1718–36.

Vaughan, W. and Weston, H. (eds) (2000) *Jacques-Louis-David's 'Marat'*, Cambridge: Cambridge University Press.

Winter, J. (1995) *Sites of Memory, Sites of Mourning: The Great War in European Cultural History*, Cambridge: Cambridge University Press.

Winter, J. and Sivan, E. (eds) (2000) *War and Remembrance in the Twentieth Century*, Cambridge: Cambridge University Press.

3

NATIONAL HOLIDAY COMMEMORATIONS

The view from below

Jon E. Fox

Introduction

National holiday commemorations have received sustained attention in the scholarship as important sites for the performance and reproduction of national attachments. Through the ritual display and performance of national symbols, holiday commemorations make the nation momentarily visible and tangible for those in attendance; these events become the living embodiment of the nation (see, e.g., Elgenius, 2011; Gillis, 1994; Mosse, 1975; Spillman, 1997; see more generally Durkheim, 1995 [1912]; Kertzer, 1988; Turner, 1969). By definition, such events commemorate the past, a specifically national past (see Chapter 2 of this volume). Historical memory imbues these public performances with depth, legitimacy and authenticity. These events do not happen spontaneously but rather are meticulously contrived to occur at regular intervals to connect the past to the present and the future (see Smith, 2009: 84–6; see also Edensor, 2006: 535–6; West, 2008: 346–9). Holiday commemorations are carefully designed, planned and staged to induce the collective experience of national belonging.

But who cares? That is, who, among the people in whose name these events are performed, actually experience these events in the national terms their elite designers intended? While the scholarship on nationalism has convincingly demonstrated how national holiday commemorations *can* generate national attachments, they have not shown how they *do* generate such attachments. No matter how carefully contrived or deftly executed, however, neither their design nor deployment alone provide a measure of the ways in which such events are received by their intended audiences. Where much of the scholarship on national holiday commemorations begins (and effectively ends) with the elite production of these events, my investigation begins (and, to be fair, also ends) at the other end: with the intended audiences of these events, 'the nation' in the broadest of terms.

Ultimately, these production and consumption perspectives are complementary. But if we are to appreciate the efficacy of production, then we need to consider the perspective of the ordinary people whose attendance – or non-attendance – has the potential to generate all manner of responses (or non-responses). My chapter will thus proceed in two parts. First, I will develop my critique of these top-down perspectives as they are manifested both in the scholarship on nationalism and the scholarship on rituals and performances. This is the view from above. Second, I will then offer my own bottom-up response to this critique: how we might begin our investigation of these events with the ordinary individuals who people them. This is the view from below. My modest contribution to this volume, and to the scholarship on these issues more generally, is to suggest that a different vantage point, that of ordinary people, might lead us to different conclusions about the meaningfulness and efficacy of national holiday commemorations.[1]

The view from above

The scholarship on nationalism has amply shown how national commemorations and holidays contain all the necessary ingredients for generating and reproducing the collective awareness of national belonging (Mosse, 1975; Smith, 1986; Spillman, 1997). Public spaces, adorned with the symbolic accoutrements of the nation – the flags, banners, songs and speeches, not to mention the pantheon of national heroes etched in the plaques, statues and monuments that form the backdrop for such events – provide explicitly national parameters to facilitate the organization and experience of national solidarities (see, e.g., Durkheim, 1995 [1912]: 231–2). These are occasions to remember, celebrate and, to a certain extent, construct a glorious (and glorified) national past, to connect the real, living nation to the mythical historical nation (Hobsbawm, 1983: 4–7; Smith, 1986: 174–83, 191–208). The national symbols displayed and performed at these events are the cultural ciphers through which national meanings and attachments are made (Mosse, 1975: 202–3). Their public performance, ritually enacted and re-enacted at fixed intervals through carefully orchestrated military parades, fireworks displays and other events momentarily fuse the imagined community of the nation into the actual community of the nation (Smith, 2009: 25, 77–8; 2013: 24, 33). With songs sung, chants chanted, banners unfurled and flags waved, all in unison, the bonds that join one another become momentarily visible and audible for all (Durkheim, 1995 [1912]: 231–4; Kertzer, 1988: 8–12, 61–76; Skey, 2006: 146–8, 151–2). Those in attendance can thus be united in the transitory awareness of heightened national cohesion. These are moments of 'hot' nationalism, connecting and spanning the national ennui that otherwise characterizes and undergirds the banality of everyday life (Billig, 1995: 43–6; Hutchinson, 2006: 298; Skey, 2006: 146–8).

For all of its merits, this top-down perspective overlooks two things. First, it does not always give sufficient attention to the diverse intents, agendas and designs of all the people involved in the production side of these events (see Spillman, 1997: 33–56). National holiday commemorations exist not as ideal types, but as sites of contention and debate, ambiguity and ambivalence. Event organizers, political and cultural elites, event designers, sponsors, work crews and the varied participants themselves all bring different understandings of – not to mention vested interests in – the particular meanings that get attached to these events (Elgenius, 2011: 20–2). The outcomes that result are thus not fine-tuned machines of nation-making, but rather a patchwork of contested and negotiated components whose functionality has been compromised long before these events are actually performed (Alexander, 2004: 555–9). Second, the meanings and uses that audiences make of these events cannot be simply inferred from the intentions, contested or not, of their elite designs (Fenton, 2007: 322–7; Whitmeyer, 2002; see also Özkirimli, 2003: 346–51; Thompson, 2001: 25–7; Uzelac, 2010: 1720–2, 1725). No matter how carefully designed or skilfully executed, the people who ultimately determine the success of these events are not their elite producers, but rather their ordinary consumers (see Hutchinson, 2006: 299).

I am not the only one to make this critique; nor am I the only one to answer it. Indeed, parallel to (but rarely in dialogue with) the scholarship on nationalism, we find a longstanding anthropological tradition, more recently picked up by cultural sociologists, that focuses on rituals and performances (Alexander, 2004; Durkheim, 1995 [1912]; Kertzer, 1988; Lukes, 1975; Turner, 1969). These accounts view rituals as important for the integrative function they serve, uniting (momentarily) otherwise atomistic individuals. As such, these perspectives are very much interested in the question of audiences and, more specifically, audience reception. Indeed, from this view, performances are successful if and only if they bind people together. This requires a good bit of help on the production side of things, but success depends ultimately on consumption. Indeed, audience reception is the *sine qua non* of successful rituals.

From this view, the audience is not simply constituted by these events, but it is a problem that needs to be overcome (Alexander, 2004: 550, 562–5). This is because audiences in the modern world are taught to be critical, reflexive and even cynical; they are thus prone *not* to reception, but to rejection (ibid.: 531, 544–5; see also Etzioni, 2000: 49; Lukes, 1975: 299–301). Most performances are therefore doomed to failure. Audiences bear witness, they even understand, comprehend what is presented to them, but they are most often unmoved and unpersuaded, and therefore unconstituted as an audience. That elusive fusion, that unity that is the hallmark of a successful performance, is seldom achieved.

This central emphasis on audiences that we find in this scholarship on rituals and performances offers an important corrective to some of the assumptions built into the scholarship on nationalism. But both perspectives are still top-heavy: they explicitly or implicitly privilege the elite designs and formal properties of the productions themselves (see, e.g., Hearn, 2007: 658–9 for a related critique). Inherent in the logic of audiences found in the scholarship on rituals and performances is this notion of reception. Audiences appear as a receptacle; they are on the receiving end of performances. As a receptacle, they are capable of doing many things: they may mix those messages up; they may conjure up new meanings and interpretations; they may therefore be critical, reflexive, even cynical; they may even ignore those messages. But, in some sense, they are still attuned to, or at least orientated to, the messages being delivered to them, poised to receive (or reject) them. The audience may hold the key to unlocking the success of these events, but it is elite producers who hold the key to unlocking the success of the audience's reception. It is thus the formal properties of the production side of these events (along with the actions of the people involved in production) that ultimately determine their efficacy (Alexander, 2004: 562–3, 566). Indeed, even the audience's critical engagement is sometimes outsourced to the production side, with its army of critics, pundits and analysts whose responsibility it is to interpret and digest these performances for the mainstream public (ibid.: 557–8).

In the language of nationalism, we are thus presented with what might be called a resonance problem (Githens-Mazer, 2008: 41–2; Özkirimli, 2003: 348–50; Smith, 2009: 31–2, 71–2). Do rituals and performances, national commemorations and celebrations work? The scholarship on nationalism assumes that they generally do; the scholarship on rituals and performances assumes that they generally do not. Both interpretations, however, are interpretations of resonance. And this question of resonance is a top-down question, a trickle-down question (though see Smith, 2009: 31, 80, who stresses reciprocity between elites and non-elites). Performances are performed, symbols are displayed, the formal properties of production are all in place. All that remains is to see if it works (Alexander, 2004: 562–3). This, of course, is a valid and important question. But by placing the audience *qua* collective actor at the end of a lengthy production chain, we are foreclosing an equally fruitful examination of the other sorts of things ordinary individuals might be doing that may or may not connect to these events.

If we begin our investigation from the perspective of ordinary people, who may or may not constitute potential audiences, who may or may not stand ready to receive or reject performances, then our findings should be more varied. The ways in which these events are produced should not be taken a priori as an indication of how they are consumed. Indeed, as has been shown in other contexts, there is not infrequently a disjuncture between elite representations of the nation and their everyday uses and understandings (Edensor, 2006: 526; Eriksen, 1993: 6; Handler, 1988: 187–96; Herzfeld, 1997: 10–21; Özkirimli, 2003: 348, 350; Skey, 2009: 342). My aim in this chapter is to invert the analytical focus, to begin with ordinary people not as consumers or even audiences (which still implies a reception disposition, a readiness to receive), but as diverse people without any inherent predisposition for being attuned to these events. By stepping out of the pathways of elite design, new avenues of investigation are opened up to ordinary people who may or may not attend these events, and who do not simply take meanings away from them, but who also generate their own meanings, which are not necessarily national (according to the logic of production), let alone nationalist (Cohen, 1996: 803; Hobsbawm, 1991: 10). This category of ordinary people need not be narrowly confined to 'organized groups' that participate 'in a ritual drama prescribed by state or other elites' (see p. 27 of this volume); rather, the category can and should include those people who do not bother assembling (or even showing up), along with those who do show up but do not partake in state-sponsored ritual dramas. I am thus interested not just in audiences or potential audiences, but in a more expansive category of ordinary people: the passers-by, the tag-alongs, the vendors, the security personnel, not to mention, of course, the activists and enthusiasts. And then there are also the legions of the nation who simply are not there, who simply are not attuned in any sense to these events, who are not facing the music. From a bottom-up perspective, we can then look for the ways people might make connections to these events in a way that does not presuppose or prefigure a logic of connections.

The view from below

In the second part of my chapter, then, I would like to begin to consider what such an investigation might look like, and what it might reveal. I will consider two meanings that ordinary people might attach to events such as national holiday commemorations. The first is what I call mixed messages, and the second is missed messages.[2]

Mixed messages

The meanings that ordinary people attach to these events, to the extent they do so at all, are, in a word, mixed. Symbols are inherently multi-vocal and multivalent; they mean different things to different people at different times (Cerulo, 1995; Eriksen, 2007; Kertzer, 1988; Turner, 1969). While event organizers may have the upper hand in affixing national meanings to the symbols they display, both their meanings and valences remain subject to critical negotiation and reinterpretation by their receiving audiences (Alexander, 2004: 531, 544–5). But these ordinary people are not simply consumers of national meanings; they are simultaneously their contingent producers (see Cohen, 1996: 803). While the meanings attached to symbols have a certain agglutinative quality, they are not too sticky to prevent them from being manipulated for different purposes. National symbols have the potential to convey national meanings, but this potential need not always be realized. Different symbols generate different meanings and different valences for different people. To what extent, then, do Fourth of July celebrations in the United States engender the sort of 'collective effervescence' imagined by Durkheim? Are the principles of *liberté*, *égalité* and *fraternité* experienced and constituted by the ordinary French citizens attending Bastille Day commemorations? These events are designed to generate national attachments, but the symbols they display and perform are subject to varied uses and interpretations: the nationalist passions of the multitudes are not always ignited by the sparks supplied by their elite designers (Elgenius, 2011: 25; Kong and Yeoh, 1997: 234–5).

So what, then, are the possibilities for what ordinary people might make of these events? One possibility, of course, at least theoretically, is that these events *are* successful in some sense: that relatively distinct and bounded audiences are momentarily united in exultation; that the imagined community of the nation becomes momentarily tangible, real, felt, experienced; that the individual is subsumed to the collective; that the nation is momentarily, or even enduringly, constituted. This, indeed, is the outcome that is inferred, and even sometimes predicted, in the scholarship on nationalism. And it is a possibility. But as the scholarship on rituals and performances reminds us, such successes are generally the exception rather than the rule in the modern world.

This is not to suggest that national solidarities are no longer publicly performed. It is to say, however, that perhaps the venue has changed (see Eriksen, 1993). While collective attachments may not be generated so often on the stage of national commemorations, they are frequently produced on the pitch of international sporting competitions. Indeed, in many countries, it is sports, not holidays, that capture the (national) imagination and inspire the (national) passions of the masses (ibid.: 9–11; Hobsbawm, 1991: 143). Shifting the analytical focus from the producers of national symbols to their everyday consumers entails a concomitant search for the sites where those symbols are wielded and manipulated by ordinary people. The international profiles of the World Cup, Olympics and other international sporting competitions provide explicitly national parameters for the organization and experience of collective belonging. As Eric Hobsbawm (1991: 143) observed, 'The imagined community of millions seems more real as a team of eleven named people'. Fans display their loyalties to their team by borrowing the symbolic repertoire of their respective nations – the flags, the anthems, the colours and even the myths. Ordinary people who might otherwise show little interest in their nations are nonetheless capable of displaying their allegiances at sporting competitions with fervour and passion. Indeed, in these and other cases, fans momentarily become the physical embodiment of the nation (Archetti, 1999: 59–70, 170–3). Singing the same songs, chanting the same chants and responding to the rhythms of the competition in Durkheimian unison – with faces painted, flags draped over shoulders, and T-shirts, scarves and jackets emblazoned in the national colours – these fans physically encapsulate and communicate national allegiances (Fox, 2006: 226–7). This is the nationalism that attracts the masses (of testosterone-fuelled young men). And here we have a case where the national meanings connected to these events are generated, for the most part, not by the event organizers, whose interest is in sport, but by the crowds themselves, whose passions are ignited in the first instance not by the nation, but by the match.

Where sports do succeed (and where holiday commemorations often fail) is in bringing about the heightened experience of collective (and perhaps sometimes national) belonging. The drama inherent in sporting competitions (but largely missing from holiday commemorations) is one important factor that helps explain this success (Elias and Dunning, 1986: 40–8; see also Archetti, 1999: 113–27, 175–7; Kertzer, 1988: 39–41, 99–101, 179–81). This drama helps ensure that those in attendance will remain singularly fixated on the action as it unfolds, providing them with a common focus for their synchronized reactions and collective engagement (all conveniently dressed in national colours; see p. 74 of this volume).

But, of course, not all rituals have to induce this sort of collective effervescence to be effective. Some rituals belong more to the realm of the ordinary than the extraordinary. Here, I am thinking of things such as flag ceremonies and school prayers, for instance, which are occasions not for the heightened experience of national belonging, but the veiled reproduction of national sensibilities (Benei, 2008: 38–50). The Pledge of Allegiance that starts the school day in classrooms across the United States relies neither on fireworks nor flamboyance, but rather on the unthinking and unquestioned collective performance of the nation. The daily repetition of this ritualized national text does not – and indeed cannot – inspire the experience of collective effervescence. Nor are such rituals designed to invite critical engagement or even conscious reflection on what the nation means (Kolstø, 2006: 677–8). Rather, its dull, rote repetition, performed mindlessly and dispassionately, is a national genuflection, instilling in the pupils taken-for-granted loyalties to the abstract notion of the nation (Benei, 2008: 24–6; Billig, 1995: 50). Its effectiveness is measured not in moments, but in lifetimes.

Combined, then, this first set of examples we have considered point to ways in which these events work in some sense, insofar as they generate some degree of collective attachment (though the actual degree or intensity of that attachment is obviously variable). But even here, as we have seen, such successes raise as many questions as they answer: for whom are they successful, what is the intensity of the solidarity they generate, and how fleeting or enduring is that solidarity (see Chapter 4 of this volume)? Even more fundamentally, we can reasonably ask what name we can give to that solidarity. The two examples I have just elaborated come with all the national trimmings and trappings, the symbolic repertoire of the nation in full display, its pageantry, its ritualized enactment in song, chant or incantation. But does the explicit national framing of these occasions generate explicitly national experiences of them? Do six-year-olds reciting the national anthem experience in some meaningful sense an abstract allegiance to an abstract symbol of the flag? What meaning does the text have for them? And does dressing up football in the national colours guarantee that it will be experienced by its spectators in the same national terms? Some studies of football fans have shown how at least some fans can and do detach their allegiances to the team from their allegiances to the nation, even when the former is expressed with the help of the symbolic repertoire of the latter (see Abell et al., 2007; Fox, 2006). Indeed, brandishing the flag in a show of support for one's football team is perhaps less of a momentary outburst of nationalist pride than an expression of football fervour, conveniently draped in the national colours. Analyses that focus exclusively on the cultural production of such events are thus unable to adequately attend to the variation in the meanings appropriated, manipulated and constituted by those actually in attendance (Eriksen, 1993: 6).

If our first conceptual possibility is some version of qualified success, our second conceptual possibility then has to be some version of qualified failure (Fox, 2011).

That is, in some sense, these events do not work, at least not in the way their elite designers would have envisioned (see, e.g., Eriksen, 1993: 5–6). To better appreciate this possibility of failure, my view is that we should consider the perspective of the ordinary people who account for failure (see, e.g., Skey, 2011: 100–5). So, it is here that we shift attention away from the enthusiastic flag-wavers and on to the enthusiastic flag-burners (Elgenius, 2011: 91–2), to the passers-by and vendors we introduced earlier, not to mention the garden-partiers (Dennis, 2002: 219–21, 281–2; Skey, 2011: 100–1) or those working at Tesco on national days, and of course to those masses of the nation who opt to exercise their national allegiances via the remote control in front of the television (see Skey, 2006: 149; see also pp. 23, 30 of the present volume). Here, we can then begin to consider a number of different conceptual possibilities for this category of 'failure' (see also Fenton, 2007; Mann and Fenton, 2009).

For one, the national meanings affixed to these events by their elite designers can be explicitly and self-consciously rejected or subverted. If, as Turner (1969) reminds us, rituals lay bare the extant social order, they also offer the potential to manipulate and transform that social order (see also pp. 69–70 this volume). Commemorations and official holiday celebrations thus can and frequently do become sites for protest and struggle, where flag-burning replaces flag-waving, inverting and therefore subverting the cherished symbols of the nation (see, e.g., Van Ginderachter, 2009). At the medal ceremony at the 1968 Olympics in Mexico City, American gold and bronze medallists Tommie Smith and John Carlos lowered their heads and raised their black-gloved fists in a powerful and very public act of defiance when the US national anthem was played. Two decades later, as state socialism's grip on Eastern Europe gradually weakened, mass demonstrations, including a number of officially sanctioned occasions for national commemoration, were transformed from public endorsements of the state's legitimacy into collective challenges to it (Pfaff and Yang, 2001: 53–6). These challenges were visually and audibly marked through the manipulation of official national symbols: holes were cut in the centre of flags in Hungary and Romania in 1989 to rid them of their communist imprint (even though, in the case of Hungary, that imprint had been officially removed 30 years hence), and ritualistic chants of adulation to Nicolae Ceaușescu in an officially orchestrated mass demonstration were overtaken by spontaneous chants of 'down with the dictator'. Indeed, Victor Turner stresses that the ritual process both depends on and produces liminality, thus allowing not only for the collective performance and ratification of the dominant social order, but also its transcendence and inversion, as that social order is laid bare for all to see (Turner, 1969: 96–7, 129). On occasions such as these, national symbols can thus be figuratively or literally inverted to reject the nation and the attachments they encourage (Elgenius, 2011: 65–6; Van Ginderachter, 2009: 65, 69–70). Symbols manufactured to convey national unity are thus capable of constructing national disunity (Kolstø, 2006).

To be sure, instances such as flag desecration or disrespecting the national anthem also suggest the presence of very strong attachments, just not the ones imagined by those supplying the flags or playing the anthems (see, e.g., Jenkins, 2007: 131–3). But many events fail to generate the same intensity of response, either through affiliation or disaffiliation; others generate ambiguous attachments at best (Van Ginderachter, 2009). Whether it is the fault of flawed design, poor execution, or whether it is because today's audiences are simply world-weary and therefore not easily impressed by a run-of-the-mill fireworks display or military parade, many events simply fail to inspire passion, let alone the heightened experience of collective forms of attachment (Alexander, 2004: 544–5).

If we begin our investigation from below, we will discover that even those attending such events engage with them (or not) in multiple ways, each capable of generating (or not) multiple (and not necessarily national) attachments (see Elgenius, 2011: 25; Uzelac, 2010: 1721). People encounter, respond to and negotiate these events in ways that have little to do with how their planners planned them (Eriksen, 1993: 5–7; Kong and Yeoh, 1997: 235–6). For one, many national holiday commemorations become occasions for family outings or consumer spending rather than the explicit public affirmations of national pride (Edensor, 2002: 81–8). Garden parties become occasions for the reaffirmation of ties with family and friends, not necessarily the nation that provided the reason for the occasion (Etzioni, 2000: 51–3; Skey, 2011: 100–1). For others, national holidays are simply synonymous with family holidays, a bit of time off work and perhaps a chance to leave the beloved homeland for a long weekend in warmer climes. And, of course, hordes of holiday shoppers might encounter national symbols that are on display to sell refrigerators and underpants as commodified accessories denuded of their officially sanctioned national venerability (Edensor, 2002: 84–8; Groom, 2007). Here, the nation is on display to spark the impulse of consumer spending, not the impulse of national adulation (see Comaroff and Comaroff, 2009). Still, others might only catch a glimpse of these events on the television before switching back to the match or their favourite reality TV programme. There are thus many ways to celebrate the nation. But the unintended and unanticipated uses of national holiday commemorations just considered call into question their ability to generate the unambiguous experience of national allegiances.

Missed messages

The nation is potentially the largest audience out there. Yet the nation is, of course, never fully realized through national holiday commemorations. The potential audience, the imagined community of the nation, thus never becomes the fully realized audience, the actual community of the nation. And this is simply because large numbers of people, indeed, probably the majority of people who potentially constitute the nation, will simply stay away. They will not go to the events, they will not go to the garden parties organized in the name of their nations, they will not buy the national refrigerators or underpants, and they will not even leave their nations on holidays. Rather, they will simply be unmoved (see pp. 56–7 of this volume; Eriksen, 1993: 6; Jenkins, 2007: 120–1). National holiday commemorations miss their mark. No matter how carefully orchestrated or creatively manipulated, national holidays are designed to engender solidarities for those who engage with them in some way.

For many members of the putative nation, then, these festive occasions are just another day, a day off work, a day *of* work; for many people, these holidays are ordinary days that are not necessarily any more national than any other day (Skey, 2006: 152–3). These are the people for whom national attachments are not and cannot be realized. The problem that rituals and performances face is thus not simply that audiences are informed and thinking, predisposed to reject the messages delivered to them, as some scholars of ritual and performances would have it (Alexander, 2004: 544–5; see also Etzioni, 2000: 49; Lukes, 1975: 299–301). The problem they face is more fundamental, that (potential) audiences are uninformed and unthinking, predisposed to ignore and deflect the messages so carefully packaged and delivered to them.

Several years ago, then Chancellor of the Exchequer Gordon Brown came up with a proposal for a British national holiday commemoration:

> Gordon Brown will propose today that Remembrance Sunday should be developed into a national day of patriotism to celebrate British history, achievements and culture . . . '[W]hat is our Fourth of July? What is our Independence Day? What is our equivalent of a flag in every garden? Perhaps Remembrance Day and Remembrance Sunday are the nearest we have come to a British day – unifying, commemorative, dignified and an expression of British ideas of standing firm for the world in the name of liberty'.
>
> (Wintour, 2006; see also Elgenius, 2011: 25–6).

Gordon Brown's proposal was not successful. But a far greater hurdle his proposal would have encountered, had he secured parliamentary backing for his plan, would likely have been a wall of popular indifference (cf. Skey, 2011: 110–14). Is Britain really ready for a national holiday-type Remembrance Sunday? Does it really want flags in all of its gardens? And, if so, which ones: the BNP's version of the Union Jack, or the football frenzy cum English Defence League Cross of St George? To be sure, traditions at the moment of invention cannot help but appear inauthentic. It is difficult to imagine a new holiday inspiring national passions or even allegiances precisely because of its newness; novelty is the enemy of authenticity (Uzelac, 2010). Such newly invented holidays necessarily appear contrived and inauthentic. But even far more established (invented) traditions still face similar problems of apathy. Established public performances can lose their power to inspire not because their authenticity is questioned, but because they are simply boring to large swaths of their potential audiences (Jenkins, 2007: 120). National holiday commemorations do not always attract the masses of the nation.

Sometimes, for instance, they attract the niche audiences of the nation, the committed: the nationalists and fringe groups, the few, the proud, the pensioners. They are in this sense like certain religious ceremonies, preaching to the converted.

Year in and year out, predictable and ultimately unimaginative variations on national holiday themes are presented to world-weary would-be nationals, inspiring them not to tune in, but to tune out. The problem is not that these people are emotionally unmoved by these events; the problem is that many of them are simply physically unmoved to attend or otherwise engage with these events (Eriksen, 1993: 5). National holiday commemorations are supposed to work because they punctuate the banality of everyday life with contrived occasions for the experience of and celebration of the nation (Edensor, 2006: 531). But their very predictability, their familiar forms, their conventional content can also be their undoing; they do not necessarily punctuate everyday life; rather, they become a part of everyday life, and, as such, are assimilated into the landscape of the ordinary. Unwatched, unnoticed, unremarked upon, many events such as these ultimately miss their mark.

But should this indifference be taken as evidence of nationalism's ineffectiveness, or of nationalism's banality in the modern world? Michael Billig, who popularized the notion of a banal nationalism, one that works not because it is celebrated, but because it is taken for granted, suggests that holidays actually do work: for these brief moments, he argues, the unselfconscious and banal attachment to the nation becomes a self-conscious and affective attachment to the nation (Billig, 1995: 45–6; see also Hutchinson, 2006: 304; Skey, 2006: 146–8). Holidays, for Billig, are not a kind of banal nationalism, but rather its antidote. They are extraordinary moments of national exultation in opposition to the ordinary perpetuity of national banality (see also Skey, 2006). But are they really? Or have national holidays also been subsumed into the banality of everyday life, a taken-for-granted fixture of our national temporalities (Edensor, 2006)? And, if they have been, is our indifference to them a sign of their failure, or the measure of their success? Perhaps these commemorations, like the flags that adorn them, do not inspire or even require displays of adulation to be effective; perhaps they are effective precisely because they do not transport us to Turner's liminality, but rather because they leave us bored, neither deserving nor even seeking our attention (Eriksen, 2007: 8; see also p. 54ff. in the present volume). 'Fixed ritual activity', writes Smith in this volume (p. 33), 'remains part of the national landscape of expectations and serves as a taken-for-granted anchor for sacred national values and traditions.' Interestingly, Billig does not consider this possibility; for him, holidays are in the business of making these things explicit, they are designed to draw attention to themselves, they are the functional equivalent not of flags hanging limply, but of flags being waved with vigour. But perhaps we ought to reconsider one measure of their efficacy as their limpness, not their vigour (see, e.g., Eriksen, 2007: 7–9).

Conclusion

In any case, the view from below certainly looks different than the view from above. This difference in fairness may be an artefact of research design (Hearn, 2007: 658–9; Lukes, 1975: 299–301). Where scholars of nationalism look for (and find) evidence of performances that work, I have looked for (and found) evidence of performances that did not work.

In his contribution to this volume, Anthony Smith (see pp. 30–1 of this volume; see also Smith, 2008: 569–71) suggests that I assume a gulf exists between elites and ordinary people on questions of nationalism. This is a fair criticism; it is possible that I have conflated the conceptual possibility for a gap with the suggestion that there is an empirically verifiable chasm. Of course, it is an interesting (and ultimately empirical) question as to how big that gap is (see Skey, 2009: 339). But it is not really size that matters here. Rather, the question that concerns me is a more epistemological question about the direction of this relationship: where does our investigation begin? Mine begins from below: rather than deducing the meaning and salience of these events from their carefully crafted and cleverly concocted elite designs, my argument has simply been that there is something to be gained by inverting the analytical lens so that we might begin our examination from the perspective of the ordinary people who might – or, crucially, might not – constitute potential audiences for these events. When we do this, we may indeed find a link between elite designs and popular consumption. But we just as easily might not, either. Just as we should not assume a gap, we also should not assume a tight correspondence.

To be fair, most scholars associated with the view from above do not discount the important role of ordinary citizens. Indeed, in this volume, Smith (Chapter 2) argues for a more balanced approach, making it clear that any analysis of the capacity of rituals to forge (and reforge) the nation must take into account the role of both elites and non-elites. And for my part, I'm not suggesting we should ignore the crucial role played by the elite designers and organizers of the events; as Smith correctly reminds us (see p. 24 of this volume), we wouldn't have much to study by way of national rituals and performances without these elites. But this is not just a question of emphasis, either. What I have attempted to do in my contribution here is to turn this resonance question on its head. The question is not in some broad sense whether nationalism works. I think it is safe to say that it does: as Billig reminds us, we know this, we all continue to live in (and reproduce) a world of nations well into the twenty-first century. The question, rather, is how does this broad relevance of the nation translate, if at all, into specific and explicit connections with the nation in and through national holiday commemorations? It is thus not whether national holiday commemorations work; it is whether ordinary people are making national holiday commemorations work for them in ways that are nationally consequential. What are ordinary people doing, or not doing, with the nation in the context of these holidays? The meaningfulness and usefulness of the nation, not to mention its meaninglessness and uselessness, are richer and more varied than we might otherwise expect (see Cohen, 1996: 803; Jenkins, 2007: 116; Skey, 2011: 95–109). If we begin our investigation from below, we may indeed find linkages with elite and structural perspectives (as certain scholars of nationalism expect). But I am guessing that we are just as likely not to find those linkages. So, rather than following those well-trodden pathways of elite design in search of these popular meanings and uses of the nation, my aim here has been to look for some of the ways in which ordinary people make connections, and, equally importantly, do not make connections, from the bottom up.

Notes

1 Smith (p. 23 of this volume) distinguishes between 'commemorations' ('rite[s] of national mourning') and 'celebrations' ('celebrations . . . of the foundation of the nation'). For him, both are 'national rites'. Alexander (2004: 528, 533–6), in contrast, distinguishes 'rituals' from 'performances'. Rituals are found only in primitive societies where they work by fusing members of those societies into an exalted sense of collective awareness. As features of modern societies, performances share much in common with primitive rituals; the key difference is that, unlike rituals, performances fail in their objective of uniting disparate elements of societies. These definitions point to important functional differences between these phenomena. My own use of these and similar terms (I favour 'commemoration', 'holiday' and the intentionally ambiguous 'event') is not functionally specific, but rather site specific. That is, I use these terms somewhat more colloquially to identify spatially and temporally bounded sites where a range of collective (commemorative/celebratory/ritual-like) activities – all with national parameters – take place.
2 This section draws from and builds on Fox and Miller-Idriss (2008: 546–9).

References

Abell, J., Condor, S., Lowe, R. D., Gibson, S. G. and Stevenson, C. (2007) 'Who ate all the pride? Patriotic sentiment and English national football support', *Nations and Nationalism*, 13(1): 97–116.

Alexander, J. C. (2004) 'Cultural pragmatics: social performance between ritual and strategy', *Sociological Theory*, 22(4): 527–73.

Archetti, E. P. (1999) *Masculinities: Football, Polo and the Tango in Argentina*, Oxford: Berg.

Benei, V. (2008) *Schooling Passions: Nation, History, and Language in Contemporary Western India*, Palo Alto, CA: Stanford University Press.

Billig, M. (1995) *Banal Nationalism*, London: Sage.

Cerulo, K. A. (1995) *Identity Designs: The Sights and Sounds of a Nation*, New Brunswick, NJ: Rutgers University Press.

Cohen, A. C. (1996) 'Personal nationalism: a Scottish view of some rites, rights, and wrongs', *American Ethnologist*, 23(4): 802–15.

Comaroff, J. L. and Comaroff, J. (2009) *Ethnicity, Inc.*, Chicago, IL: University of Chicago Press.

Dennis, M. (2002) *Red, White, and Blue Letter Days: An American Calendar*, Ithaca, NY: Cornell University Press.

Durkheim, É. (1995 [1912]) *The Elementary Forms of Religious Life*, New York: The Free Press.

Edensor, T. (2002) *National Identity, Popular Culture and Everyday Life*, Oxford: Berg.

Edensor, T. (2006) 'Reconsidering national temporalities: institutional times, everyday routines, serial spaces and synchronicities', *European Journal of Social Theory*, 9(4): 525–45.

Elgenius, G. (2011) *Symbols of Nations and Nationalism: Celebrating Nationhood*, Basingstoke: Palgrave Macmillan.

Elias, N. and Dunning, E. (1986) *Quest for Excitement: Sport and Leisure in the Civilizing Process*, Oxford: Blackwell.

Eriksen, T. H. (1993) 'Formal and informal nationalism', *Ethnic and Racial Studies*, 16(1): 1–25.

Eriksen, T. H. (2007) 'Some questions about flags', in T. H. Eriksen and R. Jenkins (eds) *Flag, Nation and Symbolism in Europe and America*, London: Routledge, pp. 1–13.

Etzioni, A. (2000) 'Toward a theory of public ritual', *Sociological Theory*, 18(1): 44–59.

Fenton, S. (2007) 'Indifference towards national identity: what young adults think about being English and British', *Nations and Nationalism*, 13(2): 321–39.

Fox, J. E. (2006) 'Consuming the nation: holidays, sports, and the production of collective belonging', *Ethnic and Racial Studies*, 29(2): 217–36.

Fox, J. E. (2011) 'When nationalist conflict doesn't happen: Romanians and Hungarians in Transylvania', Paper presented at 'Nations, States, and Conflict', National University of Ireland.

Fox, J. E. and Miller-Idriss, C. (2008) 'Everyday nationhood', *Ethnicities*, 8(4): 536–63.

Gillis, J. R. (ed.) (1994) *Commemorations: The Politics of National Identity*, Princeton, NJ: Princeton University Press.

Githens-Mazer, J. (2008) 'Locating agency in collective political behaviour: nationalism, social movements and individual mobilisation', *Politics*, 28(1): 41–9.

Groom, N. (2007) 'Union Jacks and Union Jills', in T. H. Eriksen and R. Jenkins (eds) *Flag, Nation and Symbolism in Europe and America*, London: Routledge, pp. 68–87.

Handler, R. (1988) *Nationalism and the Politics of Culture in Quebec*, Madison, WI: University of Wisconsin Press.

Hearn, J. (2007) 'National identity: banal, personal and embedded', *Nations and Nationalism*, 13(4): 657–74.

Herzfeld, M. (1997) *Cultural Intimacy: Social Poetics in the Nation-State*, New York: Routledge.

Hobsbawm, E. J. (1983) 'Introduction: inventing traditions', in E. Hobsbawm and T. Ranger (eds) *The Invention of Tradition*, Cambridge: Cambridge University Press, pp. 1–14.

Hobsbawm, E. J. (1991) *Nations and Nationalism since 1780: Programme, Myth, Reality*, Cambridge: Cambridge University Press.

Hutchinson, J. (2006) 'Hot and banal nationalism: the nationalization of the "masses"', in G. Delanty and K. Kumar (eds) *The Sage Handbook of Nations and Nationalism*, London: Sage, pp. 295–306.

Jenkins, R. (2007) 'Inarticulate speech of the heart: nation, flag and emotion in Denmark', in T. H. Eriksen and R. Jenkins (eds) *Flag, Nation and Symbolism in Europe and America*, London: Routledge, pp. 115–35.

Kertzer, D. I. (1988) *Ritual, Politics, and Power*, New Haven, CT: Yale University Press.

Kolstø, P. (2006) 'National symbols as signs of unity and division', *Ethnic and Racial Studies*, 29(4): 676–701.

Kong, L. and Yeoh, B. S. A. (1997) 'The construction of national identity through the production of ritual and spectacle', *Political Geography*, 16(3): 213–39.

Lukes, S. (1975) 'Political ritual and social integration', *Sociology*, 9(2): 289–308.

Mann, R. and Fenton, S. (2009) 'The personal contexts of national sentiments', *Journal of Ethnic and Migration Studies*, 35(4): 517–34.

Mosse, G. L. (1975) *The Nationalization of the Masses: Political Symbolism and Mass Movements in Germany from the Napoleonic Wars through the Third Reich*, New York: Howard Fertig.

Özkirimli, U. (2003) 'The nation as an artichoke? A critique of ethnosymbolist interpretations of nationalism', *Nations and Nationalism*, 9(3): 339–55.

Pfaff, S. and Yang, G. (2001) 'Double-edged rituals and the symbolic resources of collective action: political commemorations and the mobilization of protest in 1989', *Theory and Society*, 30(4): 539–89.

Skey, M. (2006) '"Carnivals of surplus emotion?" Towards an understanding of the significance of ecstatic nationalism in a globalising world', *Studies in Ethnicity and Nationalism*, 6(2): 143–61.

Skey, M. (2009) 'The national in everyday life: a critical engagement with Michael Billig's *Banal Nationalism*', *The Sociological Review*, 57(2): 331–46.

Skey, M. (2011) *National Belonging and Everyday Life: The Significance of Nationhood in an Uncertain World*, Basingstoke: Palgrave Macmillan.

Smith, A. D. (1986) *The Ethnic Origins of Nations*, Oxford: Blackwell.

Smith, A. D. (2008) 'The limits of everyday nationhood', *Ethnicities*, 8(4): 563–73.

Smith, A. D. (2009) *Ethno-Symbolism and Nationalism: A Cultural Approach*, London: Routledge.

Spillman, L. (1997) *Nation and Commemoration: Creating National Identities in the United States and Australia*, Cambridge: Cambridge University Press.

Thompson, A. (2001) 'Nations, national identities and human agency: putting people back into nations', *The Sociological Review*, 49(1): 18–33.

Turner, V. (1969) *The Ritual Process: Structure and Anti-Structure*, Ithaca, NY: Cornell University Press.

Uzelac, G. (2010) 'National ceremonies: the pursuit of authenticity', *Ethnic and Racial Studies*, 33(10): 1718–36.

Van Ginderachter, M. (2009) 'Contesting national symbols: Belgian *belle époque* socialism between rejection and appropriation', *Social History*, 34(1): 55–73.

West, B. (2008) 'Collective memory and crisis: the 2002 Bali bombing, national heroic archetypes and the counter-narrative of cosmopolitan nationalism', *Journal of Sociology*, 44(4): 337–53.

Whitmeyer, J. M. (2002) 'Elites and popular nationalism', *British Journal of Sociology*, 53(3): 321–41.

Wintour, P. (2006) 'Brown: Remembrance Sunday should become "British Day"', *The Guardian*, 14 January, available online at www.guardian.co.uk/2006/jan/14/british identity.labour?INTCMP=SRCH (accessed 11 May 2012).

4

TIME-BUBBLES OF NATIONALISM

Dynamics of solidarity ritual in lived time

Randall Collins

Nationalism is frequently explained in terms of macro-structural causes. Ernest Gellner, Anthony Smith and others have debated its relationship to modernity and to pre-modern structures. A version of that historical transformation, developed by Gellner protégés such as Michael Mann, as well as by Charles Tilly and others, may be called the theory of state penetration into society. I would put it in Weberian terms: patrimonial structures based on alliances among armed households were displaced by bureaucratic organization of the state, beginning with a permanent military and its centralized logistics, generating an expanded apparatus of tax extraction and the penetration of state agencies and laws that bring individuals into direct relation with the state.

Among the important consequences of state penetration was the invention of the social movement. In parcellized medieval society, protests could only be local and mostly ephemeral; but state penetration created both the means of large-scale political mobilization and a target to aim at. By fostering communications, transportation, education and a dynamic economy, centralizing regimes provided the material means for group mobilization; by penetrating the walls of patrimonial households to inscribe persons on the rolls of the state, not as group members but as individuals, such regimes opened up new possibilities for identity formation; by centralizing the seat of government, they provided a unifying target at which petition campaigns and revolutions alike could aim. Accordingly, as Mann (1993) and Tilly (1995, 2004) have emphasized, all kinds of social movements mobilized at the same time: classes and nationalisms, as well as a variety of reform movements ranging from anti-slavery to anti-vivisectionism. The social movement was a mould from which a variety of things could be poured. Nationalism was one of its products, just as class movements such as socialism and conservatism were likewise products of the invention of the social movement.

I would like to extend another angle of vision – the micro-sociology of nationalism. Nationalism may be defined, ideal-typically, as an intensely felt bond of solidarity. But, as Fox and Miller-Idriss (2008), Billig (1995) and others have noted, in the day-by-day experience of modern people, national identity is largely a matter of routine. Most of the time, nationalism is low-strength; latent, perhaps, but far from the thoughts and feelings of most people. The institutionalized celebrations and monuments of nationalism are, for the most part, a backdrop whose meaning is hardly reflected upon, like the statue of the victorious general in the park splattered with pigeon droppings. National holidays, to speak of the ones I have observed, such as the US Fourth of July, Mexico's Cinco de Mayo, or France's Bastille Day, are annually scheduled occasions for eating and drinking, fireworks displays or just a day off from work, and invoke little sense of national solidarity; I have never seen people on such occasions encountering strangers, or even acquaintances, and warmly addressing them as fellow countrymen. It is a danger of symbolic analysis to presume that the analyst can identify the meaning of a symbol without examining what participants actually are thinking and feeling at the moment. Symbols are alive only to the extent they are the focus of shared emotional attention; and thus symbols can be living, dead or lukewarm. What I would like to add is a mechanism determining their intensity, or lack thereof.

Even in societies where nationalism is institutionalized, it is not necessarily very strong or constant. Structural conditions are insufficient to explain the intensity of nationalism, the moments when it is indeed a living bond of solidarity, uniting strangers into a vast brotherhood, and when it is on the periphery of people's consciousness, or even non-existent in their lives. We need a dynamic theory of nationalism as a process of surges in time.

Hence my title: 'Time-bubbles of nationalism'. These are capsules of collectively experienced time, on the whole rather sudden in onset, lasting for a while, then declining back to banal normalcy. I could have used the metaphor of a balloon, getting puffed up with Durkheimian collective effervescence, floating high in the air in a mood of widespread social enthusiasm, then gradually coming down to earth as the gas slowly seeps out. Social sciences have not been very good at explaining the temporal dimension, the time-patterns of social processes. The most common metaphor, the cycle, is not strictly applicable to most important events of social life, especially social conflicts and mass enthusiasms. The metaphor of the cycle, which may be graphed as a wave, is inaccurate because most real-life social events do not show the symmetrical patterns of an ideal-typical sine wave: the ups and downs do not recur at regular intervals, nor is the amplitude of the peaks and troughs generally so regular. The metaphor of the balloon gives a better picture of the asymmetry of such collective time-dynamics, and of its capsule shape: the balloon is inflated quickly, stays high for a while, then gradually floats down; its beginning is more sudden and dramatic than its ending. A better metaphor would be a rocket zooming into the sky, exploding in an eye-catching blast, then dispersing into fallout, slowing fading from vivid to drab. But putting all that into the title would have been more mystifying than illuminating.

Let me give an empirical example. The day after the 9/11 attacks on the twin towers in New York and on the Pentagon, I realized this was an opportunity to study the long-asserted principle that external conflict brings internal solidarity. How long would solidarity last? The first two days were a time of shock, people acting bewildered about what to do collectively. On the third day, American flags started to appear; within a few days, they were sold everywhere, posted on cars and windows, and to some extent worn on clothing. All public gatherings – such as athletic events and music concerts – began with huge flag displays, generally accompanied by the other newly consecrated symbols of heroism – ranks of police officers and firefighters representing those killed in the twin towers. I surveyed the number of cars on the streets that displayed flags, as well as the numbers on buildings and windows, repeating observations of the same places at least weekly for a year (Collins, 2004a). The time-pattern that emerged was the following.

The peak level of displaying national flags was reached quite rapidly, within the first two weeks. It stayed at that peak for three months. This was also an intense period of national solidarity in other respects: political debate largely disappeared; the popularity of the president – George W. Bush – reached 90 per cent (the highest on record), a rise of about 40 percentage points from just prior to 9/11, and far above the levels to which it would fall later in Bush's administration. At around three months, political argument resumed, and articles began to appear asking, is it okay to take our flags down now? The level of flag display began to fall off, reaching a moderate level at around six months; there were brief upward blips at the one-year anniversary and thereafter, but, on the whole, we can describe the pattern of national solidarity as exploding upward rocket-like in a week or two, remaining at its balloon-like ceiling for three months, then gradually declining towards normalcy by six months. I have referred to this as the three-month solidarity-and-hysteria zone, and adduced comparative evidence that it is within such three-month bubbles of extreme collective attention upon a common identity and a shared danger that both precipitous ventures and violent atrocities are most likely to happen.

Passing by the details of the 9/11 response and similar events, I want to raise a set of theoretical issues. The shape of mass solidarity in time, the shape of the time-bubble – the rocket-like ascent, the plateau-like ceiling, the slow dissipation – is similar for the wider class of such events, although much remains to be established by comparison of cases. What varies is how long such events take; here, it appears, from cases that I will describe shortly, that the big variation is the length of the high plateau. This calls for theoretical explanation; tentatively, I will argue that societies with a high degree of state penetration, and those where symbolic mobilization is easily perceived throughout the society, sustain plateaus of national solidarity in the three-month range, but societies that are more fragmented and less state-penetrated sustain the plateau for a month or less.

A further theoretical issue concerns what happens after a collective mobilization has gone through its peak and dissipated. My hypothesis is that a refractory period follows, such that no similar mass enthusiasm can be generated for a period of time thereafter. To risk another metaphor, the nerves of the social animal are innervated after this orgy of attention upon the collectivity; once the air is out of the balloon, it cannot get it up again until after a time of rest. The Thermidorian Reaction during the French Revolution is a famous example of such exhaustion from sustained crisis. I will discuss the implications of this point presently.

I offer the metaphor of a time-bubble to emphasize that the most intense events of social life are capsules in time. Their coming is not expectable in any precise way, certainly nothing like the periodicity of sine waves; it may be a long time before another rocket goes up or another balloon is filled with similarly uplifting enthusiasm. That is why such moments in time have the emotional character of high drama, both tragic and joyous surprise. There is another and deeper theoretical reason for this sense of uniquely high experience, besides their rarity and unpredictability. What happens inside the bubble is felt as qualitatively different from ordinary life outside it. Not only is life much more intense at those times, but it has a different structure of social attention. It is rare for us, as members of large modern societies, to be in a situation in which we can be reasonably sure that most other people are paying attention to the same thing and feeling the same emotion as ourselves. When one is in a mass demonstration, crowds stretching out as far as the eye can see, and even more people beyond them, all thinking the same thought and expressing the same emotion – 'the regime must go', 'the people will triumph' – this gives a sense of the solidarity of the whole that Durkheim called collective consciousness. At such moments, it is not an abstraction or a myth, but what people feel as the highest reality. The moment does not last; but they are not thinking that now. It will not last because it takes special circumstances to create such a high degree of simultaneous focus of attention, but, while it is there, its power of shaping emotions and forming symbols is unsurpassed.

A mass demonstration or focused crowd of this sort is a large-scale version of what I have called an interaction ritual. This concept attempts to capture a generic dimension of ritualism not only in formal and traditionalized ceremonies, but running through all the activities of social life. Elsewhere, I have spelled out the ingredients and consequences of interaction rituals of varying strength (Collins, 2004b). The ingredients are: first, assembling people bodily in the same place so that they are in full multimodal intercommunication; second, focusing their attention upon the same thing, and becoming mutually aware of each other's focus, thereby generating a sense of intersubjectivity; third, feeling and expressing the same emotion. Interaction rituals can succeed or fail, can be intense or mediocre; if the ingredients pass a threshold, mutual focus and shared emotion feed back into each other, driving them upwards to high levels of rhythmic entrainment that Durkheim called collective effervescence. At these high levels, what the group focuses upon becomes symbolic, representing membership in the group, as well as depicting its boundaries and enemies; individuals are filled with emotional energy, the feelings of confidence and enthusiasm that motivate them to acts of heroism and sacrifice; and they are filled with a sense of morality, the palpable experience of good and its fight against evil. Nationalism is such a symbol.

It is through these symbols, in subsequent days, that people can recall the feelings of solidarity and morality that pumped them up at the peak moments of collective experience. The group cannot stay assembled forever; indeed, it is difficult for them to stay for as long as a few weeks. The collective emotion fades after the assembly disperses. The symbols keep it alive to a degree, but, as Durkheim recognized, periodic reassemblies and periodic rituals are needed to rejuvenate the symbols with emotion. I have added an argument about a refractory period; this holds that after an intense period of mass mobilization, people cannot experience the same intensity again for some time; they necessarily have to come down. Thus, symbols must vary over time, between moments of high-intensity significance and milder levels, even banality.

My discussion of the mass demonstration as an interaction ritual is on the micro-sociological level. Let us recombine it now with the macro-historical level with which we started, the long-term transformations of state penetration and the invention of the social movement. The modern social movement became possible because it was provided with a target, the central organization of the state. This created a physical place to assemble and a mutual focus of attention. Whether a movement wants to petition for redress of grievances, or actually to overthrow the regime and take power for itself, it focuses attention upon the state and elevates it into an image of omnipotence, an all-encompassing will or agency, which, at the moment of maximal struggle, is now endowed with the ability to carry out the will of the crowd, if it only would. This is a somewhat mythical view of the power of the state, ignoring all practical contingencies of organization and implementation, but it has very important ideological effects. The unifying focus on the state as the target of movement mobilization makes it easy, indeed natural, to invoke the unity of the people. Whatever the specific demands of the movement, it is we, the unified Durkheimian collectivity, who are demanding it. At the moment of mobilization, the sovereignty of the people is not a philosophical abstraction, but a felt experience. For this reason, mass movements engaged in state confron-tation tend towards a nationalist tone, because this is an easy identity to evoke at the moment when seemingly everyone is assembled and united in their demands. It is rituals of this intensity that make primordialism plausible, at least for their own participants.

A recent example, which I have observed from videos, photos, news reports and eyewitness accounts, is the two-and-a-half-week protest at the Wisconsin State Capitol in the US (during February and March 2011). The issue was the plan of the Republican-dominated legislature to pass a bill eliminating most of the organizing rights of public-sector employee unions. Because the State Capitol building is very close to the state university, it was easy for the teaching assistants union to mobilize a mass protest, which occupied the state building and attempted to block the legislation. The protest attracted large numbers of supporters, including even police officers – a fact that delighted the protestors. Although, in fact, it lost in the end on the legislation, it generated a mood of euphoria, with chants of 'This is what democracy looks like!' and 'We are the people!' ringing through the halls and galleries of the building. In fact, in the election three months previously, the Democrats and union supporters had lost control of every branch of the legislature and the governorship; so it cannot literally be the case that the protestors were the whole or even the majority of the people. My point is that the micro-structured experience of a mass demonstration itself generates the feeling of totality. One is aware there are enemies outside the collectivity, but they are defined away, not part of the people, but as an alien quality to be combated, much like theological views of the omnipotence of God and the shadow-reality of the devil. Thus, the Wisconsin demonstrators displayed themselves surrounded by symbols, American flags, references to democracy and the people. Although the issue was specifically the rights of labour unions, the discourse and symbolism was not largely about unions; this was played down, a particularistic interest that had to be reinterpreted in the context of an all-encompassing unity.

I have been arguing that the shape of the social movement is what creates nationalism and that this operates through a micro-sociological mechanism, the mass interaction ritual mobilized at the place of the centralizing state. Historically, we can see this same process of micro-foundations of movement mobilization in the history of nationalism, specifically in the shift from nineteenth-century elite nationalism to the mass nationalism of the twentieth century and today. It has been widely argued that nineteenth-century nationalism, particularly in less modernized states, was a matter of small numbers of intellectuals. Micro-sociologically, their chief tactic was the banquet. A few dozen gentlemen gathered in private mansions, restaurants or hotels to dine; they made speeches, drank toasts, passed resolutions. It was a banqueting campaign of this kind that led up to the French Revolution in Paris in February 1848, and that carried the nationalist revolution to Germany and elsewhere. It was a banqueting campaign that mobilized reformers in Russia in 1904 during the opening provided by the defeat in the war with Japan and prepared the way for the attempted revolution of 1905. I am drawing here on research by Stefan Klusemann (2010), who shows that the restricted settings of indoor banquets, extending the polite rituals of upper-class sociability, gave a very limited class character to nationalist mobilization; a widening came about when the labour unions in Petersburg demanded entry to the banquets, and eventually transferred such meetings to larger, more public buildings, thus setting off the movement for councils – soviets. It was the shift in the micro-organization of participation in a social movement that generated the key ideological shifts. Radicalization is a practical process and not merely an ideational one.

To summarize the key points so far: social movements were facilitated by the structural changes of modernization through state penetration; movements at their peak mobilize into huge interaction rituals directed at the central state; the micro-sociological experience at such moments is the feeling of universal solidarity in the crowd, which can be attached to a variety of ideologies but is especially compatible with ideas of popular sovereignty and the nation. These peak moments are time-bubbles, lasting for a few weeks or months, then fading, and subject to a refractory period during which they cannot be mobilized at that same intensity.

I want now to continue with the dynamics of such mobilization as they stretch out in time. A key point is the difference between the pristine experience of the Durkheimian collectivity when mass solidarity discovers itself in a large-scale mobilization, and the change that comes in subsequent mobilizations. There is a refractory period of some length after intense mobilization dissipates. Under some circumstances, the demonstrators can go home; the struggle may go on, but in a different and milder form. After their 18 days occupying the Wisconsin State Capitol, the crowds dispersed; the struggle shifted to lawsuits in the courts and electoral campaigns to recall officials. But sometimes crisis can follow crisis, and renewed mobilization may be forced upon a population, however exhausted. In 1917 Russia, there were two great peaks of revolutionary mobilization, in February and in November, separated by nine months, during which the collective identity of the people was, if not in abeyance, at least fragmented and incapable of mobilizing as a unitary or near-unity force. But, after the November revolution, all was not settled forever; in fact, there were renewed crises, with civil wars beginning already in December 1917 and continuing through 1920, a period of three years.

But these subsequent mass arousals have a different emotional atmosphere, less filled with the sense of shared solidarity and glory, more soldiering through. The peak Durkheimian moment, the fusion of the individual and the collective, is replaced by doing one's duty, going on under pressure of an organization; leaders stop being symbols of ourselves and become authorities, not part of the shared flow but a separate force impinging from outside. (The mixtures of ideological discourse and banal realities are nicely illustrated by the writings of Isaac Babel (2002 [1924–6]), based on his experiences with Red Army troops in the civil war.) There are numerous instances where revolutions or attempted revolutions follow each other in a close sequence; on the whole, the later ones have both a different tone and a different micro-sociological structure. The French Revolution of February 1848 was a quick and almost bloodless transition to popular rule; but by the time of the June insurrection, four months later, collective solidarity had split into factional conflict and a great deal of violence. National unity gave way to class conflict.

On the micro-level, interaction rituals can succeed or fail. The key variable is maintaining a mutual focus of attention, which thereby channels shared emotions into a feeling of solidarity and common identity. More precisely, the amount of mutual focus of attention is a continuum. At high levels, there is unity of one group, the people as a whole, foregrounded in the mass mobilization we see all around us, with just one goal, to win out against the enemy we are all confronting. At low levels of the continuum, people do not assemble at all, do not pay attention to much in common, but are taken up with the myriad private concerns of everyday life. In between these levels, there can be mass mobilizations, but split into factions; they cannot agree on goals, they get off into different collective actions, their discourse is splintered and off-message.

Accordingly, there are two kinds of revolutionary or peak movement struggle. One is the Durkheimian collective consciousness, stretching as far as the eye can see, and, beyond that, the sentiment that the whole world is watching. Such revolutions are often surprisingly rapid and easy. The fastest was the 1848 French Revolution: three days for the government to fall in February; five days in June for insurrection and counter-mobilization to put it down (de Tocqueville, 1987). The key mechanism is the tipping point or bandwagon effect. There is a tense period of confrontation between regime and mass uprising; there may be sporadic efforts at dispersing the crowds, a brief and hesitant use of force by authorities; but, if the crowd holds on, sustained by the courage of mass solidarity, the regime tends to split. Elites go over to the opposition; soldiers and police waver and change sides; leaders feel isolated and lose their nerve. This is the Durkheimian collective consciousness as a process in time, not a permanent entity but a forest fire, a hot centre that nothing can resist. To shift the metaphor – again! – the mass demonstration interaction ritual is like an emotional magnet; it pulls in not only those who are in the crowd, on the spot, but those who are in the opposition, tied to it by invisible lines of force that is, in fact, the common focus of attention shared by the regime and those who want to overthrow it.

Once the struggle is won, that common focus of attention is lost. The regime that is the target of protest is gone. The subsequent regime is in a different microsociological situation; that is why the post-revolutionary situation is necessarily different from those days of high euphoria and high danger when the revolutionary coalition was at its height.

The second type of revolt is one in which the unity of the revolutionists is never achieved. Instead of one central focus of mobilization, there are many; dissidents against the regime are also dissidents among themselves. Such revolutions are more difficult. They are more violent, often turning into civil wars. The regime may fall, but it is not replaced by anything of similar unity. Such revolts are characterized not by overarching Durkheimian collective consciousness, but by smaller pockets of ritual solidarity, mutually hostile. Group consciousness is split. The first type of revolt, the Durkheimian bandwagon, is maximally suited to produce moments of pure idealistic nationalism. The second type is less nationalist; that is, nationalism may be one of the ideological strands put forward during the movement, but it is contested and unconvincing, not the dominant identity. In the aftermath, a self-conscious nationalist movement may be prominent, but in the special form of a reactive nationalist militancy, struggling against other mobilized movements that are the enemy of nationalism. The White and Red factions of the Russian Civil War is an example, but there are many others.

It is dangerous to analyse events still in progress, but in the wave of Middle East revolts of 2011, we can point to the Egyptian Revolution as an archetype of the Durkheimian bandwagon revolution; and the Libyan and Yemen revolts as cases of the fragmented type, with the Tunisian Revolution combining elements of both. (The Syrian Civil War, growing out of the Arab Spring uprisings in 2011, strongly underscores the pattern of protracted violence when there is no central organizing place and no possibility of a rapid tipping point revolution. Since it is still ongoing at the time of this writing, it will not be treated here.) Let me review a few salient points, chiefly their time-dynamics, micro-interactional patterns and the situational evocation of nationalist symbols. The sources of all information in the following account are reports from the BBC, Associated Press and al-Jazeera.

The Egyptian Revolution covered 18 days of mass demonstrations, from 25 January 2011, when the first big crowd gathered in Cairo's Tahrir Square, to the fall of Mubarak on 11 February 2011. Actually, there was a preliminary period of a week, beginning 17 January, the day of one-month remembrance of the self-immolation that set off the Tunisian protests; a man attempted to set himself on fire in front of the Egyptian parliament, and five others made similar attempts, all stopped by the police. This week-long lull before the storm was given over to organizing, so what we count as day one – 25 January – had prearranged wide support from many political, civil and ad hoc groups. The date was chosen to take advantage of a national holiday in honour of the police. Hijacking a national holiday is not an unusual tactic in authoritarian regimes that allow no other way to assemble, turning a banal mechanism of national solidarity into a mobilizing device for revolt. A similar tactic was used to set off the Tiananmen Square democracy demonstrations in China in 1989, using the occasion of a state funeral for a CCP leader.

The Egyptian police were also ready, and violence quickly escalated, beginning with tear gas and water cannons against crowds wielding rocks and firebombs. For the first four days, violence took place at demonstrations not only in Cairo, but Alexandria, Suez and several other cities. An important swing occurred on day five: the army was called out but refused to intervene between police and protestors; by day seven, the army was announcing it would not hurt the protestors. At the same time, violence in other cities fizzled out; attention was centred on Tahrir Square in Cairo, where crowds now reached 250,000, while in Alexandria they had fallen to hundreds. As of day five, Mubarak began offering concessions, but these were not accepted.

By day eight, the Tahrir Square protest had grown to a million, and had become mostly peaceful. There was one more important episode of violence, the 'Battle of the Camel', when Mubarak supporters invaded the square, causing many injuries and several deaths, while the army attempted to separate the sides. This was day nine; from day ten onwards, there was no notable violence in Cairo and most of the rest of the country. A sign of the tipping point was visible already on day 16, when a small demonstration in a provincial town was attacked by the police, killing several; but the following day the police were arrested. Mubarak, on the defensive, offered more concessions, which were rejected as unacceptable, and he finally resigned on day 18. This led to one last big day of rejoicing in Tahrir Square (with imitations in other cities), then the square was cleared. In following days, there were demonstrations in various places, but no longer big heterogeneous crowds; instead, separate occupational groups pressed their specific demands. The honeymoon was over, replaced by interest-group politics.

The period of violent contestation was brief, almost entirely in the first four days, and spread among many different sites around the country. After that, the Durkheimian collective consciousness became an overwhelming centre of attention, as virtually all other action stopped to focus on Tahrir Square. (The chief exception is after the last big violent episode, the 'Battle of the Camel' on day nine; this was followed by a brief upsurge of violence and looting in Alexandria.) The massive assembly, unmoved by the violent attack, soon broke the will of the regime; the army had shifted to the crowd's side and ended up in charge of the transitional regime. The Durkheimian solidarity of the assembled crowd was so great that the revolutionaries' self-image – and their image in the eyes of its international supporters – was as a non-violent, virtually bloodless revolution. This was not strictly true; altogether, about 400 were killed and 6,000 wounded, most of them in these first four days when fighting took place in many different cities, before Tahrir Square had established its primacy in the attention space.

On the whole, violence disperses and solidarity concentrates. We see this also in photos, as I have shown in comparative study of violent behaviour (Collins, 2008): when demonstrations are peaceful, they are compact crowds; when violence is happening, people are running around, widely spaced apart.

It was in the gatherings at Tahrir Square that expressions of Egyptian national unity were most in evidence. Many women took part, some in full abaya, others flaunting Western styles, even smoking and kissing. Christian and Muslim clerics ostentatiously appeared together expressing religious unity. These sectarian and gender divisions soon reappeared after the euphorious mass demonstrations had broken up. Some women were sexually molested and assaulted in the vast crowd on victory celebration day, day 19. When Egyptian women assembled again in Tahrir Square for International Women's Day (8 March, three-and-a-half weeks after the downfall of Mubarak – i.e. day 43), they were heckled and threatened. On the following day, Muslim/Christian violence broke out again in the Cairo suburbs, killing 13 and wounding 140. During subsequent months, Tahrir Square was used as a symbolic rallying point, but, on the whole, the huge crowds of the peak period were not reassembled. Intermittently, from April to July 2011, militant crowds demanded speeding up the process of transition from military control, and stronger prosecution of the old regime; on 23 July, a violent crowd attacked the defense ministry building. By 1 August, when military forces cleared Tahrir Square of hold-out demonstrators camping there, most Egyptians appeared to be tired of the conflict and supported their removal. The old regime as an opponent diminished as a focal point holding together a unified opposition; in the remaining months of 2011, and through 2012, intermittent clashes among Muslim, Coptic Christians and secularists came increasingly into the centre of attention. Egyptian nationalism was no longer a symbolic weapon with any potency either to generate solidarity or to overcome opposition. The ostentatious waving of Egyptian flags and signs referring to the unity of the people of Egypt was largely confined to the high points of collective assembly, inside the time-bubble of nationalism. For the Egyptian Revolution, the time-bubble was 18 days (or 26 days if we include the previous week of initiation, the time it took to first inflate the balloon).

In Tunisia, there was a mixture of violent conflicts dispersed around the country, and the eventual formation of a peaceful revolutionary crowd in the capital city. The revolution in Tunisia took four weeks in December and January 2010–11, with an additional two weeks of demonstrations after the president fled, while protestors pressed for further changes. The first week began with two spectacular public suicides in an outlying town, spreading to protests in other small towns within a 30-mile radius of the capital. Since there was news censorship, probably these first protests spread by word of mouth, like traditional protest movements such as the rural arson campaign in England in 1830 called the Captain Swing Rebellion (Collins, 2008: 248; Tilly, 2003: 178–87). The first killings of demonstrators by the police happened on day 8, as demonstrators became increasingly destructive, burning tyres, police cars and public buildings. In the second week, protests spread to the three second-rank cities of the country, as the national labour union became involved; in the capital, two days of relatively small and peaceful protests were organized by the lawyers' association. Bigger and more modern organization was now becoming involved. Apparently this is when the ultra-modern internet social media began to make a buzz – not organizing the revolt on the internet alone, but adding to existing forms of organizational mobilization on the ground. (According to the BBC, 34 per cent of the population of 10 million were internet users; probably mostly in the coastal cities, as half the population lives in the impoverished countryside.)

During days 18 to 27, violent protests occurred in still other provincial towns, especially in the remote western region near the Algerian border. Here, violence became increasingly two-sided, as police escalated from tear gas and water cannon to live ammunition; crowds threw stones and petrol bombs, and snipers fired from rooftops. Simultaneously, in the Mediterranean coastal cities where labour and professions were well organized, more peaceful tactics were used, including protest marches, strikes and blogging. The combination of street fighting in the small towns and the provinces, plus more peaceful, politically sophisticated demonstrations in the urban centres, created an omnipresent sense of crisis. On days 29 and 30, the tipping point came: the president attempted to impose a state of emergency, the military staged a coup, and the government fell. Thereafter, almost all the action was in the capital city itself, as demonstrations kept up pressure for a more radical change in the transitional government; at this point, the demonstrations were, on the whole, more peaceful, and the police were eager to accommodate their demands. Here, the time-bubble was little more than a month.

We see a contrast between the tactics and levels of violence in the two kinds of sites of confrontation. In the small towns where the protests began, and the remote provincial regions where it escalated to guns, bombs and arson, it is likely the police had only small detachments; the fact that the violence spread from one town to another – rarely in the same place more than a few days (like the pattern of the Paris Banlieu riots in 2005, Collins, 2008: 492) – meant that the police were always heavily outnumbered and on the defensive; when their forces were beefed up by reinforcements, protests moved somewhere else. In the big cities, with their Westernized cosmopolitan style, protests had more centralized organization behind them; violence was restrained on both sides, and the protestors generated a better sense of legitimacy and responsibility – creating a magnetic attraction for government officials who would move across the line in a tipping point for regime change. These big coastal cities are the main tourist route, touted in the West for their beaches, ancient ruins, colourful but tamed Islamicism and cafe enjoyments. The Tunisian Revolution, on the whole, did not make much use of nationalist slogans and symbols. The revolution was made possible by the temporary unity against the regime, as common enemy, between the Arab underclass in the hinterlands, and the liberal cosmopolites of the tourist zone. The contrasting directions of orientation between the two components of the team tended to keep nationalism out of the centre of attention.

In Libya and Yemen, revolutionary struggle was much more dispersed and prolonged, both in time and space. This pattern in itself is enough to limit the strength of Durkheimian collective consciousness, and to prevent resolution of the conflict by a tipping point abdication of power and flight to the winning coalition. In Libya, the revolt broke out almost immediately after the success of the Egyptian Revolution, taking it as a sign that the unravelling of authoritarian regimes would proceed across the Arab world like a worn-out sweater. It might also be regarded as the transmission of Durkheimian collective consciousness vicariously, by the mass media and by the new electronic social media. The nationalism of such collective high points is propagated as a kind of generic enthusiasm for the nationalist tactic, not for any nation in particular but as a device for generating the experience of the people united in action.

In Libya, the spread of popular enthusiasm went on for about eight days (beginning 16 February). Gadhafi's forces did not crumble, but took the time to mobilize their superior weaponry. At first, military repulses of the rebels were attributed to an anti-national force, foreign mercenaries; during the second week, as rebels began to be pushed back, African guest workers in rebel-held territory were attacked in a wave of xenophobic nationalism. Hysteria about alien mercenaries settled down in the third week, when it became apparent that Gadhafi had tribal support of his own, an apparatus of clients, and a military force much better organized than the almost completely spontaneous rebel army. There were no equivalents of Tahrir Square; even in rebel strongholds such as Benghazi, quick success meant there was no need or purpose in prolonged crowd assembly, and the revolt soon turned into a civil war spread out across 500 miles of battle. In March, just as the militarily superior regime forces were about to extirpate the rebel centre four weeks after the revolt began, international military intervention by largely NATO-membership air power, along with covert ground support, turned the military balance. The Gadhafi regime was finally overthrown when its military strongholds were captured in late August 2011. Stable government was not restored. Within six weeks, rival militias were fighting in Tripoli, the old capital; clashes also went on in remote areas of the south during 2012, with attacks even in revolutionary Bengazi. Efforts failed at disarming and unifying the various rebel groups, adherents of the old regime, and regional tribes. Neither monopoly over the means of force, nor a focal centre of government, was re-established.

For such cases, revolution is the wrong word; a unified regime is replaced by a fragmented one, and no revolutionary policy or restructuring can be carried out. Although nationalist slogans and symbols were displayed early in the revolt, the bubble of nationalism was hardly inflated at all, at most a popular mood in a limited part of the territory and lasting little more than two weeks.

In Yemen, there were indeed versions of crowd solidarity assembling heroically against the regime, especially in the capital city; but struggles took place in several cities, many of them already strongholds of rival factions. Although the Tunisian Revolution provided a catalyst for a new round, it merely added to long-standing and multi-sided conflicts: a 50-year history of civil war, partition and reunification, and ongoing wars against secessionists, religious and ideological enemies. Although there were instances of heterogeneous crowds assembling in temporary unity against the regime of President Saleh, there is no unifying axis of conflict. No predominately peaceful tipping-point transition was possible. Fighting took place in the three major cities, among coalitions of tribes and militia; splits within the army produced further battles; secessionist movements and de facto autonomous regions split the structure of political control. President Saleh manoeuvred and backtracked among numerous deals, withdrew to Saudi Arabia after an assassination attempt, returned unexpectedly, and finally in February 2011 – thirteen months after the 'Arab Spring' period of demonstrations began – agreed to step down in favour of the vice president. But the presidency had never been strong enough to serve as a revolutionary turning point; decentralized and fragmented conflict cannot be resolved by replacing a token individual in such a structure.

Symbols of popular unity, under such circumstances, do little to galvanize a movement for taking power. A momentary scene is described in an Associated Press report from the capital of Yemen, 22 March 2011, when protests had been going on for about 40 days:

> Protesters massed by the tens of thousands in the downtown Sana'a plaza they have dubbed 'Change Square'. Crowds ululated, chanted and painted each other's faces in the red, white and black colours of the national flag. Conservative tribesmen brought their wives to the protest, and the women brought their children, all basking in a carnival atmosphere.

Similarly, one can view photos of supporters of the Libyan rebels with flags of the old monarchist pre-Gadhafi regime, or their faces painted with that particular brand of nationalist colours. Similar uses of national symbols are seen in revolts all over the Middle East. It is striking how many of these photos are of women. I read this as a strategic use of nationalism: women in the Arab world are taking advantage of mass political mobilization to take part in public life; unity of the people is of special concern for them, since they have been most excluded from the arena in which peoplehood is enacted. Perhaps shared memories of participation in these revolts will help – a little. It needs more structural transformation for women to be accepted, not as militant nationalists but as banal, taken-for-granted citizens.

The overwhelming conclusion one takes away from such cases is the illusory quality of nationalist time-bubbles, if the structural conditions for national unity, the state penetration and economic and cultural integration articulated by Gellner, Mann and Tilly are not present. This is certainly the case with revolts such as Yemen and Libya.

The Egyptian Revolution, even with its greater success in assembling a massive collective consciousness, does not appear to have had more integrating consequences, as seen two years after the event.

To be sure, there is also a calmer, everyday nationalism than the impassioned displays of revolutionaries at the height of mass mobilization, what Michael Billig (1995) has dubbed banal nationalism. But national identity is important in ongoing social relations chiefly when it is not the default setting, the unmarked case, but the foregrounded gestalt that immediately strikes the eye. The national identities of self and other are most inescapably present when there is a conflict or at least latent hostility founded on palpable differences in privilege: British or French or Dutch colonialists in their day, or American soldiers abroad in the early twenty-first century, irrevocably marked off by their intrusiveness, hence gathered together in consciousness of their nationality. National identity is most salient in everyday life when it is divisive. Wars, too, heighten nationalism, although chiefly in the first three months or so after breaking out. Banal nationalism may not be much, but on the whole it reflects better conditions of everyday life than the contentious mobilizations and violence that are the platforms on which stronger national identities are staged.

To end with a methodological exhortation: nationalism is visible; it is measurable. It is a varying quantity of emotion-laden belief during the rising and falling intensities of interaction rituals in everyday life. Many scholars are now engaged in close observation of nationalism. What is needed is more detailed attention to the dynamics that generate locally successful or unsuccessful ritual solidarity: what conditions exist for assembling or disassembling crowds; how much mutual focus of attention, and what breaks up attention; what kinds of emotions; what degree of intensification through rhythmic entrainment; how long solidarity rituals can be sustained. Our theoretical frontier is to explain their trajectories in time.

References

Babel, I. (2002 [1924–6]) 'The red cavalry stories', in *The Collected Stories of Isaac Babel*, New York: Norton, pp. 19–27.
Billig, M. (1995) *Banal Nationalism*, London: Sage.
Collins, R. (2004a) 'Rituals of solidarity and security in the wake of terrorist attack', *Sociological Theory*, 22: 53–87.
Collins, R. (2004b) *Interaction Ritual Chains*, Princeton, NJ: Princeton University Press.
Collins, R. (2008) *Violence: A Micro-Sociological Theory*, Princeton, NJ: Princeton University Press.

de Tocqueville, A. (1987) *Recollections of the French Revolution of 1848*, New Brunswick, NJ: Transaction.

Fox, J. E. and Miller-Idriss, C. (2008) 'Everyday nationhood', *Ethnicities*, 8: 536–76.

Klusemann, S. (2010) *After State Breakdown: Dynamics of Multi-Party Conflict, Violence, and Paramilitary Mobilization in Russia 1904–1920, Germany 1918–1934, and Japan 1853–1877*, PhD dissertation, University of Pennsylvania.

Mann, M. (1993) *The Sources of Social Power, Vol. 2: The Rise of Classes and Nation-States, 1760–1914*, Cambridge: Cambridge University Press.

Tilly, C. (1995) *Popular Contention in Great Britain, 1758–1834*, Cambridge, MA: Harvard University Press.

Tilly, C. (2003) *The Politics of Collective Violence*, Cambridge: Cambridge University Press.

Tilly, C. (2004) *Social Movements, 1768–2004*, London: Paradigm.

5

COMPETITION AS RITUAL AND THE LEGITIMATION OF THE LIBERAL NATION STATE

Jonathan Hearn

Introduction: nationalism, ritual and competition

One of the main puzzles in the study of ritual, symbolism and nationalism is establishing how we know that national rituals and symbols are having a significant effect, and not just being routinely observed, indifferently, out of habit. How do we know whether the Fourth of July is being experienced as an intensification of national identity or just a picnic? In their contributions to this volume, Jon Fox and Anthony Smith articulate opposing views on this question, Fox advocating a sceptical view from below and caution about assuming the deep effects of national rituals, and Smith arguing that we should take such rituals as evidence as of a discursive frame shared between elites and non-elites around the significance of the nation. My approach to this question is to worry less about who is sending and who is receiving the messages that rituals generate, and to ask rather: what do rituals do? How do they contribute to a social order that is national? I address this question about the process of ritual and performances by exploring the role and features of competition within liberal forms of society. This problem of assessing the impact of national rituals is even more acute when considering those of liberal societies, where states and governments, as a matter of principle, make milder demands on identity and solidarity, allowing considerable degrees of disengagement and dissent. My argument is that the ritualization of competition in liberal societies plays an important role in fostering national identity and cohesion, and, perhaps more importantly, in legitimating the general system of power relations and authority that undergird such societies.

Before proceeding, let me clarify how I am using the terms 'competition' and 'ritual'. I take competition in its broadest sense to indicate the organic struggle for existence that so fascinated Charles Darwin (1998 [1859]), and, more narrowly, the struggles over resources and supremacy that have gone on within and between societies for millennia. But I want to make a key analytic distinction between the brute fact of what we might call 'natural' competition and competition as 'artifice'. There is a difference between people and other life forms competing over limited goods due to the sheer force of circumstance, and the conscious cultivation and formalization of competition, as a way of addressing certain issues, and pursuing deliberate ends. It is this 'artificial' kind of competition that is my concern here. But it must be recognized that artificial forms of competition are perceived against the backdrop of more natural forms of competition; that the boundary between the two is sometimes difficult to parse, and that this has the ideological effect of naturalizing artificial forms of competition, making them seem more inevitable – part of the natural order of things.

'Ritual' is a word that simultaneously risks meaning too much and too little. At one extreme, it gets attached strictly to efforts, mainly religious, to establish a relationship between profane and sacred spheres, through stylized, symbol-laden actions. At the other, it gets attached to any trivial, routine, repetitive behaviour, such as a particular way of preparing one's breakfast, or getting one's desk in order before beginning a task of writing (Kertzer, 1988: 8–9). In the former, we commune with the supernatural; in the latter, we perform mindless habits. This banal sense of ritual is basically irrelevant to the present discussion. But I do want to stress the importance of looking beyond particular, elaborate, large-scale rituals to a much wider ritual complex, in which a range of similarly formalized and symbolically underpinned rituals run from the grand to the minute, from holy Mass to the odd 'hail Mary'. Moreover, we may need to think of ritual as not so much a matter of kind as of degree. The sacred may shade into the mundane, and ritual may run the gamut from profound to banal. Be that as it may, while exploring a basically secular form of ritual, I nonetheless want to maintain the idea that, in this sense of 'ritual complexes' that pervade society (cf. Collins, 1994: 232–4), ritual does provide clues to 'cosmology'; that is, underlying, taken-for-granted beliefs about the social and natural orders, which help sustain the organization of social power (cf. Rappaport, 1999; Wolf, 1999: 279–91).

In the Durkheimian tradition, ritual is primarily associated with the formation and consolidation of social solidarity and group identity (Durkheim, 1965). The ritual and its symbols instantiate the group and its relations, both internally between members and externally with the supernatural. Durkheim placed great emphasis on ritual as marking the boundary between the sacred and the profane, and I have just questioned that premise. In addition, while not entirely rejecting Durkheim's insights, I would put more emphasis on the power dimension, which was often neglected in his thought. I see ritual as centrally concerned with the definition, dramatization and legitimation of power in society, not just the affirmation of identity and social solidarity. Thus, methodologically, I am inclined to argue that we should proceed by identifying core power processes, and looking for the corresponding rituals, rather than identifying intriguing rituals, and then seeking explanations for them. My basic contention here is that beginning with power structures in society will help us distinguish important from unimportant rituals.

I am sympathetic to Robert Wuthnow's broad definition of ritual as 'a symbolic-expressive aspect of behaviour that communicates something about social relations, often in a relatively dramatic or formal manner' (Wuthnow, 1987: 109). However, I am inclined to argue that the most important, culturally central rituals are not just 'about social relations', but more specifically about how power is socially organized, either affirming or challenging the state of affairs, and sometimes doing both at once (cf. Gluckman, 1954).

The performative aspect of ritual is crucial to my argument. Rituals are performative in at least two senses. On the one hand, they dramatically communicate messages to participants and wider audiences. They say something about society to society. On the other, they perform acts (Austin, 1975), effect transformations, classic examples being weddings and initiation ceremonies, which alter the social statuses of the participants – the doing makes it so. Competitions exhibit both of these aspects, at once dramatizing a key aspect of the social order while also effecting and validating a change in social statuses, separating winners and losers, and apportioning rewards accordingly. They not only dramatize social order, they are an active element in its reproduction. I am sympathetic to Roy A. Rappaport's argument that much of the force of ritual lies in how it links the concrete specificity of individuals to invariant canonical and liturgical forms, seeming to infuse the particulars of life with transcendent order, with eternal truths (Rappaport, 1999: 23–58). I think that in modern liberal society, competition provides a central guiding principle, which is continually being affirmed through ritualized forms that legitimate actual outcomes and real distributions of power and rewards.

In sum, to really understand nationalism and national identity in liberal nation states, we need to look beyond the more overt civic rituals that affirm national identity and social solidarity (e.g. national days, funerals of public figures, pilgrimages to historic sites, etc.) and look for those rituals that, in their very form and performance, affirm and dramatize the constitution of society. Examining the ritualization of competition helps us do this.

The problem of national ritual in a liberal context

First, another clarification: by 'liberal society' or 'the liberal nation state', I indicate the complex interdependency between *capitalist* economic systems, *democratic* political institutions and *cultural values* stressing individual freedom and autonomy, all generally bound together by a single *state and legal system*. It is an emergent historical form, not a philosophical ideal. The role of national ritual in this context is particularly complicated.

Ritual, especially in Durkheimian terms, is often seen as intrinsically conservative, its basic function to reaffirm the given social order. Of course, this is often the case. But we should not forget rituals can also play a more generative role in challenging old orders, as in the recent public demonstrations against authoritarian regimes sweeping the Arab world from 2011, and in establishing new orders, as in the wave of new symbols and rituals that followed the French Revolution of 1789 (Kertzer, 1988: 12). Liberal nation states, based on capitalist economies and democratic political institutions, pose a certain paradox here. Because the form of social order itself is premised on maintaining considerable economic and political dynamism, but also stability, the conservative and innovative functions of ritual are strangely fused. It is in this light that the ritualization of competition is particularly important for understanding the workings of the liberal nation state, because it is competition that simultaneously propels and regulates, however imperfectly, core political and economic activities. Competition is conflict controlled. It is a 'hot', dangerous object at the heart of daily life.

Mary Douglas once commented on the tendency, especially during the radical 1960s, to equate ritual with empty formalism, with the social control of more natural and authentic impulses (Douglas, 1973). She felt this view underestimated the important function of rituals in dramatizing social order for its participants. Nonetheless, the view from which she was dissenting is somehow diagnostic of liberal society, in which the privileging and maximizing of individual autonomy, at least as an ideal value, grinds against the idea of ritual as something that brings people into conformity, in which the collective subsumes the individual. There is a certain dissonance between the ideas of ritual and liberalism.

This is not to deny the many public civic rituals found in liberal nation states, whether commemorations of national suffering and loss in war, celebrations of national triumph, or more simply of national cultural identity (or identities). These clearly have some role in affirming and consolidating national identities and solidarities. But, as I suggested at the outset, there are questions about the exact purchase of public rituals on individual consciousness in relatively liberal forms of nationalism. In some ways, the efficacy, or at least attempted efficacy, of political ritual is more apparent in authoritarian regimes and forms of intensified ethnic politics. In these, the participants are in some sense obliged to buy into national rituals, or keep their dissent from and resistance to the ritual hidden. Liberal society, on the other hand, by its nature allows citizens much more scope to opt in or out of public rituals, to engage with them deeply, superficially, or not at all. General privatization, affluence and cultural and ideological diversity weaken the conditions for intensifying national rituals. Because of this difference, I think there is a danger of reading too much meaning, and too much effect, into relatively overt public, civic rituals in liberal nation states.

My basic point here is that rituals will operate differently in different societal contexts, which provide the conditions for their functioning. Where power and authority are tightly focused in the state, a single ruling party or a single leader, the conditions for participating in and interpreting the national rituals on offer are very different from more liberal forms of society. In liberal societies, power and authority, as a matter of principle, are understood as more diffused and multi-centred (even if this may, to some degree, obscure actual concentrations of social power). We should not assume that national rituals are 'one size fits all', but rather that they will take on forms specific to certain types of political environment and social order. It is not sufficient to ask, 'How do rituals work?' We must also ask how they might work differently in different contexts: conservative, revolutionary, authoritarian, liberal and so on.

Competition: institutional embedding and ritual forms

Despite its ubiquitous presence in modern liberal society, sociologists have paid relatively little attention to competition. The florescence of 'conflict theory' in the 1960s (Collins, 1975; Coser, 1956) nonetheless failed to produce a specific line of inquiry about competition as a social institution. Of course, the concept looms larger, but is also more restricted in its application, in economics and politics. Among the classical sociologists, it is really only Simmel who gave the concept special attention, emphasizing its formal qualities and socially integrating function (Helle, 2008; Simmel, 1955). There are some exceptions, not surprisingly in the field of economic sociology (Burt, 1993; Podolny, 2005), and perhaps less expectedly in the study of religion, where there have been debates about whether competing religious institutions (churches) tend to drive up religious participation (Finke and Stark, 1998; Trejo, 2009). Closer to the study of nationalism, there is a well-established argument that the formation of the modern state in Europe was accelerated by military-imperial competition between dynastic states (Mann, 1988; Tilly, 1975). While all are important, none of these approaches really get at the analysis of competition as a systemic feature of the liberal nation state that I advocate. Simmel's rather abstract ruminations come closest, but are very speculative and not embedded in a thoroughgoing social analysis.

This deficit is odd, because the reflexive cultivation of competition is a defining feature of liberal society. The great modern shift in political authority and legitimation, from a heritable right of landowning elites, to a collective right of a people – a 'demos' (Bendix, 1978; Wood, 1991) – poses a fundamental problem: how are 'the people' to agree who, in practical terms, does the day-to-day ruling? The revolutionary-authoritarian answer has been for a single political party and leader to claim to effectively represent the totality. But the liberal-democratic answer has been to gradually build up institutional mechanisms to guide the controlled, systematic contest for political leadership; that is, to make factions and interest groups compete for power through various models of democracy. These developments have corresponded with the rise of the market economy, in which open competition between economic actors, within various legal frameworks, has been encouraged. There is a basic complimentarity between the organizing rationale of competition in both the political and economic spheres. The legitimacy of activities in these spheres rests on the principle that they are subject to true competition. Of course, these institutions and their principles of competition are imperfect and often corrupted. But this does not alter competition's *de facto* role in the legitimation of outcomes in the practical distribution of power.

However, there is an inherent ambiguity in turning to competition to help resolve power conflicts and distributional problems, which hinges on the distinction between natural and artificial forms of competition raised at the outset. As a social form, competition ambiguously fuses principles of 'might' and 'right'. On the one hand, outcomes get resolved through the demonstrated capacity to prevail and dominate, through sheer competitive might, within the rules of a given 'game' (be it political, economic or even aesthetic). On the other, many contests are ultimately resolved by 'experts' with a socially constituted right and authority to make relevant allocative judgements. Some competition rituals are simply won in the act of contest, while others are won by being judged the winner. And there are hybrid forms that combine these two principles for resolving outcomes. This (con)fusion of natural order and social artifice in the resolution of outcomes is part of what gives ritualized competition its ideological spread, bite and force.

For heuristic purposes, although I have acknowledged that competition is a very general, ubiquitous phenomenon, and that highly formalized competition shades into a broader social environment of competition, I develop an idea of competition as a ritual form. I suggest we conceptualize *competition rituals* as distinct from a more general competitive environment, as *formalized procedures for channelling conflict and resolving the allocation of limited goods, in ways that are often dramatically and symbolically elaborated and heightened.* How we harness, structure and manage competition through ritual is contextually varied, achieving effects through different context-specific rules and cultural understandings. Nonetheless, these variations weave together into a wider social fabric, in which formalized competition forms part of a common sense, or folk, wisdom about how distributional issues are best resolved. We can begin mapping the complexity of ritual form and function by abstracting certain 'ideal types' (Swedberg, 2005: 119–21), which reflect the tensions between might and right, nature and artifice, noted above. Consider the diagram in Figure 5.1.

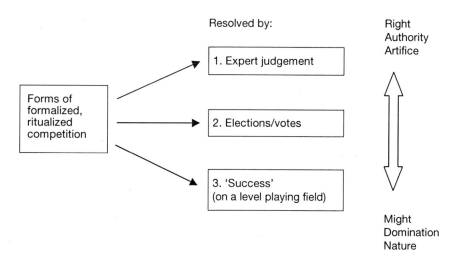

FIGURE 5.1 A typology of competition rituals.

To elaborate briefly on the three boxes in the middle column:

1   Some competition rituals are resolved by the judgement of an expert or panel of experts. This is especially typical of academic and arts competitions (e.g. the Booker Prize), but also plays a role in some kinds of sporting competition, such as gymnastics or boxing, and various kinds of appointment procedures. This form assumes the existence of authorities that are competent to judge, and the process can be undermined and invalidated by corruption or incompetence on their part.

2   Some competition rituals are resolved by winning votes in elections. The paradigm here is, of course, competition for political office. This type of competition ritual is absolutely central to the legitimation of democratic political systems, with electoral corruption and low voting participation raising problems for the legitimacy of the political system (cf. Beetham, 1991: 117–60).

3   This is the most enigmatic and perhaps significant type of competition ritual, paradigmatically represented by many kinds of sports. Here, the competition is resolved by the outcome itself, realized by one party (individual or team) achieving the target goal over the competitor (e.g. over the finish line first, the most points when time is up). To be legitimate, the outcome must be achieved within the rules, on a 'level playing field', with no unfair advantage given to any competitor. But judgement and decision, while they may help regulate (i.e. referee), do not determine the final outcome – if they do, something has gone wrong with the ritual. Ideally, the outcome should reflect only differences in the qualities of the players/contenders.

There are, of course, hybrid combinations of these types. For instance, some groups of experts will seek consensus, while others will resort to voting. (An example from popular culture is the television series *The X Factor*, which combines panel judgements with audience voting to determine which contestants are knocked out in successive rounds.) Nonetheless, I suggest these ideal types highlight three very distinct mechanisms for determining outcomes – expert judgement, majority opinion and performative success – which nonetheless all get framed within ritualized forms of competition and presented as variants on the same thing.

There is an important 'elective affinity', or underlying analogy, between type 2 rituals and politics and type 3 rituals and the economy. Resolution of competition by popular vote is uniquely suited to mass democratic politics, providing a mechanism for aggregating broad public opinion into support for contenders for power and leadership. There are obviously elements of type 1 in the selection of candidates to put forward by the party core. And there is a sense in which the sheer winning of the political contest, above and beyond the electoral mandate, stands as a demonstration of political skill, bringing in elements of type 3. But the process of democratic competition is anchored in the popular vote, and simply could not exist without it. Type 3 rituals have a particular affinity with the much less bounded, but still formalized, and, in many respects, rule-governed competition in the economy, in which the outcome of the contest is its own validation. Contenders (corporations, companies, entrepreneurs, etc.) compete for advantage in markets, and can be knocked out of the competition (i.e. fail, go bankrupt). They must, in theory, 'play by the rules' (no industrial espionage, rigging of contracts, etc.). And there is a cultural fiction of a 'level playing field', often problematically presented as intrinsic to market relations (see Crouch, 2011). There is sometimes a rough argument that consumer purchasing power functions rather like the popular vote, endorsing certain companies and their products, thus introducing an element of type 2 into the realm of economic competition. Nonetheless, the defining feature of economic competition, which is highly naturalized in the popular imagination, is precisely that its outcomes are validated not by a small group of experts, nor by the aggregation of collective will, but rather by sheer success in the satisfaction of private demand.

In addition to this deep affinity between ideal types of competition rituals and the core social domains of politics and economy, there is a penumbra of competition rituals that saturate popular culture. I have already mentioned the obvious arena of sports, and *The X Factor*, but of course we could add a whole series of award ceremonies for the popular arts, and (cheaply produced) television shows premised on participants competing to win prizes for their cooking skills, or ability to remain locked inside a house, in a jungle camp, or on a coach tour (again, with a mixture of procedures for resolving outcomes). At this level, we move well beyond competition rituals as a functional device for legitimating the allocation of social goods, and into the realm of society representing itself back to itself, almost as parody. I suggest that there is more to this than simply low-cost mass entertainment. The very fact that this appeals as a form of entertainment suggests it resonates with basic, mass-level experiences and understandings of how society works. The ancient Roman crowd was entertained by bloody, life-and-death gladiatorial contests that encapsulated the martial infrastructure that underpinned the empire's expansionist dynamic. Similarly, we are entertained by a steady stream of over-the-top competition rituals, which reaffirm the general social order while also raising it to a level of absurdity.

Let me suggest, more generally, how 'high' competition rituals merge by degrees into a more general social environment of competition. An indicator that we are dealing with competition in one of its more highly abstracted and ritualized forms is that the 'good' or 'goal' that is the object of competition is constituted by the ritual itself. Without the competition ritual, the award, the prize, the status of being 'winner', could not exist. But in more mundane forms of competition that are nonetheless highly ritualized, the 'good' exists independently of the contest, and the contest serves precisely as a legitimate mechanism for allocating that scarce good. Access to political office, jobs, places at university, government and business contracts, homes, and so on ad infinitum, are normally regulated through formal procedures of competition. And the formalization of the competition is a sign of the high social value placed on the good being allocated. Further down, routine advancement in all kinds of middle-class careers is regulated by competitive procedures for promotion, outside funding and other forms of recognition. Finally, that most basic of social goods, employment, is almost always an object of competition to some degree. I am not saying that we are all enthusiastic competitors – we often play our appointed roles reluctantly, by force of circumstances rather than choice. But avoiding competition altogether is rarely an option. What I am saying is that competitive procedures are pervasive, and they run the gamut from highly stylized rituals that are almost ends in themselves (e.g. sports, entertainment), through major public dramas that allocate crucial public goods (e.g. political elections), down to the myriad everyday contests we are all personally subject to.

I would like to make two final points to this section. First, the anthropologist Max Gluckman referred to 'rituals of rebellion' (Gluckman, 1954), arguing that the ritualization of conflict can actually have socially integrating functions. While he had more a traditional sense of ritual in mind, my argument tends to concur with his. I see the ritualization of competition as, in a sense, one of the most refined developments of this principle. It is not just that certain rituals allow the expression of underlying social tensions, enabling participants to 'blow off steam', and thus re-equilibrating the social system. Competition rituals explicitly embody a socially approved method for channelling conflict and adjudicating distributions of limited goods. Competition rituals do not just contain social conflict; they harness and direct it (cf. Gluckman, 1955). Second, I have emphasized paradigmatic types within what I am calling 'competition rituals' to highlight what I see as basic characteristics and variations within the broader social form. However, unlike many arguments about ritual that emphasize its sharp separation from daily life (again, Durkheim, 1965), mine emphasizes precisely the opposite, that these paradigmatic forms simply augment and exaggerate ways of formalizing competitive behaviour that permeate society. They take normal, everyday competition, abstract it and raise it to a high dramatic pitch, and, at the same time, that high drama reflects back on, and in a sense endorses, the more mundane and routine forms of competition.

Connections to nationalism and national identity

It could reasonably be objected that what I am describing here is a phenomenon characteristic of liberal societies in general, and what this has to do with nations, nationalism and national identity in particular is not immediately obvious. There is some truth to this. I am trying to analyse a feature characteristic of a general type – but type of what? I would say a type of nation state. Just as certain rituals, say of the investiture of a monarch, were characteristic of a range of European feudal societies, the same can be said of competition rituals in regard to liberal society. But the focus on the more general sociopolitical form does not preclude attention to its more nation-specific functions. I elaborate, first by addressing the general relationship between the nation state and competition, and then returning to the notion of ritual in this context.

The nation state has an external, geopolitical face, and an internal, domestic face, and principles of competition operate differently on the inner and outer slopes of the modern state, while also interacting and reinforcing one another. It is conventional to imagine the global, international arena as one of economic competition, both between states and between more purely economic actors such as major corporations. As Liah Greenfeld (2001) has argued, economic competition among nations is one of the crucibles for the formation of modern national identity. Particularly in leading capitalist nation states such as the Britain and the US, but also in quasi-capitalist countries such as China, economic might, exhibited in the international arena, has strongly shaped notions of national greatness, pride and purpose. Even Iceland's recent unfortunate venture into the realms of high finance and international banking was driven by a reinvigorated national pride, a belief that new economic circumstances would allow a tiny country to punch way above its weight (Boyes, 2009). (National feelings swirling around various 'tigers', Asian and Celtic, could also be explored here.) The economist Paul Krugman (1994) has challenged much of the economic ideology around the idea of international competitiveness, arguing that countries are often in less direct competition than is suggested, and viewing the language of international competition as ideological cover for national policies weakening the bargaining strength of ordinary workers. But this does not really go against the thesis presented here. The mere presence of a powerful, normalizing language of competition, however misleading it may be in regard to reality, is evidence of the deep embedding of competition as a way of making sense of how the world operates.

Whatever the limits of notions of international economic competitiveness, the more general geopolitical view still holds: that states find themselves in an arena of international relations that involve competition. Much of the twentieth century after the Second World War was fundamentally shaped by the geopolitical struggle for global influence and hegemony between 'communism' (the USSR) and 'democracy' (the US). That the respective elites construed their situations in this way, and much of the populations they led during this period followed in this view, is readily apparent. Going further back, any quick review of the diverse discourses of fascism (e.g. Griffin, 1995) that preceded the Second World War reveals a language saturated with the idea that nations and nation states are fundamental social units locked in an inevitably militarist zero-sum struggle for supremacy. And, of course, one can go back even further to the contests between competing European imperialisms and mercantilisms. The point here is not to go into any great detail, but simply to remind ourselves that the economic struggles and transformations that have so preoccupied students of globalization in recent decades, and perhaps currently dominate our thoughts on competition, have their correlates in more strictly geopolitical struggles of long historical standing.

On the inner, domestic slope of the nation state, competition operates somewhat differently. It is not just a condition of existence, but also more fully a matter of law, of the rules of the game. Competition is a morally binding force legitimating power distributions among a body of citizens. Central here are the competition rituals of national politics itself. By legitimating political leaders through the competitive electoral process, the nation state itself is affirmed, as grounded in just principles of rule. And when that process appears corrupted, not genuinely competitive, its capacity to validate the national system of political power is called into question. On the economic front, although increasing 'global' competition is a factor, a great deal of the competition that small- and medium-sized enterprises engage in is framed within the nation state, which, through its laws and policies, sets much of the basic conditions for that competition (e.g. interest rates, monopoly and merger regulations, etc.). Although perhaps only implicit (cf. Billig, 1995), the legal regulation of competition in both economic and political spheres reinforces the national frame as a rule-bounded moral universe.

However, it is not just that people are bound together by their shared observance of principles of competition, but also that modern, market-driven societies identify much of their national strength and virtue, their 'national character', with the value of competitiveness (again, see Greenfeld, 2001). Competition is a purifying process that 'brings out the best' in the population, cultivating its strengths, and, in a word, its competitiveness. Endless anxieties about the competitiveness of workers, and declining educational standards, are symptomatic of this post-fascist, economically globalist preoccupation with national fitness. Competition within society, within the state's boundaries, is a proving ground for the unavoidable arena of competition beyond its boundaries, with other nation states. Finally, 'competition' itself becomes a kind of national value put on international display (often somewhat hypocritically, as when contradicted by government protection of agriculture in the US and the EU). Thus, when liberal democracies call for 'free and fair elections' in authoritarian regimes or newly formed states, or make arguments against the dangers of protectionism in the current global economic downturn, they present themselves as defenders and promoters of 'properly constituted' competition in the international arena.

Returning to ritual, it is apparent that what I have called 'competition rituals' are developed only to a limited degree in the international arena. While there are transnational bodies, such as the World Trade Organization, with a remit to regulate and promote competition to a degree in the international arena, this is a matter of tenuous inter-legal negotiations at a high governmental level, not of public ritual. The cases of transnational ritualized competition that immediately come to mind – the Olympics, the World Cup in football, perhaps the Eurovision Song Contest – are notable precisely for their marginal relationship to real geopolitics. They run alongside this as a diverting sideshow, on the one hand suggesting an international community of mutually respectful competitors, but also sometimes serving as proxies for underlying geopolitical rivalries (consider Olympic judges of gymnastics during the Cold War, or the national voting patterns of Eurovision). The predominance here of sports, and what I have called 'type 3' rituals, resolved by sheer performance, seems to correspond to a view of the international arena as one of naturalized competition, in which matters are resolved by the demonstration of might. Eurovision is the exception, but this is related to its perennially comical, slightly absurd air. It is within the bounds of the nation state that we find all three types of competition ritual highly elaborated in multiple forms. That is because it is within this frame that the main struggles over the allocation of key resources takes place, and has to be resolved and legitimated. Citizens are called to compete with each other over the resources that determine their fates (e.g., jobs, education, political representation), and simultaneously their cultural environment normalizes and routinizes competition through myriad rituals that both entertain and allocate more trivial resources.

I underscore the preceding argument with a brief illustrative contrast between two rituals, as I have defined them. As I write this in the UK, the Queen's Diamond Jubilee has just passed, an event that marked and celebrated her 60th year on the throne. As a celebration of the formal head of state and embodied symbol of the British nation, the event clearly ritualizes principles of national solidarity. By contrast, the next UK general election in 2015 will be a grubbier affair, involving cold electoral calculations and public disparagement of opponents. But I want to suggest that it is perhaps a better example of ritual, and one more closely integrated with sinews of society than the Queen's Diamond Jubilee.

The main celebrations of the Queen's Diamond Jubilee took place over the extended weekend of 2–5 June 2012. In addition to being a national holiday and celebration, it was also a major tourist attraction and opportunity for merchandising across the UK. On Saturday 2 June, the Queen attended the Epsom Derby. On Sunday 3 June, there was a boat pageant on the Thames and a festival celebrating 'design, music, art, film, fashion and food' in London's Battersea Park. On the same day, participants in the fourth annual 'Big Lunch', a civic project designed to enhance civic solidarity by encouraging citizens to hold local street parties, were invited to link this up with the Diamond Jubilee celebrations. Thus, the Big Lunches provided a more local link-in to what, as with other major events in the UK, might inevitably have become a somewhat London-centric event. On Monday 4 June, the Queen and Royal Family attended a BBC-organized concert, followed by the lighting of Diamond Jubilee beacons across the world in Commonwealth countries. Finally, on Tuesday 5 June, the celebrations culminated in a service of thanksgiving at St Paul's Cathedral, including a choir made up of children from across the UK. This was followed by a carriage procession from Westminster Hall to Buckingham Palace, capped off by the Royal Family observing an RAF fly-past from a balcony (see Directgov, 2012).

The accent here is on celebrating Britain, not just the Queen, in as diverse and inclusive a way as feasible. A recent Guardian/ICM poll found that '67 per cent of all people – including 73 per cent of women and 57 per cent of 18–24s – think the monarchy is relevant to life in Britain today' (Glover, 2011). So, although it is uncertain how Britons see the monarchy as relevant – whether as a spur to tourism, as an element in the constitution, or otherwise – there appears to be general support and willingness to identify with the Diamond Jubilee as a national celebration (perhaps more strongly in the south-east of the UK). But the key question in relation to my argument is this: how important is it for the reproduction of British society and its political system? However the event may enhance general social solidarity and be symbolically necessary, given that there is a monarchy, it is difficult to argue that it is essential to the workings of society, or that it could not be dispensed with. Despite its many stylized elements and vocabulary of core national symbols, it does not appear to be doing much of the work of affirming the everyday social order. It is rather more like mass entertainment, as distraction, than the inner workings of society dramatized.

Following legislation in 2011, UK parliamentary elections have been set on a fixed five-year cycle, the next one scheduled for 7 May 2015. It will generally follow the established sequence of stages. Once the current session is concluded, on 13 April parliament will dissolve, a proclamation will set the date of the sitting of the next parliament and the Queen's opening speech, and writs will be issued for elections in the UK's 650 constituencies. A date will be set by which citizens 18 and over wishing to vote must register, candidates must submit their nomination papers to returning officers and election agents must be appointed. In terms of public political discourse, the campaigning will have already begun in some sense, but the formal campaign begins at this point. On 7 May, polling booths will be open between 7 a.m. and 10 p.m. at various public locations (usually schools). Counting begins when the polls close and continues through the following day. All of this is conducted under the scrutiny of an electoral commission, an independent body set up by the parliament that insures the integrity and legitimacy of the process. On a date previously designated, parliament returns and is sworn in, and the Queen's speech and formal opening follows soon thereafter (Parliament, 2012).

Within this formal, rule-governed framework of procedure, the cut and thrust that citizens normally recognize as the 'real' process will take place: hustings and campaign speeches, journalistic blasts and counter-blasts, paid political advertisements, and party activists handing out leaflets on street corners and going door to door. In the 2010 general election, the overall turnout of the electorate was 65.1 per cent, almost 4 per cent higher than the previous election, with constituency turnouts running from 77.3 per cent in East Renfrewshire to 44.3 per cent in Manchester Central (Cracknell *et al.*, 2010: 23). Thus, it is fair to say there is wide participation. Like many rituals, there is a core, scripted part and a penumbra of more spontaneous activity. There is a complex hemming in by ceremony of a somewhat dangerous period of liminality in which the nation is without government. There are ritual experts appointed to insure that things go according to the rules. And there is the mounting drama up to election night, when many people will stay up late glued to their television sets, enduring punditry, rooting for their side and awaiting the final results. Some are indifferent to this drama and its outcome, but many will consider it of the utmost importance for the health of the nation and its future fortunes. To drive home the point I am making, the Queen's Diamond Jubilee, for all its national symbolism and celebration, is largely a matter of performance, entertainment and recreation. The general election, on the other hand, precisely because it is built around competitive procedures that have the manifest effect of reconstituting government, reassigning social roles and reapportioning the core social good of state power, with an element of obligatory participation by all qualified members of society, much more fully exemplifies a 'ritual' in the classic, anthropological sense.

Conclusion

There is a tendency in the study of nationalism to a divide between those who focus on culture, symbols, discourse and meaning, and those who prefer power, institutions, organization and resources, in their efforts to understand nationalism. The broader implication of the present argument for nationalism studies is that some of the most interesting questions involve the crossover between these approaches. The idea of competition as ritual implies that the organized allocation of power relies on, indeed is saturated with, symbolism and meaning. It also suggests that liberal forms of society, while more weakly defined in terms of ethnicity and its symbols, are nonetheless fruitful for investigating the interactions of power, symbol and ritual in the constitution of nations.

In his major study of ritual, Roy A. Rappaport argues that athletic contests are not rituals in the proper sense (Rappaport, 1999: 37–46). I disagree, and the reasons, which hinge on different understandings of 'performance', are perhaps instructive for summing up the present argument. For Rappaport, rituals are essentially about the unification of those involved, through shared participation in relatively invariant and formalized sets of canonical acts, at least partly inherited by the actors, which override social divisions. For him, athletic events, by contrast, involve a fairly sharp division between audience/fans and contestants (the true participants), are unpredictable in their outcomes (part of the point), and have disjunctive effects, separating winners from losers. Leaving aside his highly elaborated theory of ritual and focusing only on this distinction, it seems to me he fails to appreciate the peculiar nature of formalized competition. First, he underplays the binding power of competition, which distinguishes it from mere conflict. It is not just that players are bound together by rules of fair play, but also by more complex commitments to the game itself, as such, and to each other as worthy opponents, as the loyal opposition, on which the entire activity depends. Moreover, the audience of fans and supporters partakes, however vicariously, in this same experience of unity through rivalry. Second, while on one level the outcome and winner(s) are undetermined in advance and unprescribed by the ritual, that there will be winners and losers is prescribed, and at the very heart of the ritual. If this fails to happen, something has gone wrong. Finally, and most importantly, ritual in the sense associated with religion, which is Rappaport's main concern, purports to put people in touch with fundamental cosmological principles that order the universe. I would argue that competition rituals such as athletic ones also, and for many profoundly, appear to say something about, and put participants experientially in touch with, what are understood as basic organizing principles in their reality. Such competitions appear to abstract out, distil and highlight underlying principles of life and social order, in often intensely compelling performances, which both dramatize and effect social statuses. Needless to say, what I have argued here in regard to the interpretation of athletic events as ritual applies more generally to competition rituals as I have defined them.

To avoid confusion, I am not arguing that competition is an entirely artificial social construct. There is a sense in which we find competition in nature, in processes of biological evolution, and the general course of non-biological human social evolution can usefully be conceived as a process of competition and selection among social forms (Hodgson and Knudsen, 2006). But neither am I trying to suggest that competition rituals are simply a manifestation of this underlying 'natural' substrate. They are indeed highly artificial, infused with human intent, full of historical contingencies, an imposition of a particular strategy for generating social order out of much wider possibilities. That is the point, and part of what makes them so effective. They offer up an approach to making social order, as if it emerged directly and unproblematically out of the natural order. But no such option is available to humans.

The central thrust of this chapter has been that, when it comes to understanding the role of ritual in the modern nation state, too much emphasis on a Durkheimian concept of ritual modelled on religion can be partial and misleading. While not denying this aspect, I suspect that such rituals do only a part of the overall work of validating and integrating social relations, of legitimating power. I have argued that we need to examine the network or 'complex' of rituals that permeate society, running the gamut from intense and elaborate performances to much more mundane procedures. Competition rituals are particularly significant for analysing the workings of the liberal nation state because they encode certain core values, certain notions of fairness, justice and identity. They do the work not just of symbolizing authority and the nation, but of actually apportioning power and other social rewards. Competition, and its ritualization, takes us to the heart of liberal culture and its embedding in the modern nation state.

References

Austin, J. L. (1975) *How To Do Things With Words*, 2nd edn, Cambridge, MA: Harvard University Press.

Beetham, D. (1991) *The Legitimation of Power*, Basingstoke: Palgrave Macmaillan.

Bendix, R. (1978) *Kings or People: Power and the Mandate to Rule*, Berkeley, CA: University of California Press.

Billig, M. (1995) *Banal Nationalism*, London: Sage.

Boyes, R. (2009) *Meltdown Iceland: How the Global Financial Crisis Bankrupted and Entire Country*, London: Bloomsbury.

Burt, R. S. (1993) 'The social structure of competition', in R. Swedberg (ed.) *Explorations in Economic Sociology*, New York: Russell Sage Foundation, pp. 65–103.

Collins, R. (1975) *Conflict Sociology: Toward an Explanatory Social Science*, New York: Academic Press.

Collins, R. (1994) *Four Sociological Traditions*, New York: Oxford University Press.

Coser, L. A. (1956) *The Functions of Social Conflict*, London: Routledge & Kegan Paul.

Cracknell, R., Berman, G., Bolton, P., Booth, L., Hardacre, J., Keep, M., Keith, K., Tetteh, E., and Thompson, G. (2010) 'General Election 2010, preliminary analysis', Research Paper 10/36, House of Commons Library.

Crouch, C. (2011) *The Strange Non-Death of Neoliberalism*, Cambridge: Polity.

Darwin, C. A. (1998 [1859]) *The Origin of Species*, Ware: Wordsworth Editions.

Directgov (2012) 'The Queen's Diamond Jubilee – celebrations and events', available at: www.direct.gov.uk/en/Nl1/Newsroom/Features/DG_WP200687 (accessed 14 May 2012).

Douglas, M. (1973) *Natural Symbols: Explorations in Cosmology*, New York: Vintage Books.

Durkheim, É. (1965) *The Elementary Forms of the Religious Life*, New York: Free Press.

Finke, R. and Stark, R. (1998) 'Religious choice and competition', *American Sociological Review*, 63(5): 761–6.

Glover, J. (2011) 'Monarchy still broadly relevant, Britons say: support for royals remains constant but royal wedding greeted by tolerant scepticism, Guardian/ICM poll finds', *The Guardian*, 24 April, available at: www.guardian.co.uk/uk/2011/apr/24/monarchy-still-relevant-say-britons (accessed 14 May 2012).

Gluckman, M. (1954) *Rituals of Rebellion in South-East Africa (The Frazer Lecture, 1952)*, Manchester: Manchester University Press.

Gluckman, M. (1955) 'The peace in the feud', *Past and Present*, 8(1): 1–14.

Greenfeld, L. (2001) *The Spirit of Capitalism: Nationalism and Economic Growth*, Cambridge, MA: Harvard University Press.

Griffin, R. (ed.) (1995) *Fascism*, Oxford: Oxford University Press.

Helle, H. J. (2008) 'Soziologie Der Konkurrenz – sociology of competition by Georg Simmel', *Canadian Journal of Sociology*, 33(4): 945–78.

Hodgson, G. M. and Knudsen, T. (2006) 'Why we need a generalized Darwinism, and why generalized Darwinism is not enough', *Journal of Economic Behavior and Organization*, 61: 1–19.

Kertzer, D. I. (1988) *Ritual, Politics and Power*, New Haven, CT: Yale University Press.

Krugman, P. (1994) 'Competitiveness – a dangerous obsession', *Foreign Affairs*, 73(2): 28–44.

Mann, M. (1988) *States, War and Capitalism*, Oxford: Blackwell.

Parliament (2012) 'General Election timetable 2015', available at: www.parliament.uk/about/how/elections-and-voting/general/general-election-timetable-2015/ (accessed 14 May 2012).

Podolny, J. M. (2005) *Status Signals: A Sociological Study of Market Competition*, Princeton, NJ: Princeton University Press.

Rappaport, R. A. (1999) *Ritual and Religion in the Making of Humanity*, Cambridge: Cambridge University Press.

Simmel, G. (1955) *Conflict and the Web of Group-Affiliations*, New York: Free Press.

Swedberg, R. (2005) *The Max Weber Dictionary: Key Words and Central Concepts*, Palo Alto, CA: Stanford University Press.

Tilly, C. (ed.) (1975) *The Formation of National States in Western Europe*, Princeton, NJ: Princeton University Press.

Trejo, G. (2009) 'Religious competition and ethnic mobilization in Latin America: why the Catholic Church promotes indigenous movements in Mexico', *American Political Science Review*, 103(3): 323–42.

Wolf, E. R. (1999) *Envisioning Power: Ideologies of Dominance and Crisis*, Berkeley, CA: University of California Press.

Wood, G. S. (1991) *The Radicalism of the American Revolution*, New York: Vintage.

Wuthnow, R. (1987) *Meaning and Moral Order: Explorations in Cultural Analysis*, Berkeley, CA: University of California Press.

PART II

Applications

6

RITUAL IN THE EARLY LOUVRE MUSEUM

Carol Duncan

My topic focuses on the early years of the Louvre Museum as a ritual of national identity, and, more broadly, on the terms by which art museums and galleries may be considered as ritual sites.[1] The officials who shaped the museum in the two decades immediately following the French Revolution created a ceremonial space designed to make the new relationship between the nation and its citizenry come alive as a symbolically lived experience. It should be noted at the outset that the idea of the nation implicit in the galleries of the early Louvre Museum was the civic nation, a political concept structured in what were understood to be universal terms. In theory, the museum programme was equally uplifting to all of its visitors; in practice, it constructed the viewer as belonging to the educated and self-educating strata of French society. And while it celebrated the advantages of being a French citizen, it also asserted French pre-eminence within a community of nations that shared a common elite art culture. In all this, the Louvre's managers created a prototype for national art collections that was followed throughout Europe and beyond.

The rise of the public art museum

Galleries decorated with art collections have a long history in Europe. Displays of objects now regarded as works of art were common in both classical and medieval times in the treasuries of temples, churches and palaces. Modern art galleries – spaces that we would recognize today as art galleries – have their beginnings in Renaissance palaces, where displays of art treasure were assembled as monuments to the great princes of church and state. Contributing to this development was an emergent secular culture that began elaborating a modern concept of 'art', one that put increasing value on the quality and uniqueness of an artist's mental labour as distinct from the quality and quantity of his manual skill and the cost of his materials.

Public art museums – art collections that in some way belong to a community or nation as a whole – appear in the late eighteenth and early nineteenth centuries, the era that brought into being the modern nation state. Indeed, national galleries were and still are prized attributes of modern states, thanks to their ability to make manifest what Benedict Anderson (1991) called the 'imagined community' of the nation and to confirm its international prestige vis-à-vis other nations. The most dramatic demonstration of this power of the museum was in revolutionary France, where the new republican state seized what had been the art collection of a royal palace and declared it the property of the nation, henceforth open to all comers. In doing so, the Revolution appropriated a type of ritual space that had evolved over preceding centuries as an accessory of princely splendour, and turned it into a setting for the ritual celebration of the new state.

Among the Louvre's majestic halls is the Apollo Gallery (Figure 6.1), once Louis XIV's reception hall and the ceremonial heart of the seventeenth-century royal palace. Throughout its interior, an elaborate decorative scheme of gilded, carved

FIGURE 6.1 Apollo Gallery, Louvre Museum.

and painted surfaces celebrates the glories of Apollo, the deity with whose radiance Louis XIV sought to identify his royal person. The Revolution overlaid that meaning with a new one and spelled it out on the lintel over the gallery's entrance. On it is inscribed the Revolutionary Assembly's decree of 1792 ordering the creation of a national museum as a commemorative monument to the fall of the monarchy (Figure 6.2). The Assembly also ordered this monument to be open to all. In an instant, the gallery was made to salute the existence of 'the nation' and its principle of equal citizenship. From now on, a public art museum or national gallery could be taken as proof that the ruling power of a state was committed to serving its 'people' by making the nation's cultural treasures public property, or at least accessible to all. Museum fever quickly spread throughout Europe as monarchs hastened to declare their royal collections national galleries. In several instances, these new galleries were 'public' institutions in name only, since the 'publics' in

FIGURE 6.2 Entrance to the Apollo Gallery.

question were often subjects of a crown, not citizens with rights. (The painting collection in the Dulwich Picture Gallery, discussed below, was originally assembled for just this kind of 'national gallery'.) However they were brought into being, the new museums were almost always housed in palatial buildings. Whether installed in former palaces or in purpose-built structures, their grand halls and galleries were scaled for large public gatherings, processions and ceremonies, and could give visitors a sense of presence in the 'imagined community' of the nation even when actual visitors were few in number.

Art galleries as ritual spaces

I will return to the early Louvre Museum presently. First, I want to touch on the antecedents of the public art gallery and the kinds of rituals they accommodated. I will also say something about how art galleries and museums in general may be considered as ritual sites.

The history of art galleries hinges on the ways art audiences of the past experienced and thought about art. Well before the eighteenth century, European elites were collecting it, displaying it with particular effects in mind and devoting ever-greater attention to its study and criticism. Accompanying these developments was a burgeoning philosophical interest in aesthetics, an interest that flowered in the writings of David Hume, Edmund Burke and Immanuel Kant. Although these men did not write about individual art works as such, they asked new questions about taste and beauty, and gave new import to sensual and imaginative experience. The appearance of art galleries together with the emergence of philosophical aesthetics testifies to an increasing expectation that looking at art not only was pleasurable, but also could have great cognitive and moral value. Or, to put it another way, art galleries and museums developed as ancillary to the growth of an aesthetic cult, providing it with its own type of ritual precinct.

By the late eighteenth century, enlightened opinion agreed that the most appropriate thing to do with an art object is contemplate it aesthetically. It followed from this that the type of place where this activity can best be done is in a gallery designed for the display of art objects, since there is little or nothing else to do in such a place, little or nothing to distract one from looking at art. Gallery space was recognized as a kind of lens that focuses the viewer's attention on a work's aesthetic meaning and pushes aside as extraneous any other meanings or uses it may once have had. Statues and paintings originally meant to fill viewers with thoughts of divinity or sacred narratives now became examples of the artistic genius of individual masters and/or their art-historical epochs. By the early decades of the nineteenth century, European high culture accepted museums as the most 'natural' of places in which to keep and look at art. This opinion became so uncontested in modern culture that one can easily lose sight of what historical oddities art museums once were: structures that are consecrated to a transcendent but not recognizably religious function, and that have no purpose other than to shelter objects that have no use-value other than to be looked at. It is this new activity of looking at things in art museums that I want to consider as a ritual activity.

From the perspective of Enlightenment thought – and, if anything, museums came into being under the aegis of Enlightenment rationality – it might seem contradictory to identify ritual experience with visits to museums. In their effort to undermine the authority of the church, Enlightenment philosophers were more likely to couple ritual with barbaric beliefs, superstitions or magical practices – irrational goings on that could hardly be identified with the contemplation and learning that museums supposedly foster. As modern anthropology has taught us, however, rituals can be unspectacular, even casual moments of contemplation or recognition, and our supposedly secular culture is full of ritual situations and events, very few of which take place in religious contexts. Like other cultures, we too build sites that represent dominant beliefs about the order of the world, its past and present, and the individual's place within it. Museums of all kinds provide excellent examples of such microcosms and often equip visitors with maps to guide them through the universes they construct.

Guidebooks almost always represent museums as the sum total of their collections and treat a museum visit as a series of individual encounters with rare and precious objects. To be sure, some museum settings – beautiful old palaces or glittering new structures by star architects such as Gehry or Liebeskind – may be as much or even more of a draw than their art collections, but most museum settings are the products of earlier periods and were designed to be impressive, albeit appropriately dignified, backgrounds for contemplating art objects. To understand museums as ritual settings, one must approach them as complex totalities comprising everything one sees, including architectural details, spatial sequences, the order in which collections are presented, the iconographic programs they realize and the way in which objects are installed and lit. Together, these elements may be seen as forming a ritual script, scenario or dramatic setting that prompts visitors to enact a performance of some kind – whether or not actual visitors would describe it as such and even if only some of them are educationally prepared to do so. This is not to imply that all art museums are equally coherent or effective as ritual sites; much depends on the particulars of the collections, the architectural possibilities of the setting, and the knowledge, skill and imagination of the curatorial staff.

In many traditional rituals, participants perform or witness a drama collectively. But a ritual performance may be something an individual enacts silently and alone by following a prescribed route, repeating a prayer, recalling a narrative, or engaging in some other programmed experience that relates to the history or meaning of the site or to some object or objects on the site. In art museums, it is the visitors who enact the ritual even when they are watching performance artists. In this, museums are comparable to older ritual sites such as monuments in which pilgrims follow a route, stopping at prescribed points for prayer or contemplation. The ambulatories of medieval churches are familiar instances of sites with built-in ritual routes. In them, the symbolic meaning of the pilgrim's walk around the altar is often articulated in images, reliefs or paintings; for example, carvings on choir screens that narrate a sacred story of sacrifice and salvation. Art museums, too, provide narratives that unfold through space and structure ritual performances. Even when visitors enter museums to see only selected works, the museum's larger narrative programme stands as a frame and gives meaning to individual works.

Implicit in every museum programme is an ideal visitor who is optimally prepared socially, psychologically and culturally to enact the museum ritual. Museums construct their ideal visitors with varying degrees of effectiveness, specificity and relevance to the experience and education of actual visitors. Inevitably, there will be visitors who are not prepared to 'get' all of the museum's ritual prompts, people who 'misread' or scramble or critically resist the museum's cues or who actively invent, consciously or unconsciously, their own programmes according to all the historical and psychological accidents of who they are. Visitors may fail to identify with or reject the social or cultural roles a scenario offers them (for example, when, as tourists, we visit religious monuments to faiths we do not share). But then, the same may be true of any situation in which cultural products, ancient or modern, are performed or interpreted. I make no attempt to construct an 'average visitor' or 'sample' of visitors. I work much like those art historians who study iconographic programmes in Renaissance chapels or other ritual sites and who interpret the ritual functions of a monument in the light of relevant cultural and historical contexts.[2]

Practiced museum-goers resemble users of traditional ritual sites in that they have learned to shift into an appropriate state of receptivity. Like many older ritual sites, museum space is marked off as a precinct reserved for a particular kind of contemplation. Monumental, costly architecture, grand entrances, pairs of lions, few or no windows – these are some of the features, many of them borrowed from ceremonial sites of the past, that help establish a boundary between museum space and the ordinary space outside. Such features cue visitors to put aside their everyday concerns and prepare for a different kind of experience. 'Liminality', a term used to describe the state of mind of a ritual performer, comes closest to the quality of attention art museums elicit. First used by the Belgian folklorist Arnold van Gennep, the term was adopted by the anthropologist Victor Turner to indicate a mode of consciousness outside of normal, day-to-day social and cultural states. Turner realized that the category of liminality had strong affinities to modern Western concepts of aesthetic experience, and he recognized aspects of liminality in such activities as attending the theatre, seeing a film or visiting an art exhibition (Turner, 1977a, 1977b). These cultural situations, he argued, could open a space in which individuals may step back from the practical concerns and social relations of everyday life and look at themselves and their world – or at some aspect of it – with different thoughts and feelings. Given that Turner's concept of liminality was developed out of anthropological categories and was based on data gathered mostly in non-Western cultures, he was cautious about superimposing it on to Western concepts of art experience. He characterized Western art experience as 'liminoid' rather than 'liminal', perhaps out of a reluctance to jettison entirely the Enlightenment dichotomy between the civilized and the savage.

Turner's caution notwithstanding, I find a striking affinity between philosophical notions of aesthetic experience and the liminality of ritual. The resemblance appears even in the presumed outcome of both phenomena. According to their advocates, museums give their visitors the same spiritual benefits as traditional rituals: a feeling of revelation or uplift and a sense of being mentally nourished, restored or refreshed. In other words, aestheticians gave the phenomenon of liminality a new philosophical formulation, recognizing it as a state in which the normal business of life is suspended – most famously encapsulated in Kant's notion of 'aesthetic disinterestedness'. Considered in historical perspective, the rise of aesthetics is a good example of the secularization of Western culture, a process in which various qualities of feeling and thought were moved from the religious to the secular sphere, put into new social and cultural settings, and given new theoretical formulations.

Over the past two centuries, writers have often described museum space in terms that come strikingly close to Turner's notion of liminality. I will cite only two such observers. In 1824, the English critic William Hazlitt visited the recently opened National Gallery in London, then installed in a house in Pall Mall. Hazlitt comes close to being an ideal gallery visitor; he was psychologically, philosophically and culturally prepared to enter a state of liminality, and he left a vivid account of his experience of it. Time and space in the gallery, he wrote, have an entirely different feel from time in the bustling world outside. The gallery's space is a 'sanctuary', a 'holy of holies'; to enter it

> is like going on a pilgrimage – it is an act of devotion performed at the shrine of Art! [It makes the] business of the world at large, . . . even its pleasures, appear like a vanity and an impertinence. [Inside,] we are abstracted to another sphere: we breathe empyrean air . . .
>
> (Hazlitt, 1824: 2–60)

A century and a half later, Sir Kenneth Clark, director of the same National Gallery and host of the much-aired BBC series of the 1970s *Civilization*, made the same claim for the liminality of museum space:

> The only reason for bringing together works of art in a public place is that . . . they produce in us a kind of exalted happiness. For a moment there is a clearing in the jungle: we pass on refreshed, with our capacity for life increased . . .
>
> (Clark, 1954: 29)

From the princely gallery to the connoisseurial hang

Beginning in the late eighteenth century, a variety of urban elites in both England and France – artist-academicians, *philosophe* journalists, enlightened connoisseurs and reform-minded government officials – began urging greater public access to art collections. In the same spirit, some aristocratic and bourgeois collectors began to make their collections more accessible to an expanded, albeit still selective, public.

In France, in the years prior to the Revolution, the crown itself was moving in the same direction. By the time of the Revolution, access to art's spiritual treasures came to be seen, at least by some, as a natural right, one that could even become symbolic of other rights. In this view, which was embraced by the revolutionary government, a national art museum that gives everyone access to the nation's riches is visible proof that the state is delivering on its promise of *égalité*.

This brings us back to the creation of the Louvre Museum, or, to put it more exactly, the creation of a museum within certain sections of the Louvre Palace. It would take some time to transform those spaces into a setting for a public art museum. The ceremonial halls of the old palace had been designed as backdrops for monarchical power. The most opulent of them, the Apollo Gallery (Figure 6.1), was not simply a state reception hall; it was the reception hall of an absolute monarch. It was meant to awe all who entered with the glory and might of the prince, a message painted and carved on to every surface through a complex iconography and countless symbols and insignia. When it was created in the seventeenth century, the Apollo Gallery was not an art gallery in the sense we use that term today; its decorations, commissioned for that specific site, did not incorporate a pre-existing art collection. But its baroque style of decoration became the authoritative style for princely reception halls across Europe, many of which were built to house art collections.

The hall represented in Panini's *Interior of a Picture Gallery with the Collection of Cardinal Silvio Valenti Gonzaga*, 1749 (Wadsworth Athenaeum, Hartford, Connecticut), more than equals the baroque excesses of the Apollo Gallery. Although it was based on an existing gallery, Panini greatly enlarged its scale and the extravagance of its ceiling decorations. I refer it here because, like other seventeenth- and eighteenth-century paintings of imaginary art galleries, its exaggerations make plain features that powerful men wanted their galleries to have, in this case splendour beyond belief and as much of the world's movable art as one could get hold of and cram on to a wall. This style of hanging pictures frame-to-frame with no visible wall surface is called a 'tapestry' or 'wallpaper' hang and was common in the baroque era. A thriving international market in oil paintings made such accumulations of art possible. Clearly, galleries such as this were not designed to facilitate the quiet contemplation of individual paintings.

In the later eighteenth and early nineteenth centuries, various European collectors began installing their galleries in new ways. The change was partly brought on by the decline of late baroque decorative fashions, but there were also new ideas afloat about what a visit to an art collection should entail. Installation styles were developed that prompted visitors to focus more on the art and less on the razzle-dazzle of the setting or the costliness of the collection. Collectors also adopted ways to draw attention specifically to their judgement as art connoisseurs. The tapestry hang was gradually discarded, and more wall space was allowed between works, enabling viewers to concentrate on one painting at a time. It became the fashion to hang pictures in groups or sequences that enabled viewers to better compare and contrast the styles of the principal schools of painting – Italian, Flemish,

Dutch and French – and their leading masters (by the later eighteenth century, the Spanish School was added). Accordingly, a portrait or religious subject by an Italian or French master might be paired with a painting of the same size and subject by a Flemish or Dutch master. Of course, these connoisseurial installations would have been intelligible only to those with some knowledge of the critical code underpinning them. And since tutoring in that code figured as part of the education of aristocratic young men from the wealthiest families, a gallery organized around its precepts could function as a test of one's class standing. A visit to such a collection could be an opportunity to display one's mastery of the code, and hence one's aristocratic refinement, by recognizing the various 'manners' of Titian, Rubens or Claude without the help of labels and by pronouncing the correct appreciative clichés before their works. Such exercises in class identity could be performed both domestically and internationally – class, not nation, is what mattered here. Ownership of and familiarity with art culture was so important that men of power, or men aspiring to more power and social standing than they already had, found it expedient to buy properly constituted collections of art wholesale and to retain experts to install them. In ritual terms, the connoisseurial gallery provided a stage enabling both host and visitor to perform as refined and noble individuals regardless of their actual origins. No doubt, as in art museums today, there were visitors not prepared to respond to the galleries' cues, people who came away with a sense of their inferior social standing or lack of refinement compared to their host's, or people who simply experienced themselves as outside the social and cultural orbits mapped out by the ritual. Women, rarely schooled in matters of art before the nineteenth century, might well have experienced themselves in these ways. Other viewers may have refused their assigned role on moral or aesthetic grounds – Puritans, for example, who frowned upon the sensual allure of the visual arts, or art professionals, who disdained the ruling taste of the day.

Dulwich Picture Gallery in south London (Figure 6.3), opened in 1817, is a good example of a connoisseurial collection. It was originally assembled by the English art dealer Noel Joseph Desenfans for King Stanislas Augustus of Poland, who planned to make it the core of a Polish national gallery. However, Stanislas was forced to abdicate while the collection was still in London, at which point efforts were made to keep it in London and open it as a public gallery. Eventually, it was given to Dulwich College in South London, where it was installed in a new, purpose-built structure designed by Sir John Soane (Waterfield, 1985). Today, the gallery is hung in the style of an early nineteenth-century connoisseurial collection, and, while its walls are less crowded than they were originally, the scale of the rooms in combination with the isolating function of the large frames promotes the intimacy that someone such as Hazlitt so savoured before paintings.

A civilizing ritual

I return now to the creation of the Louvre Museum. By the time of the Revolution, the Louvre had largely given up its palace functions to the nearby Tuilleries and

FIGURE 6.3 Dulwich Picture Gallery.

the more distant Versailles. But because the building was encrusted with historical memory, both figuratively and literally, it remained a potent icon of French state authority. To appropriate even a portion of the site for a national museum was to appropriate some of that authority and attach it to the new state. In both the Revolutionary period and the Empire, the government requisitioned several of the building's most magnificent rooms, turned them into museum galleries and opened them up to the public. (The 'museumization' of the palace would be completed in 1993, when the last government office moved out.) Thus, the old palace was brought back into service as a setting for state ceremonies. However, it is one thing to seize a palace and a royal art collection and declare them property of the nation and quite another to transform them into a site that convincingly says something to its visitors about the new French state and the place of citizens within it. Before the palace could be a museum of the French people, it had to undergo extensive alterations, both architecturally and symbolically.

The overthrow of the monarchy had created a compelling mandate to break with the symbols and rituals of the old regime and replace them with ones that could teach and celebrate the values and ideals of the new order. Officials of the Republic created new ritual sites, redesigned old ones and replaced the ceremonial paraphernalia of the old church-state order, borrowing heavily from classical mythology and history. During the Empire, despite the return of crowned heads and titles, the state maintained much of the rationalism, rhetoric and classicizing symbolism of Republican culture. So, in the Louvre Museum, beginning in the 1790s and continuing through the Empire, museumized rooms were given new iconographies or existing decorations were reinterpreted and reframed by means of new symbols and inscriptions.

Some of the museum's earliest exhibitions presented works of art as so many war trophies of the victorious French army.[3] Displays of looted treasure may have been crowd-pleasing, but they did not satisfy the need for a dignified presentation of the nation's art treasures. Indeed, government officials were anxious to demonstrate to foreigners and educated Frenchmen alike that, even in the midst of its revolutionary struggle, the state does not neglect '*le culte sacré des arts*'.[4] The task given to the museum's organizers, themselves sophisticated art professionals, was to produce a coherent and enlightened museum programme that would win international respect and make visible the values and ideals of a new order. The museum, wrote Minister of the Interior Roland, 'must attract the attention of foreigners, satisfy art lovers, and nourish a taste for the fine arts. In short, it must be one of the most powerful ways of illustrating "La Républic française"' (cited in Blum, 1946: 151–2). How to accomplish all of this posed difficult questions. The managers of the new institution engaged in protracted debates about what works should be put on display and how they should be ordered. There were often disputes about how much and in what ways the installations should look different from (or resemble) contemporary connoisseurial hangs. There were risks either way. If the new museum looked too much like the collections of the old nobility, it could be accused of perpetuating the corrupt and corrupting values of the old regime. But an installation that completely ignored the aesthetic character of the art in favour of educational goals could look monotonous and make the state appear ignorant of art's finer points. The discourse around these issues was often conditioned by shifts in the political scene, some of them violent, and changing ideological pressures, developments that could precipitate fierce power struggles and intrigue among the museum's administrators.

Nevertheless, and despite the turns and twists of political life, the Louvre's successive administrators developed a body of enduring musicological principles and practices. Already in 1794, an official report stated what would become the core of the museum's ritual scenario. The state's collections, it said, should show visitors 'the progress of art and the degrees of perfection to which it was brought by all those peoples who have successively cultivated it' (cited in Landais, 1981: xxv). The statement is based on a view that was advocated by many critics and art professionals of the time. In this view, progress in art can be measured by a single, universal standard: the *beau idéal*. The assumption was that all societies inexorably evolve towards this ideal, but that ancient classical sculpture, epitomized by the *Apollo Belvedere* and the painting and sculpture of the Italian Renaissance (especially the work of Raphael), achieved this ideal most fully. Beauty was not simply a matter of aesthetic judgement. It was a kind of moral elixir that lifted the spirit, instilled in one a love of reason and justice and, ultimately, worked to regenerate society. In the art culture of the museum and the state-run art academy, artistic style was an indicator of how far a people or epoch evolved towards the highest level of civilization. It also revealed the degree to which a society may have fallen away from that ideal, as seen, for example, in the degenerate works of artists such as Boucher or Van Loo, the darlings of wealthy patrons in the old regime. A museum worthy of the French nation would have to be much more than a pastime for dilettante aristocrats. It must be an instrument of moral and social regeneration. It must teach its visitors to recognize and appreciate the *beau idéal* in the art of the present as well as the past (Tuetey and Guiffrey, 1909).

In 1810, after undergoing extensive renovations and drawing from almost two decades of museological experience, the museum, renamed the Musée Napoléon, reopened. Newly hung and renovated sections together with galleries installed some years before were unified within a coherent programme that took visitors through what had become – and would remain – the museum's core ritual scenario. As in connoisseurial hangs of the past, the museum differentiated the principal 'schools' of painting and sculpture, but rather than emphasize the distinctive manner of each school, the installation emphasized the progress towards ideal beauty within each school. Compared to past practices, the installation gave more attention to chronological order, sometimes, as certain critics complained, at the expense of aesthetic quality.[5] By and large, the museum staff endeavoured to balance respect for the quality of outstanding masterpieces with the mandate to teach the story of art's progress. Visitors could see an outline of that story on the ceiling of the museum's 1800 entrance, the Rotunda of Mars.[6] In its centre is a mythological account of the origins of sculpture, surrounded by four ovals, each depicting a female personification of one of the four principal schools of sculpture: Egyptian, Greek, Italian and modern French. Each of these figures holds a key example of its school: Egypt, a cult statue; Greece, the *Apollo Belvedere*; Italy, Michelangelo's *Moses*; and France, Puget's *Milo of Crotona*. The ceiling thus represents key points in the history of Western sculpture, beginning with its antecedents in Egypt, continuing through its first flowering in classical antiquity, followed (after a dark age) by the rebirth of the classical spirit in the Italian Renaissance and concluding with the reflowering of that spirit in modern France. In the galleries beyond, visitors literally walked through this history of art, and, while doing so, it was presumed, relived step by step the progress of civilization, absorbing its civilizing, morally transforming charge.

As a ritual setting, the museum's galleries called upon the visitor to enact a persona very different from the one implicit in the nobleman's connoisseurial gallery. The latter set a stage for visitors to perform themselves as cosmopolitan *amateurs* of art, conversant with an international discourse of art criticism. The visitor to the Louvre was not a guest of royalty or aristocracy. He was there by right, as a citizen, come to the museum for enlightenment, aesthetic stimulation and self-improvement. No doubt, many if not most noblemen, French or otherwise, and even some women, could have enacted the museum's ritual, but the persona written into the script came closest to an idealized version of a self-improving French bourgeois male. The museum's programme, spelled out on the ceiling of the entry hall, invited him to savour (and foreigners to take note of) his place as a member of a nation that, more than any other, was heir to the classical spirit of the great civilizations of the past.[7] The museum's galleries were thus conceived as so many chambers of ritual transference wherein the progress of art became part of the historical and nationally specific heritage of the visitor. In time, the cult of classicism in art would turn into a stifling academic dogma and, finally, a superficial historicism, but in the Revolutionary and early Empire periods, it spoke not of slavish imitation of a dead past, but of regeneration of the classical spirit, a fresh engagement with reality and possibilities for a new future. Finally, whatever else one found there, passage through the galleries was a prolonged encounter with the French state, the power that organized and managed the nation's cultural life and that programmatically identified with the spirit of classical civilization more thoroughly and vigorously than any other nation at that time.

The history of the Louvre after the Empire lies outside the scope of this chapter, but it can be said, I think, without risking too much that throughout its long history, despite periodic reinstallations and expansions, the museum largely kept to its core narrative of the history of Western art, with emphasis on its classical heritage.[8] At times, this narrative has been reaffirmed with great effect. One such moment was the 1884 reinstallation of the *Victory of Samothrace* (Figure 6.4), a Greek work of the second or third century BC. Visitors first saw it not far from the museum's main entrance at the end of a dimly lit hall of classical sculpture. At that point, the great Daru Stairway leads visitors out of the dark ground floor into the brightness above (Figure 6.5). On the stair's central landing, bathed in natural light, the *Victory*, wings still spread, alights on the prow of her vessel. Until the Louvre's main entrance was moved in 1993, she stood as the culminating point in the museum's opening act, brilliantly summarizing the narrative's central thesis: the triumph of the classical spirit in French culture.

FIGURE 6.4 *Victory of Samothrace*, second century BC, marble, 8′½″, Louvre Museum.

FIGURE 6.5 The Daru Staircase with the *Victory of Samothrace*, Louvre Museum.

So great was the prestige of the Louvre Museum that every regime after the Empire, be it republican, monarchical or imperial, wished to leave its signature somewhere in the building. This wish often materialized as a new suite of galleries or the renovation of one or more old ones. You can still see symbols and insignia of regimes past on the museum's ceilings and walls – Napoleonic bees, Bourbon *fleurs-de-lis*, the initials of Louis Napoléon or Charles X, or the Second Republic's RFs – reminders of the frequent shifts and reversals in nineteenth-century French political life. Indeed, despite the museum's inception as a monument to republican *égalité*, some of those regimes sought to awaken the building's royal memories and bring back its palace functions. Their lingering symbols or initials – and traces of some that were subsequently scraped away – should remind us that the meanings a museum generates may mutate considerably.[9]

Foreigners in the museum

I have focused mainly on the museum as a ritual of French nationalism, concentrating on its character as a post-revolutionary monument. However, it should also be remembered that, from the start, the Louvre's brilliance was meant to radiate internationally and augment France's reputation as a great nation among nations. Minister of the Interior Roland had been emphatic that the new institution *must* impress foreign visitors, by which he meant emissaries from other lands and people of education, means and influence – the tourists of that era. Just as the Apollo

Gallery had once been the reception hall of the monarchy, so the museum would be the reception hall of the republic, a place where foreign visitors would encounter the French nation's highest ideals. To fulfil this order and to command the international prestige that Roland and his successors desired, the museum's programme had to be convincing to the foreign social and professional elites most likely to visit it. The Louvre's key organizing thesis – the advancement of civilization as manifested in progress towards the *beau idéal* – met this demand. Originating in an international discourse conducted by eighteenth-century enlightenment intellectuals, the thesis was fast becoming the dominant critical outlook among educated elites throughout Europe. The Louvre's ritual scenario was crafted as much for such foreign visitors as for domestic ones. Yet, while foreigners could retrace the museum's story of progress, they could do so only as onlookers or guests of the nation, not as citizens exercising their right to the civilized pleasures offered by their state.

As Roland wished, the Louvre Museum instantly became an object of intense international admiration and has remained so to this day. To cite just one instance of this: in 1866, a group of well-to-do Americans celebrating the Fourth of July in the Bois de Boulogne heard a speech by John Jay, a prominent New Yorker. Jay proposed the creation of a new art museum for New York, the nation's biggest city. He hoped it would one day rival the Louvre and thus make clear the importance of New York. Back home, he organized committees of rich and influential men, and in due time the Metropolitan Museum of Art was brought into existence (Howe, 1912; Lerman, 1969; Tomkins, 1973). It was quickly followed by similar institutions in Boston, Chicago, St Louis, Philadelphia, Detroit and other major American cities. Testifying to the powerful influence of the Louvre, the Art Institute of Chicago was given a grand stairway with multiple flights and a prominent central landing. On it was placed a plaster copy of the *Victory of Samothrace*, signifying in Chicago – as in Paris – the achievement of civilization.

Notes

1   This chapter is a condensed version of the first two chapters of my study of public art museums (Duncan, 1995). It also draws from an earlier article I co-authored with Alan Wallach (Duncan and Wallach, 1980). Readers interested in a full accounting of the research on which the present text is based should refer to those publications. In this text, I refer only to sources actually cited or works not cited in these earlier writings.

2   The work of Pierre Bourdieu and Alain Darbel (Bourdieu, 1984; Bourdieu and Darbel, 1969) supports the notion of art museums as ritual settings, but the performance they identify is understood almost wholly as an exercise in class identity, whereas I treat museums not only as socially distinguishing forms, but also as structures with substantive cultural content, a content that is not always, or not entirely, an ideological instrument subject to sociological or political description.

3   Thanks to systematic looting by the French army, the government amassed colossal stockpiles of art treasure taken from the churches and palaces of conquered nations. Works of art were also confiscated from French churches and monasteries. For a detailed history of the early Louvre Museum, see the important book by Andrew McClellan (1994).

4   From a statement by Dominique-Joseph Garat, Minister of the Interior in 1793 (cited in Tuetey and Guiffrey, 1909: 112).

5   I am simplifying a complicated story here. During the Louvre's early years, the museum staff tried various ways to meet demands for both educational and aesthetic interests.
6   Although the room no longer functions as an entrance, its ceiling is still intact. Its painted panels were completed in 1799, but the stucco decorations surrounding them, executed in a baroque style, date from the seventeenth century (Aulanier, n.d.: 76–7; Blum, 1946: 162).
7   The claim to be the principle heir of the classical tradition was hardly new to this era. Well before the Revolution, French cultural officials and academicians asserted French high culture's distinctive affinity to the spirit of the classical past. However, ideas about what that spirit actually amounted to and which cultural products of the past most exemplified it could change radically.
8   The museum has maintained this focus partly by moving collections extraneous to its central narrative off site into separate or semi-autonomous institutions. Impressionism, post-Impressionism and modern art, as well as collections of Asian and African art, have all been given homes outside the walls of the Louvre. The Department of Near Eastern Art, created in 1881, was the last new department until 2003, when Islamic Art was given its own department.
9   In this regard (although it may be a coincidence), it is worth wondering how much the placement of the *Victory of Samothrace* on the Daru Stair in 1884, during the Third Republic, was meant to reconnect the Louvre to its republican origins. Museum curators reinstalling the collections after the Second World War left little doubt about their intention to reaffirm the Louvre's original programme by highlighting the classical tradition in Western art history and the prominent place within it of French art (Charbonneaux, 1948–9: 98, Huyghe, 1948–9: 17–18; Salles, 1948–9: 92).

References

Anderson, B. (1991) *Imagined Communities: Reflections on the Origin and Spread of Nationalism*, London: Verso.

Aulanier, C. (n.d. [after 1945]) *Histoire du Palais et du Musée du Louvre*, Paris: Editions des Musées nationaux, 5, pp. 76–7.

Blum, A. (1946) *Le Louvre: Du Palais au Musée*, Geneva/Paris/London: Milieu du monde.

Bourdieu, P. (1984) *Distinction: A Social Critique of the Judgment of Taste*, trans. R. Nice, London and New York: Routledge & Kegan Paul.

Bourdieu, P. and Darbel, A. (1969) *L'Amour de l'art: Les Musées d'art européens et leur public*, Paris: Editions de minuit.

Charbonneaux, J. (1948–9) 'Reinstallation of the collections of Greek and Roman antiquities', *Museum*, 1–2: 24–97.

Clark, K. (1954) 'The ideal museum', *ArtNews*, 54 (January): 29.

Duncan, C. (1995) *Civilizing Rituals: Inside Public Art Museums*, London and New York: Routledge.

Duncan, C. and Wallach, A. (1980) 'The universal survey museum', *Art History*, 3(4): 447–69.

Hazlitt, W. (1824) *Sketches of the Principal Picture-Galleries in England*, London: Taylor & Hessey, pp. 2–6.

Howe, W. E. (1912) *A History of the Metropolitan Museum of Art*, New York: Metropolitan Museum of Art, 1, pp. 95–111.

Huyghe, R. (1948–9) 'Changes in the department of paintings and the Grande Galerie', *Museum*, UNESCO serial articles, 1–2: 17–18, available at: http://unesdoc.unesco.org/Ulis/cgibin/ulis.pl?catno=9984&set=4C577A08_0_0&gp=0&lin=1&ll=1 (accessed 25 July 2013).

Landais, H. (1981) 'Preface', in Y. Cantarel-Besson (ed.) *La Naissance du musée du Louvre. La politique muséologique sous la Révolution d'après les archives des musées nationaux*, 1, Paris: Ministère de la culture, Editions de la Réunion des musées nationaux.

Lerman, L. (1969) *The Museum: One Hundred Years and the Metropolitan Museum of Art*, New York: Viking Press, pp. 11–15.

McClellan, A. (1994) *Inventing the Louvre: Art, Politics, and the Origins of the Modern Museum in Eighteenth-Century Paris*, Cambridge: Cambridge University Press.

Salles, G. (1948–9) 'The museums of France', *Museum*, 1–2: 92.

Tomkins, C. (1973) *Merchants and Masterpieces: The Story of the Metropolitan Museum of Art*, New York: Dutton.

Tuetey, A. and Guiffrey, J. (1909) *La Commission du Muséum et la Création du Musée du Louvre, 1792–1793*, Documents collected and annotated by A. Tuetey and J. Guiffrey, *Archives de l'art français*, 3, p. 181.

Turner, V. (1977a) 'Frame, flow and reflection: ritual and drama as public liminality', in M. Benamou and C. Caramello (eds) *Performance in Postmodern Culture*, University of Wisconsin-Milwaukee: Centre for Twentieth Century Studies, pp. 33–55.

Turner, V. (1977b) 'Variations on a theme of liminality', in S. F. Moore and B. Myerhoff (eds) *Secular Ritual*, Assen/Amsterdam: Van Gorcum, pp. 36–52.

Waterfield, G. (1985) 'Introduction', in *Collection for a King: Old Master Paintings from the Dulwich Picture Gallery* (exhibition catalogue), Washington, DC and Los Angeles, CA: National Gallery of Art and Los Angeles County Museum of Art.

7

INVENTING OR REVIVING THE GREEK IDEAL?

Forging the regeneration of the French nation in the art of Paul Cézanne after the Franco-Prussian War*

Athena S. Leoussi

Introduction

This chapter explores the national significance of the classical imagery that emerged in the art of the French avant-garde in the late nineteenth century. It shows how the traditional, classical motif of the nude in a landscape was modernized and became a national symbol for modern France. More generally, this chapter shows the role of culture, and especially that of the visual arts, in defining and projecting visions of national identity. By staging and enacting the national identity, and especially the national way of life, in a shorthand and stylized manner, art can capture and crystallize this life, give it definite form, and thus make it visible – 'real' – and an object for public reflection (literally, a *denkmal*). Indeed, art can also act as a medium for communicating, propagating or reinforcing visions of national identity to the wider public. This chapter thus shares common ground with Carol Duncan, whose contribution to this volume shows both the centrality of classicism in French culture, and the role of art and of the art museum in nation-building.

This chapter focuses on the classicism of the French avant-garde artist Paul Cézanne. It examines Cézanne's engagement with the classicist movement for national regeneration that followed French defeat in the Franco-Prussian War of 1870–71. In the context of racial interpretations of national identity and history, national regeneration came to mean physical regeneration through care for the body, in imitation of ancient Greece, in its 'golden age'. Racial interpretations of national identity came to dominate European opinion from the second half of the nineteenth century until the end of the Second World War. They set up the Greek body as the ideal human body, and focused attention on the bodies of nations.

* I should like to thank Professor Andrew F. Knapp for his comments and suggestions, which helped me convey a more accurate, nuanced account of nineteenth-century French culture.

The body-centred, ethno-classical revival that marked French society at the turn of the nineteenth century became intimately connected and was often combined with a Catholic revival. This reaffirmed chastity and motherhood and celebrated another 'golden age'. This was the age of the Gothic cathedrals, which was seen as a period of great moral virtue, a golden age of Christianity. Classical civilization and medieval Catholicism thus provided the resources for the reconstruction of national identity in France after the German assault on it. For German unification, which was completed in 1871, was achieved, at least partly, at France's expense (Breuilly, 1996). By affirming their part (and, indeed, leading part) in these 'golden ages' of European culture, and by reviving and combining particular motifs from these rich repositories of ideas and values, French intellectual elites led the way to French national regeneration from the destruction of war. And this national redefinition and reincorporation in the two core European cultural traditions brought about a new and modern French Renaissance. Like its sixteenth-century predecessor, the French Renaissance of the late nineteenth century revived the ancient world and, at the same time, revitalized Catholic Christianity. But it did this through reconstructing, recombining and remoulding them both to the demands of modern, post-war France.

I have examined elsewhere the ways in which the classical and Christian traditions were combined in late nineteenth-century French society and artistic culture (Leoussi, 2009). In this chapter, I focus, first, on the ways in which the revival of the classical physical ideal became a central component of a *variety* of French nationalist movements, both official and unofficial, which were concerned with the autonomy, unity and identity of France (Smith, 1991: 73). Second, I focus on *how* the French artistic avant-garde (1) became associated with these nationalist movements, and (2) through their works made this ideal visible and tangible. I shall here concentrate on one of these rebellious and forward-looking French avant-garde artists, the Impressionist (and later post-Impressionist) artist Paul Cézanne (1839–1906). In his later paintings, and especially those from the 1880s until the end of his life, Cézanne oriented his creative energies to the *mise-en-scène* (the staging) of the new French national ideal: the healthy, strong and beautiful body – the classical Greek body.

The present consideration of the Greek revival in France after the Franco-Prussian War has an additional theoretical concern. It examines the role of the past in modern, post-Enlightenment societies. Drawing on the work of Anthony D. Smith, John Hutchinson and Steven Grosby regarding the uses of the past in post-Enlightenment societies, this chapter offers an empirically based critique of Eric Hobsbawm's notion of the 'invention of tradition' (Hobsbawm and Ranger, 1993 [1983]).

Past and present: revisiting the 'invention of tradition'

Smith, Hutchinson and Grosby have all stressed the importance of the past for human societies as a repository of ideas and values that may guide the present.

More specifically, Smith and Hutchinson have emphasized the importance of revivals of past 'golden ages' in movements of national and especially *cultural* renewal (Hutchinson, 1992: 100–17, 2005: 74; Smith, 1999: 263–4). Furthermore, and according to Smith and Hutchinson, revivals of past 'golden ages' do not simply imitate earlier periods, but are innovative, transmuting selected aspects of the 'golden' past into novel creations, adapted to modern problems. Similarly, Grosby, in his own analyses of 'the bearing of the past on the present', has stressed the importance of the past as a constitutive element of the present in all human societies. And this, not only as a source of categories for *Kulturgeschichte* (i.e. for historiography and historical interpretation), but also, perhaps more importantly, as a component of the living culture of the present, influencing the thought and conduct of individuals (Grosby, 2001: 128, 2011a: 73–96). At the same time, Grosby has recognized, following Edward Shils, the 'contingent character' of the reception of tradition, as each generation reconsiders its past in the light of changing circumstances (Grosby, 2001: 128; Shils, 1981). It is in accordance with this overarching theoretical framework that this chapter explores the revival of the physical ideal of the 'golden age' of Greece in *fin-de-siècle* France. It is also in opposition to Eric Hobsbawm's influential notion of a market-driven and invented past – 'the invention of tradition' – that this chapter assesses late nineteenth-century French attachment to the classical Greek body.

Hobsbawm has described the nation as a modern creation: 'a very recent newcomer in human history', and no older than the eighteenth century (cited in Grosby, 2001: 126). He has also referred to nations as 'pseudo-communities', in his phrase, 'all-embracing pseudo-communities (nations, countries)' (Hobsbawm and Ranger, 1993 [1983]: 10). Hobsbawm has further interpreted references to the past, in late nineteenth- and early twentieth-century industrial and industrializing European societies claiming to be nations (i.e. ethno-cultural communities preserving and/or reviving age-old traditions into the new industrial present) as mostly forgeries (Grosby, 2001; Hobsbawm and Ranger, 1993 [1983]: 8). For Hobsbawm, European revivals of the past in the period 1870 to 1914 are ideological inventions, belonging, in the Marxian sense, to the 'superstructure' of European bourgeois societies (Hobsbawm and Ranger, 1993 [1983]: 3, 263–307). They are mechanisms (or opiates, to use a Marxist image) for creating identity and social cohesion among masses of people who possess neither and who are brought together by the bourgeois modern state, pursuing its class interests. Finally, Hobsbawm has claimed that the 'term "invented tradition" is used in a broad, but not imprecise sense' (Hobsbawm and Ranger, 1993 [1983]: 1). Here is Hobsbawm's definition of 'invented tradition': 'Invented tradition' is taken to mean a set of practices, normally governed by overtly or tacitly accepted rules and of a ritual or symbolic nature, which seek to inculcate certain values and norms of behaviour by repetition, which automatically implies continuity with the past. In fact, where possible, they normally attempt to establish continuity with a suitable historic past' (Hobsbawm and Ranger, 1993 [1983]: 1).

The first observation that needs to be made regarding the above summary of Hobsbawm's views is that Hobsbawm's key notion of 'invented tradition' is so broad and imprecise that it is rendered methodologically weak and untestable. The second observation is that it is, as Steven Grosby has persuasively argued, exaggerated (Grosby, 2001: 128). For, as Smith has remarked, even if modern elites and intellectuals do, indeed, 'deliberately select and rework old traditions', they have to do this within limits (A. D. Smith, 1998: 129). These 'limits are set by the culture, or cultures, of the public in question' (A. D. Smith, 1998: 129). They must have some pre-existing foundation either in empirical (e.g. archaeological) reality, or in the spiritual and social reality (social practices) of the popular psyche in order to be accepted. Hobsbawm himself recognized the need for 'genuine popular resonance' (Hobsbawm and Ranger, 1993 [1983]: 264). And it must be stressed that this need is particularly crucial in 'open', democratic societies, ruled on the basis of public debate and consent. In addition, given the rapid development of evidence-based historiography and historiographic debate in Europe, from the eighteenth century onwards, myth-making (as well as myth-preserving), or the 'invention of the past', was, in fact, limited even further (rather than expanded). It is worth noting, in this respect, that not only Hegel, but also Marx were major contributors to this explosion of history writing and, indeed, to the historicism (historical determinism) with which it became associated.

What makes Hobsbawm's term 'invention' especially meaningless is the fact that it refers both to forged claims about the past *and* to any 'conscious invention' or 'construction' of new social institutions or practices (including symbolic and ritual practices) (Hobsbawm and Ranger, 1993 [1983]: 263, 1). This is a misunderstanding of human societies and social change. First, it is in the nature of human beings to have consciousness, and thus to think or deliberate about the ways in which they lead their lives; second, all forms of human life in common are socially constructed and reconstructed, as Berger and Luckmann have shown in their classic book, *The Social Construction of Reality* (Berger and Luckman, 1984 [1966]); and third, as Karl Popper has observed, accepting the possibility of 'false consciousness', knowledge in democratic, 'open societies' (i.e. most western European societies, as these have been developing from the late eighteenth century onwards, albeit with some totalitarian, 'closed' detours), is the result of 'conjectures and refutations' – of making or inventing a theory or hypothesis, and then either matching it with reality (i.e. empirical evidence, or submitting it to public criticism) (Popper, 1989). Danger lurks, as Popper pointed out, when such conjectures (in this case, theories of the past) are removed from the realm of 'open', critical debate, and become objects of legislation, as absolute truths, and thus state policy, as they did in Nazi Germany.

In order to empirically assess Hobsbawm's notion of 'invented tradition', this chapter questions Hobsbawm's fundamental assumption that the supposed 'modern world', a world of 'constant change and innovation' (Hobsbawm and Ranger, 1993 [1983]: 2), cannot coexist with elements of the pre-modern (Grosby, 2011b; A. D. Smith, 1995, 1998). Indeed, Hobsbawm has claimed the 'long-term inadaptability of pre-industrial ways to a society revolutionized beyond a certain point' (Hobsbawm and Ranger, 1993 [1983]: 8). In contrast to this claim, this chapter, in its analysis of the art of the avant-garde, will show modernists' disenchantment with the culture of modernity, and their efforts to find a balance between modernity and tradition. It will thus show, first, following Grosby, that values need not be confined to one historical period; and, second, following Hutchinson, that cultural revivals are 'a recurring force, often re-emerging in modern societies to have a long-term effect on the status order' (Grosby, 2011a: 91; Hutchinson, 1992: 111). Finally, it will show the adaptability of pre-modern solutions to the problems of the modern present. These adaptations of the past cannot be considered inventions in any sense of the term. Indeed, the modification and reinterpretation, in varying degrees, of past values and practices by later generations is a characteristic of most traditions; traditions themselves have a history – and this history is one of change over time (Grosby, 2012).

As far as Hobsbawm's claim that traditions are invented for the purpose of securing the interests of the ruling classes, this chapter will try to show the positive and popular aims of French classicism: not only to re-moralize, but also to achieve the health, beauty and strength of the French people. This perspective is based on the concept of transcendence, taken from Durkheim's sociology of religion (Durkheim, 2008 [1912]) and applied by Shils to understand the nation (Shils, 1997). The chapter will try to show that French nineteenth-century classicism, as a cultural movement, was not invented for the lower classes, but rather generalized the traditional and revived classical ideals and aspirations of French elites and intellectuals to the entire population. It was an attempt to rebuild the French nation. This nation rebuilding set out to homogenize the masses by morally uplifting and physically improving them, and by instilling in them a national consciousness. This consciousness was the belief that they belonged to a wider and cohesive, national collectivity, and one of which they could be proud, as it was moulded on an image of France as classical Greece (see Figures 7.1 and 7.2).

Revanchisme and the competition between civic and ethno-racial definitions of France

French ethnic (genealogical) and physical identification with the ancient Greeks emerges most potently as a dominant national narrative after French defeat in the Franco-Prussian War of 1870–1. The war resulted in the loss of the French territories of Alsace and of half of Lorraine to a coalition of German states led by Prussia. It also resulted in the 'completion' of the Prussian Prime Minister Otto von Bismarck's plan to create a united Germany – the Second Empire (Breuilly, 1992: 12–13). This plan included the forced annexation of French territories (Alsace and part of Lorraine), which contained sizeable German-speaking populations.

It was this bitter national experience that formed the background to Ernest Renan's famous lecture at the Sorbonne, on 22 March 1882, 'Qu'est-ce qu'une nation?'. In this lecture, Renan, now in his democratic phase, denounced Germany's forced annexation of the French provinces on the basis of linguistic affinity, demanding that the principle of social and political belonging is the individual will and that it should be consulted when establishing the frontiers of a political community. Thus, for Renan,

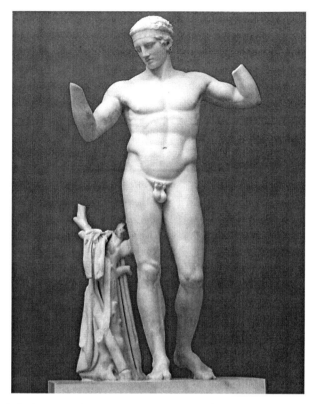

FIGURE 7.1 Polycletus, Diadoumenos, Roman copy of about 100 BC, of a bronze original of about 430 BC, National Archaeological Museum, Athens, Greece.

Dans l'ordre d'idées que je vous soumets, une nation n'a pas plus qu'un roi le droit de dire à une province: «Tu m'appartiens, je te prends».Une province, pour nous, ce sont ses habitants; si quelqu'un en cette affaire a droit d'être consulté, c'est l'habitant.[1]

[According to the ideas that I am outlining to you, a nation has no more right than a king does to say to a province: 'You belong to me, I am seizing you'. A province, as far as I am concerned, is its inhabitants; if anyone has the right to be consulted in such an affair, it is the inhabitant.][2]

In his 1882 lecture, Renan defined the nation, the type of human community that he considered to be 'good and necessary' – *'bonne, nécessaire même'* – for his era, the nineteenth century, seeing it, the nation, as *'la loi du siècle où nous vivons'* [the law of the century in which we live], in both historical and republican terms. Nations were old, historical communities that were held together in the present and the future by the sheer will of their members: *'L'existence d'une nation est (pardonnez-moi cette métaphore) un plébiscite de tous les jours'*[The existence of a nation is (forgive the metaphor) a daily plebiscite]. These ideas about the nation that he knew would be condemned by an international audience as 'French ideas' – '*idées françaises*' – were rooted in the ideas of the French Revolution, with its universalism, voluntarism and humanism. They offered a conception of '*le peuple*' united into a nation that we now call 'civic'. This conception was the opposite of the German conception, which was ethno-cultural, with an emphasis on language and the linguistic community; a conception that had shaped nineteenth-century German state-building (Brubaker, 1992; Schnapper *et al.*, 2010). Renan rejected racial, linguistic, cultural and geographical definitions of the nation, which he found too deterministic of what he believed to be the free will of the individual human being:

> *L'homme n'est esclave ni de sa race, ni de sa langue, ni de sa religion, ni du cours des fleuves, ni de la direction des chaînes de montagnes. Une grande agrégation d'hommes, saine d'esprit et chaude de cœur, crée une conscience morale qui s'appelle une nation. Tant que cette conscience morale prouve sa force par les sacrifices qu'exige l'abdication de l'individu au profit d'une communauté, elle est légitime, elle a le droit d'exister. Si des doutes s'élèvent sur ses frontières, consultez les populations disputées. Elles ont bien le droit d'avoir un avis dans la question. Voilà qui fera sourire les transcendants de la politique . . .*[3]

> [Man is a slave neither of his race nor his language, nor of his religion, nor of the course of rivers nor of the direction taken by mountain chains. A large aggregate of men, healthy in mind and warm of heart, creates the kind of moral conscience that we call a nation. So long as this moral consciousness gives proof of its strength by the sacrifices, which demand the abdication of the individual to the advantage of the community, it is legitimate and has the right to exist. If doubts arise regarding its frontiers, consult the populations in the areas under dispute. They undoubtedly have the right to a say in the matter. This recommendation will bring a smile to the lips of the transcendants of politics . . .][4]

As noted above, Renan defended the integrity of the French state, shrunk by German occupation, by reference to 'civic' principles of sociopolitical formation that went back to the French Revolution. In this chapter, I examine the post-1871 emergence and practical implications of ethno-racial conceptions of the French nation. These conceptions of the French nation competed and coexisted with the earlier, civic conceptions throughout the Third Republic, which replaced Louis Napoleon III's Second Empire after the disaster of the Franco-Prussian War. The ethno-racial conception of the French nation was epitomized most dramatically in the anti-Semitism that manifested itself in connection with the Dreyfus Affair that began in 1894 and divided the nation in complex ways (Harris, 2011).

At the centre of the new, ethno-racial visions of France that were combined with a strong militarism was the Greek physical ideal (see Figure 7.1 and 7.2). French adoption of the Greek physical ideal as a national ideal served the same goal as Renan's civic exhortations: *revanchisme*, or the recovery of the lost territories of

Alsace and Lorraine, as illegitimately German domains. Greek ethnic and physical identification gave the French a sense of status superiority over the Germans. It also provided a means whereby the French believed that they could become militarily superior to the Germans and thus defeat them *en revanche*: a Greek body would give them the physical strength that they needed and would replace the degenerate and feeble body of the soldiers who were defeated at Sédan on 1 September of *l'année terrible*, the year 1870, so poignantly recounted by Victor Hugo in his poem of that title, published in 1872 (Hugo, 1986). French hostility was to haunt Germany and threaten peace on the European continent, until the provinces were finally returned to France in 1918 (Tombs, 1992: 713–19).

The idea of race and the Greek identity of the French

French physical identification with the ancient Greeks belonged to the new, scientific and physical approach to national identity, which became a central preoccupation in nineteenth-century Europe. Its key concept was the idea of race. Through the idea of race, human physical appearance acquired a power it had never before possessed:

1   It classified and divided humans into distinct physical types, whose character-istics were transmitted from one generation to the next through biological inheritance. The evolutionary accounts of the multiplicity of human races (speciation) found not only in Darwin's *On the Origin of Species by Means of Natural Selection* (1859) and *The Descent of Man* (1871), but also in Gregor Mendel's earlier observations did not affect the belief in fundamental differences dividing the varieties of mankind.
2   On the basis of predominantly European aesthetic and cultural criteria (or prejudices) and traditions, it organized racial types into hierarchies of superior and inferior races.
3   It was used as an explanation for cultural differences among humans through the theory of racial determinism (Banton, 1990; Bulmer and Solomos, 1999).

Although there was a proliferation of racial classifications of humans among European and American anthropologists, there was wide consensus on the superiority in beauty, intelligence, morality and strength of one race: the white race, also called *Homo europaeus*, or Indo-Atlantic race, or Indo-European, or Aryan or Caucasian race, the latter a term still in use today, and an invention of Johann Friedrich Blumenbach (1752–1840). Blumenbach was a German anthropologist, physiologist and comparative anatomist of the University of Göttingen, and is frequently called the 'father of physical anthropology' (Bulmer and Solomos, 1999).

There was similar consensus that inside the white or European race, the ancient Greeks, or 'Hellenes', reigned supreme as the fullest embodiment of this superior white race. Evidence for the appearance of the ancient Greeks was taken primarily from Greek figural art, and especially the naturalist sculpture of the fifth century

BC, the 'Pheidian' age of Greek sculpture. This was supposed to have recorded the actual appearance of Greek men and women as they reached that moment of unsurpassed physical perfection, their youth. Indeed, it was because of its models, the young men and women of Greece, that Greek art of the 'golden' or classical age was supposed to owe its supreme beauty.

The Greeks were generally described as having an oval head, symmetrical features and proportions, and muscular, strong and healthy bodies (Leoussi, 1998: 3–24). And what we find, in the context of nineteenth-century rivalries among the leading European nations, and especially among the English, French and Germans, is the development of new conceptions of modern European national identities. These theories resulted in competing claims as to who was more Greek. This was because: (a) all European nations were supposed to belong to the white or Indo-European race; and (b) these leading European nations had all contributed to the development of the idea of race and of Greek physical perfection. They thus shared a common conceptual framework. And in these competing claims to Greek identity, we also find competing and thus diverse descriptions of the physical characteristics of the Greeks.

In post-1871 France, the claim to a Greek physical identity and the need for all French men and women to have a Greek body was widely accepted. One of the most influential exponents of these beliefs was the historian, critic and admirer of England, and, until the Franco-Prussian War, of Germany too, Hippolyte Taine (1828–93). Napoleon III had appointed Taine professor of aesthetics and of the history of art at the École des Beaux-Arts in 1864. He held this post for 20 years. During this time, Taine developed his theory regarding the determination of cultural production by '*race, milieu et moment*' (Lacombe, 1909). This theory informed his analysis of Greek art, which he published in 1869 as *Philosophie de l'art en Grèce*. This book, and the others that had preceded it (including *Philosophie de l'art*, 1865, and *De l'idéal dans l'art*, 1867), had been based on his lecture courses at the École des Beaux-Arts.

Taine believed in the theory of the Aryan race. This theory, especially in its Indo-Germanic version, set the typically blonde, Germanic nations (including the Anglo-Saxon English and Americans) and, more generally the north European nations apart from the other Indo-European or Aryan nations as the perfect Aryans, and thus as the real descendants of the ancient Greeks (Poliakov, 1974). Aryanism had many followers in France, especially before the outbreak of the Franco-Prussian War. The war inevitably dampened French admiration for the Germans. It also produced new and negative accounts of the Germans, and especially the Prussians. For example, the Aryanist doyen of French physical anthropology, Armand de Quatrefages, described, in 1871, what he called '*La race prussienne*' not as Germans, but rather as belonging to the semi-barbarous 'Finnish race' that had inhabited Europe before the Aryan colonization, or as mixed Finno-Slavs (Poliakov, 1974). It must be noted, however, that racial interpretations of French defeat in the Franco-German war, which were widely spread in both France and Germany, had its detractors. Among them, was not only Ernest Renan, whom we have already discussed, but also Georges Clémenceau. Clémenceau, a Republican député, who became France's premier in the period 1917–20, denounced the very idea of race and racial hierarchy in his famous '*débat colonial*' with Jules Ferry, which took place in the Chambre des députés on 31 July 1885:

> *Races supérieures! races inférieures! c'est bientôt dit! Pour ma part, j'en rabats singulièrement depuis que j'ai vu des savants allemands démontrer scientifiquement que la France devait être vaincue dans la guerre franco-allemande parce que le Français est d'une race inférieure à l'Allemand.*
>
> (Clémenceau, 1885: 1677 ff.)

The most influential representative of Aryanism, both inside and outside of France, was Count Arthur de Gobineau (1816–82), the 'father of racist ideology' (Biddiss, 1970). Being close to Alexis de Tocqueville, who, it must be noted, was to disapprove of his friend's illiberal, deterministic, racial theories, Gobineau was appointed by Tocqueville *chef de cabinet*, when Tocqueville became, for a short time (June to October), Minister of Foreign Affairs in 1849. This appointment opened up for Gobineau a diplomatic career that enabled him to travel abroad, including Athens and Teheran, and develop his ethnographic interests, and with them his version of the theory of the Aryan race.[5]

Gobineau's admiration for the Germans is most evident in the dedication of the first edition of his major book on race, *Essai sur l'Inégalité des Races Humaines* (1853–5), to a German sovereign, '*sa Majesté Georges V, Roi de Hanovre*'. In this book, Gobineau described the Aryans as blonde. He thus described the Aryan Greek woman as follows: '*cheveux blonds, aux yeux bleus, aux bras blancs . . .*' (cited in Leoussi, 1998: 19).

Taine shared with Gobineau many of his ideas. And, like Gobineau, and also Winckelmann, the great eighteenth-century German leader of neoclassicism, he believed that the beauty of Greek figural art was due to the actual beauty of Greek youth. Taine explained the beauty of Greek youth as the result of race and athletics (see Figure 7.1). Greek physical education – '*la culture musculaire*' – developed and perfected the innate, inherited characteristics of the race. On this basis, Taine advocated '*la culture musculaire*' for modern France, in imitation of the ancient Greeks, for the purpose of French physical regeneration (Taine, 1872: 163). In his *Notes sur l'Angleterre* of 1872, Taine had praised modern English public school and university education for its Greek-inspired emphasis on athletics and sport (Taine, 1872: 148). For Taine, the transformation of French youth into Greek athletes, which the English had seemed to him to have already achieved for themselves, was possible because the French, being a European nation, belonged to the same Indo-European or Aryan race as the Greeks, an identification that Taine ardently advocated (Taine, 1905: 358). Taine was not alone in his admiration for the physical aspects of English middle- and upper-class education. Baron de Coubertin, who successfully revived the Olympic Games in 1896, thereby positing the classical Greek physical ideal as a universal ideal, was another influential admirer of English education (MacAloon, 2009; Yalouri, 2004). Coubertin was particularly attracted to Dr Arnold, headmaster of Rugby School. Thomas Arnold's educational principle was the classical principle, *mens sana in corpore sano* (Hobsbawm and Ranger, 1993 [1983]: 300; Leoussi, 1998: 120–3).

Taine's ideas from the 1860s and 1870s, and especially his philosophy of Greek art, acquired a new urgency after the Franco-Prussian War. And they became hugely influential well into the 1890s and beyond. We find them in 1898 in the work of the distinguished French anatomists Mathias Duval and Édouard Cuyer. In their book written for the anatomical education of artists, *Histoire de l' Anatomie Plastique*, Duval and Cuyer would reiterate Taine's belief that a healthy body was as important for modern societies as it had been for the ancient Greeks. Duval and Cuyer also emphasized the importance of a *balanced* development of both the mind and the body, in accordance with the classical Athenian educational formula, *mens sana in corpore sano*. They thus criticized modern life as follows:

> . . . *au lieu de réaliser l'antique et classique formule qui demande une intelligence saine dans un corps robuste (*mens sana in corpore sano*), nous voyons trop souvent l'humanité dite civilisée tendre comme type vers un corps débile* . . .

> [. . . instead of realizing the ancient and classical formula that requires a healthy mind in a healthy body (*mens sana in corpore sano*), we see, too often, so-called civilized humanity, tend towards a weak physical type . . .]
>
> (Duval and Cuyer, 1898: 9)

Following Taine, Duval and Cuyer further emphasized in their 1898 book '*ces conditions du milieu*', the social institutions that had shaped the Greek body. The most crucial of these institutions was the system of open-air physical exercises that Greek teachers had developed. And they quoted Taine's observation that:

> *les maîtres, en véritables artistes, exerçaient le corps pour lui donner non seulement la vigueur, la résistance et la vitesse, mais aussi la symétrie et l'élégance.*

> [the teachers, like real artists, exercised the body in order to give it not only vigour, resistance and speed, but also symmetry and elegance.]
>
> (Duval and Cuyer, 1898: 15)

Similar ideas regarding the importance for modern French men and women of physical exercise in imitation of the ancient Greeks can also be found in the writings of the anti-Darwinian, ardently Roman Catholic and nationalist anthropologist-cum-artist, as well as teacher at the École des Beaux-Arts, Charles Rochet (1815–1900). In his immensely popular public lectures at the Sorbonne, between 1869 and 1872, and in his book *Traité d'Anatomie d'Anthropologie et d'Ethnographie appliquées aux Beaux-Arts* of 1886, Rochet claimed that the French were similar to the Greeks in that both nations were southern – '*Bruns méridionaux*'. The Germans, by contrast, were different from both the French and the Greeks on account of

FIGURE 7.2 Visit of the shah of Iran in France, 1873: Nasser al Din in front of the statue of the *Venus de Milo* in the Museum of Antiques in the Louvre (*Visite du shah de Perse en France, 1873: Nasser al Din (Nasser-al-Din) devant la statue de la Venus de Milo au musée des Antiques du Louvre*).

their blonde hair: '*Le blond est avant tout Allemand, Scandinave, Anglo-Saxon*'. And as original mankind had also had '*les cheveux d'un beau noir*', the French were superior to the Germans because the latter's blonde hair was a deviation from original perfection: '*le Brun . . . est l'homme supérieur*' (Rochet, 1886: 222, 223, 235). And here we find the adaptation of the Greek physical ideal to French national interests, and, most notably, to French desire for national pride. For Rochet's account of the Greek physical type as dark haired is at odds with the more widely accepted classification and description of the ancient Greeks as '*blonds*', which we found in the theory of the Aryan race.

As an ardent Catholic, Rochet also rejected Darwin's accounts of the descent of mankind from the apes and considered the body of '*la belle race des Hellènes*' as the body of the men and women of creation. For Rochet, statues such as the Discobolus or the '*beau torse de Ilissus de Phidias*' exemplified the physically perfect Greek male adult, and the *Venus de Milo* and the *Crouching Venus* the female (see Figure 7.2). On this basis, Rochet advocated the imitation of the Greek cult of physical health and beauty as the will of God, who had made original mankind perfect in his image, which the Greeks had managed to preserve:

> *Tout Être humain doit avoir un beau corps, comme il doit avoir une bonne santé; le Créateur ne reconnaît comme étant son oeuvre que l'Être beau et en bonne santé.*

> [Every human being must have a beautiful body, as well as good health; the Creator does not recognize as being His Creation other than beautiful and healthy beings.]

> (Rochet, 1886: 262)

For Rochet, by imitating '*la vie naturelle*' of '*la belle race des Hellènes*' [the natural life . . . of the beautiful Hellenic race], the French could also achieve the colour of perfect humanity whose skin was '*rouge*' or '*cuivré*' [red or bronze] – bronzed by the sun. For, according to Rochet, '*les hommes du beau soleil*' were the '*vrais enfants de Dieu*' [the people of the sun . . . were the true children of God] (Rochet, 1886: 232, 246).

'Dans la Provence d'or flotte l'air de l'Hellade': *French nationalism and Provençal regionalism*

Greek identification was justified not only morphologically (i.e. by similarity in physical appearance between the ancient Greeks and the modern French), but also historically and ethnically (genealogically). This was done through reference to archaeological remains, and to historical, literary accounts of Greek Phocean settlements in Provence from the sixth century BC, which also involved inter-marriage between the local Gauls and the Greek colonists. This Mediterranean identity rejected the north with its centre in Paris (Leoussi, 2009). Rejection of the north as the source and centre of French national life reinforced the view that the majority of the French people were Gallo-Romans and thus distinct from the

Frankish aristocracy, an idea that went back through Abbé Sieyès' revolutionary pamphlet of January 1789, 'Qu'est-ce que le tiers état?' to the sixteenth century (cited in Bulmer and Solomos, 1999: 49). To this, Roman, and already classical connection of the Gauls, was now added a specifically Greek connection. Greek ethnicity was already cultivated in the 1850s and 1860s, during the Second Empire, a regime that took the populist, Gallo-Roman line. Art, including public monu-ments, was a direct and visual way of propagating this national identity, based on ethnicity and the past; hence, the proliferation of official commissions and public displays of statues of Gallic heroes – warriors and defenders of national autonomy such as Vercingétorix (Grand Palais, 1986: 50, 374). Indeed, Napoleon III took a personal interest in the archaeological and ethnographic reconstruction of the '*passé national*', and especially the Gallic past. In 1862, for example, he launched the excavation of Alesia, the Gallic fortress that Caesar besieged, and where he captured Vercingétorix in 52 BC.

The Greek genealogical connection was proclaimed, most significantly, in the 1865 competition for the Rome prize (*Prix de Rome*), a major official competition that enabled the winning artists to study in Rome, the centre of 'high art'. The subject of this competition was *La fondation de Marseille*. This subject was, most significantly, the story of the marriage, in the sixth century BC, of the Gallic Princess Giptis to Protis, one of the Greek founders of Marseilles who had come as 'colonists' (in the sense of peaceful settlers, requesting permission to found a city) from Phocaea. Phocaea had been an Ionian city that lay on the coast of Asia Minor. Significantly, entries for this famous art competition were intended for public display at the 1867 Universal Exhibition in Paris. This would enable the French to proclaim to the world, by using the directness and effectiveness of the visual arts, their Greek ancestry (Grand Palais, 1986: 50–2). The Greek association of Provence remained a potent theory well into the twentieth century. This is evident in the sculptural decorations of the monumental staircase of the railway station Marseille-Saint-Charles. Conceived in 1911, the monumental staircase was completed and inaugurated on 24 April 1927. It figures an allegorical representation of '*Marseille, colonie grecque, . . . vêtue d'une chlamyde*' (Wikipedia, n.d.).

The transformation of Southern France into the source and centre of modern French national life also strengthened the revivalist movement of Provençal language and culture that had started in the 1850s as a result of the efforts of prominent Méridional regionalists such as Frédéric Mistral and the Félibres. These affirmed the Greco-Latin ethnic and cultural roots of modern Provence (Athanassoglou-Kallmyer, 2003). As Joachim Gasquet, another Provençal poet poetically put it in his poem 'Chant filial' of 1899,

> *Les hommes de ma race à leur sang sont liés.*
> *Dans la Provence d'or flotte l'air de l'Hellade . . .*

> [The men of my race are linked to their blood.
> In the golden Provence floats the air of Hellas . . .]
> (cited in Athanassoglou-Kallmyer, 2003: 292, 216)

According to Athanassoglou-Kallmyer, the Méridional regionalists regarded a 'historically Greco-Roman Provence as the region (and the race) destined to spearhead a cultural and national renewal for France' (Athanassoglou-Kallmyer, 2003: 216). She has located the origins of this new and ethnically justified classical revival in the wake of the Franco-Prussian War, becoming especially potent in the 1890s. This was a time of mounting French resentment against German Imperialism. In this context, the Greco-Latin ideal posited French supremacy over 'inferior' and 'barbaric' Anglo-Germanic cultures (ibid.: 216).

Opposition to Germany and identification with the Mediterranean and classical civilizations of ancient Greece and Rome were also expressed in another literary movement, Naturism (also known as Naturalism). This was based in Paris. Naturism's origins lay in Hippolyte Taine's 'scientific' and, indeed, deterministic theories of history ('race, milieu et moment'), of the 1860s. The spiritual leader of literary Naturism was the eminent Parisian intellectual, novelist, and ardent anti-Dreyfusard, who grew up in Aix-en-Provence, Emile Zola (1840-1902). Zola was also a particular kind of Republican, whom he called a 'naturalist or scientific Republican' (*The New York Times*, 4 May 1879). The aesthetic ideals of Naturism consisted essentially of a rejection of Romanticism and symbolism as foreign, Anglo-Germanic imports: '*L'esprit germanique ne nous séduit plus*' [The Germanic spirit does not seduce us anymore] (Athanassoglou-Kallmyer, 2003: 293, 217).[6] Instead, the Naturists advocated classicism, '*La Renaissance classique*', whose sense of order they viewed as the essence of Frenchness, '*l'esprit national*' (ibid.: 294, 219). Belief in the specifically ethnic–genealogical connection between the French nation and the classical spirit was clearly expressed by the Naturist Louis Bertrand. In his important preface to the collection of poems by Joachim Gasquet, whom I mentioned above, *Les Chants séculaires* of 1903, Bertrand stressed the fixity and continuity of biologically inherited physical and intellectual characteristics, a principle that supported the belief in the Greco-Roman identity of modern France. In this same preface, Bertrand also urged the French to rise against barbarity, meaning Germany, and to be proud of themselves because, as direct heirs of Rome and Athens, they are carriers of civilization. Finally, he pointed to the importance of healthy and beautiful Provence for the recovery of ailing France. Thus:

les dispositions innées et héréditaires . . . ne sont pas seulement physiques, elles sont encore intellectuelles . . . Affirmons-nous encore une fois en face de l'univers, car il est trop sûr que nous Latins, héritiers directs de Rome et Athènes, nous sommes la civilisation! En ce moment, le Barbare, qui en est le pire ennemi, est dressé contre elle . . . Si le corps de la patrie est gangrené, quelques membres sont restés sains . . . en terre provençale, – je le sais ! – il est encore de beaux fils de France . . . qui sont avides de continuer la vie des ancêtres selon son idéal de gloire, justice et raison.

[innate and hereditary inclinations . . . are not only physical, but also intellectual . . . Let us assert ourselves, one more time before the world, for it is absolutely certain that we, Latins, direct inheritors of Rome and Athens, represent civilisation! At this moment, the Barbarian, who is the worst enemy of civilization, has risen against it . . .

If the body of (our) homeland is gangrenous, some parts of it have remained healthy . . . in the land of Provence, – I know it! – there are still some beautiful sons of France . . . who are eager to continue the life of their ancestors according to its ideal of glory, justice and reason.]

(P. Smith, 1998: 23, note 69)

Greek identification had far-reaching and specifically *practical* consequences in post-war France. In order to regain their lost Greek body, the French had to change their ways: they had to care for their body as the Greek ancestors had done. They should do gymnastics, and make trips to the Mediterranean south of France, and especially Provence, where the roots of France were supposed to lie. Contact with the Mediterranean sea, sunshine, open air and way of life of Provence was expected to revive the nation, just as contact with his mother Earth (Gaia) had given strength to the mythical Antaeus who was defeated when Hercules, using a bear hug, lifted him in the air, uprooting him.

Before 1871, and despite efforts by both the state, especially by Napoleon III's minister of education, Victor Duruy (1811–94), and individuals such as Hippolyte Taine, who, as a positivist and, as noted above, an Aryanist, and the arch-champion of classical Athenian notions of physical strength – '*la force*' – French opinion had resisted the idea of race and the care for the body that it implied. Indeed, gymnastics were seen as 'unseemly or degrading activities', especially by Parisian Salon society, devoted to 'mind gymnastics' (Holt, 1981: 42). French Catholic opinion, on its part, had been either indifferent to modern science or opposed to its rationalism and secularism – '*la religion et la science en désaccord*' (Lacombe, 1909: 240–62).

After the French defeat in 1871, and the explanation of this defeat as the result, at least partly, of national physical degeneration, all this changed. The ideas of people such as Taine, who had advocated the cultivation of bodily strength and health as well as beauty, became hugely influential, permeating French popular culture and shaping French daily life. As Tamar Garb has shown, journals such as *La Revue Athlétique*, founded in 1890, or *La Culture Physique*, founded in 1904, with their illustrations of statues of ancient Greek athletes, indicate not only the spread of the cult of the body in France after the Franco-Prussian War, but also its Greek models (Garb, 1998: 55–7). The proliferation of voluntary gymnastic associations during this period was another manifestation of the new physical concerns of the French, which Flaubert satirized in his *Bouvard et Pécuchet*. In addition, the names of these associations bear witness to the patriotic and specifically *revanchiste* motives that lay behind their formation: *La Régénératrice*, *L'Alsace-Lorraine*, *La Revanche* (Holt, 1981: 47). Gymnastics also acquired an official and, indeed, obligatory status on a national scale: they were introduced, by law, into French state schools. They became part of the transformation of 'peasants into Frenchmen'. Indeed, as Evgen Weber has remarked, 'Gymnastics were meant to "develop in the child the idea of discipline, and prepare him . . . to be a good soldier and a good Frenchmen"' (Weber, 1976: 333). It was the 1882 law of Jules Ferry that made primary education obligatory, as well as '*laïque*' for both boys and girls – '*Loi du 28 mars 1882 sur l'enseignement primaire obligatoire*' – made, in article 1, '*La gymnastique*' obligatory in primary education. It also made obligatory, in the primary education of boys, military exercises – '*Pour les garçons, les exercices militaires*'.[7] Thus, after 1871, there was 'broad agreement' in France that 'the country must work to outstrip the Germans in the very areas in which Germany excelled: warfare, science, and the education of its citizens', which emphasized gymnastics (Revel, 1995: 5).

The Greek physical ideal in the art of the avant-garde

The post-war Greek physical ideal found cultural expression in French art. Indeed, the desire for the Greek body, as a national ideal, was so powerful that it engaged even the artistic avant-garde. One of the artistic consequences of this was a reconciliation of modernity with tradition, as the artistic avant-garde turned their eyes to nudes in landscapes. This supremely classical and academic motif was reanimated by the energies of the avant-garde, becoming the central object of their artistic creativity. It was in this post-war context that Paul Cézanne, and other Impressionist artists, such as Pierre-Auguste Renoir, abandoned their earlier commitment to '*la vie moderne*' [modern life] and turned, from the 1880s onwards, to the revival of '*la vie ancienne*' [ancient life] (Dymond, 2003: 353–70; House, 2010: 28–43). They also became involved in nationalist circles, and especially in the revivals of the Greek heritage of Provence that were led by Provençal intellectuals. These gained momentum under the Third Republic (Athanassoglou-Kallmyer, 2003, and see below).

There were additional links between the avant-garde and Provence. Cézanne was a native of Provence. Having been born and schooled in Aix-en-Provence, he returned to live and paint there permanently. This he did in the late 1880s, after the death of his tyrannical father in 1886, and after having made his artistic debut in Paris, where, during the 1870s, he had become associated with the Impressionists. Indeed, Cézanne called himself a 'man of the South' (Krumrine, 2000: 35). Renoir, for his part, made frequent travels to the Mediterranean South of France, from 1882 onwards, finally relocating in Cagnes in 1908 (Grand Palais, 2010: 379). His landscapes and bather scenes of this later period of work are marked by the sunlight, sites and vegetation of the South in which he immersed himself, transmuting his impressionism into a colourful and vibrant classicism. And, as John House has observed, Renoir's travels to the Mediterranean South of France, and his final relocation in Cagnes, together with the changes in his art towards 'the Classicism of the Mediterranean', were associated with mainstream French ideas about 'the revival of Provençal culture' (House, 1985: 268). These ideas were part of the 'collective cultural consciousness of late nineteenth-century France', which insisted 'that France itself embodied a living part of classical antiquity' (House, 1998: 25). Robert Herbert, too, has seen in Renoir's move to Cagnes where he bought an estate, Les Collettes, and had a house built, 'no longer just the act of an aging artist', but his participation in 'new attention to the Mediterranean as the resort of France's Greco-Roman origins' (Herbert, 2000: 81). It was this 'potent myth', as House has described it, which pulled to the South, along with masses of French men and women seeking regeneration, not only Renoir, but also Matisse, Signac, Seurat and many other non-native artists of the avant-garde (House, 1998: 25). These artists revived and renewed the image of the 'golden age' through the invention of radically new artistic styles. In so doing, they also realized with paint and colour, the visions and hopes for their own modern age – an age that was to be built on the principles of an earlier 'golden age'.

In the images of the South of France that were created at the turn of the nineteenth century by the Impressionist and post-Impressionist avant-garde, we find the French body removed from the city, and especially Paris, and placed in sunny Mediterranean landscapes, on riversides and coastlines, bathing, wrestling, running or resting after physical activity. These new, idyllic Mediterranean paintings of strong and healthy male and female nudes, in sunbathed landscapes, echoed the shift in geo-cultural and geopolitical focus away from what was seen as the grey, sterile, demoralizing and disfiguring industrial and urban Parisian north, and towards the natural, healthy and chaste Mediterranean south. They were imaginings of a new, regenerated France, recreated in the image of Greece.

Cézanne's bathers and the Greek physical ideal

Cézanne engaged with the Greek physical ideal of his time through a new and much more luminous and calm series of images of modern Provençal young men and women bathing in, playing or resting by Provençal rivers or the Mediterranean sea (see Figures 7.3, 7.4, 7.5, 7.6). These nudes contrasted with his earlier renditions of the nude. As Lawrence Gowing has observed, Cézanne's later bather compositions contrasted sharply with his earlier Romantic, thickly painted, dark, passionate and embattled male and female nudes engaged in *La Lutte d'Amour* (*c*.1875–6) (Gowing, 1988: 18). These end in the mid-1870s when Cézanne began painting a different kind of nude, the bather, which was to become a constant preoccupation, giving rise to a whole series of bathing scenes (Krumrine, 1988: 27). In this series, the two sexes tend to be separated in alternate images of *Baigneurs* and *Baigneuses*, ending in *Baigneuses* (Krumrine, 2000: 33).

Often sexually indeterminate and thus without sexual motive, these later young bodies of bathers show a more innocent, brighter and calmer image of human life and of the human body, which almost echoes Winckelmann's classical ideal, '*edle Einfalt und stille Grösse*' [noble simplicity and calm grandeur]. Through this series, culminating in *Les Grandes Baigneuses* of *c*.1895–1906 in Philadelphia, his final statement, Cézanne finally came to 'worship at a classic shrine' (Gowing, 1988: 17–18) (see Figure 7.5).

The male and female nudes of this later period, with their broken contours, lack of naturalist beauty and, increasingly, their tension between realism and abstraction, do not exactly achieve the classical physical ideals of wholeness, symmetry and elegance. Nevertheless, in their statuesque grandeur and simplicity, their healthy nudity, swelling with muscle, and their warm Mediterranean flesh tones, these figures in landscapes hark back to the classical tradition. This tradition is not absorbed passively or imitated slavishly; instead, it is updated and creatively remoulded in images that show the direct relevance of tradition to modern times. Indeed, Cézanne's bathers are presented, through references to modern life, such as the swimming trunks that we see in *Le Grand Baigneur* of 1885 or the *Baigneurs* of 1890–94, as modern (see Figure 7.4). They are the modern descendants of the Greek ancestors of the region. At the same time, their classicism is unmistakeable. The massive square chest of the male bather facing the spectator in *Les Baigneurs au repos* of 1875–6, in the Barnes Foundation, repeated in *Le Grand Baigneur* of 1885 in the Museum of Modern Art, New York, reproduces what, in Winckelmann's neoclassical tradition had been described as the 'grand and square' style of fifth-century BC Greek art. This type of chest also conforms with the national campaign for strong, square chests for French men. As noted above, this campaign was led by French anatomists and medical doctors, as well as Taine. Indeed, the link between Cézanne's bathers and Taine was explicitly made by Cézanne's

FIGURE 7.3 Cézanne, Paul (1839–1906): *Bathers (Baigneurs)*, *c.*1890, oil on canvas (54.2 × 66.5 cm), St Petersburg Hermitage Museum.

Source: © 2013. Photo Fine Art Images/Heritage/Scala, Florence.

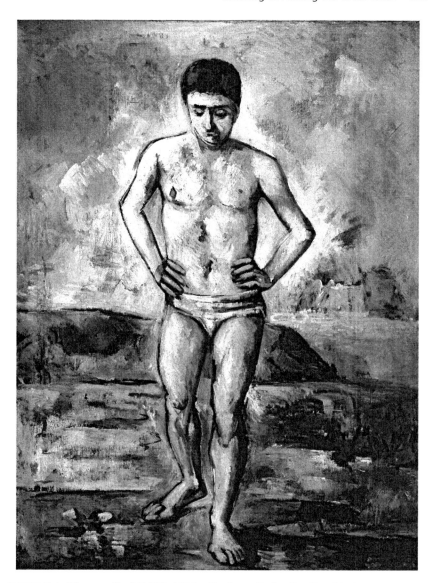

FIGURE 7.4 Cézanne, Paul (1839–1906): *The Large Bather (Le Grand Baigneur)*, *c*.1885, oil on canvas (127 × 96.8 cm), New York, Museum of Modern Art (MoMA).

Source: © 2013. Digital image, Museum of Modern Art, New York/Scala, Florence.

contemporary and friend, the Provençal poet, Joachim Gasquet, mentioned above. In his book about the artist, called *Cézanne*, of 1921, we find Gasquet making frequent and positive references to Taine, and quoting Cézanne as having said: 'I like muscle, beautiful tones, blood. I'm like Taine . . .' (Kendall, 1989: 306).

We find a variety of classical physical types among Cézanne's male bathers: not only the 'grand and square', but also the still muscular and naturalist but more

FIGURE 7.5 Cézanne, Paul (1839–1906): *The Large Bathers* (*Les Grandes Baigneuses*), 1906, oil on canvas (210.5 × 250.8 cm), Philadelphia Museum of Art.

Source: © 2013. Philadelphia Museum of Art/Art Resource/Scala, Florence.

elongated and slender type of Lysippus' athletes, as in the three bathers on this side of the river in the Hermitage *Baigneurs* (*c.*1890–91) (see Figure 7.3). The standing figure on the right also seems to replicate the attitude of Michelangelo's *Dying Slave* (Krumrine, 2000: 168). In contrast, the deeply tanned figure seated facing us on the opposite bank of the river has a more compact body with a massive square chest. According to Conisbee, Cézanne's reliance on second-hand images for his bathers instead of models increased towards the last years of his life. Significantly, these included 'his drawings after old master paintings and especially sculptures in the Louvre, from antiquity through Michelangelo to the Provençal Pierre Puget' (Conisbee, 2006a: 238). Conisbee further emphasizes the personal significance of the bathing theme for Cézanne as a nostalgic recollection of the artist's youth as well as 'a key expression of his own experience of, attachment to, and vision of, Provence' (ibid.: 233). The Greek associations of Cézanne's bathers, and especially their links with Greece's golden, 'classical' age of the grand and calm images of gods, heroes and athletes, were recognized early on by the critic Georges Rivière. Rivière commented on *Les Baigneurs au repos* of 1875–6, shown at the second impressionist exhibition of 1877, as follows:

M.Cézanne est, dans ses œuvres, un grec de la belle époque; ses toiles ont le calme, la sérénité héroïque des peintures et des terres cuites antiques, et les ignorants qui rient devant les Baigneurs, par exemple, me font l'effet de barbares critiquant le Parthénon . . .

[M. Cézanne is, in his works, a Greek of the great period; his canvases have the calm and heroic serenity of the paintings and terra-cottas of antiquity, and the ignorant who laugh at the *Bathers*, for example, impress me like barbarians criticizing the Parthenon . . .]

(Conisbee, 2006a: 233)

In addition to the bathing motif, it is important to note, in the case of the Baltimore *Baigneurs*, another Greek athletic motif, that of wrestling, in the two crossing figures on the right (see Figure 7.6). These young men of Provence who had preserved their Greek ethnic and cultural inheritance are the few remaining healthy men of France, whom the Naturists had praised and expected to lead the regeneration of the body of France, temporarily '*gangrené*'.

Cézanne's *baigneuses* also show healthy and muscular bodies in natural surroundings, with allusions to the physical – and classical – activity of bathing. However, as Garb has observed, they tend to be presented in more static attitudes, while the *baigneurs* 'seem poised in frozen movement' (Garb, 1998: 211). In *Les Grandes Baigneuses* of 1906 in Philadelphia, the pinnacle of his series of male and female bathers, Cézanne's classicism is evident in the abundance of reproductions

FIGURE 7.6 Cézanne, Paul (1839–1906): *The Bathers* (*Les Baigneurs*), 1898–1900, oil on canvas (27 × 46 cm), Baltimore Museum of Art.

Source: © 2013. The Baltimore Museum of Art: The Cone Collection, formed by Dr. Claribel Cone and Miss Etta Cone of Baltimore, Maryland, BMA 1950.195.

of Greek statues of Venus – the muscular torso and draped lower parts of the *Venus de Milo*, the folded figure of the *Crouching Venus*, the *Vénus à la coquille* and the *Vénus de Vienne* – and of *L' Hermaphrodite endormi*, itself an offspring of Venus (see Figure 7.5). The *Diane chasseresse* in the Louvre can also be recognized in the striding figure on the left.

Cézanne and the Provençal revival

It is important to consider Cézanne's association with the regionalist and nationalist movements of the Third Republic more closely. Nina Maria Athanassoglou-Kallmyer has traced Cézanne's regionalist sympathies and their expression in his art in her award-winning book, *Cézanne and Provence: The Painter in His Culture* (Athanassoglou-Kallmyer, 2003). According to Athanassoglou-Kallmyer, Cézanne shared with Gasquet, and other prominent Méridional regionalists such as Mistral and the Félibres, their belief in the Greco-Latin ethnic and cultural roots of modern Provence. Cézanne also shared the similarly classicist ideas of the Naturists and their identification of Provence with ancient Greece (ibid.: 221). This is evident, for example, in the fact that in1900, the names of Cézanne and Renoir, as well as Monet, featured among the honorary members of the Collège d'esthétique moderne, the art school of the Naturists (ibid.: 221).

The classical characteristics of Cézanne's later paintings were an artistic expression of *enracinement*, of ethnic attachment to the native land that was Provence. And this classical interpretation of Provence and of its inhabitants was amplified by his intimate knowledge of ancient Greek and Latin writers. He had read these Greek and Latin writers as a part of his classical education at the Collège Bourbon in Aix, and, during these youthful years, he had deeply identified with them. His memories of this experience were revived by his friendship with Joachim Gasquet, who was involved in a number of classicizing nationalist and regional (Provençal) cultural circles, including the literary circle, the 'Symposiasts' (P. Smith, 1998: 11–23; 2006: 59–74, 69). Cézanne had met Gasquet in April 1896 in Aix. Gasquet, much younger than Cézanne, was then studying philosophy at the University of Aix (Gowing, 1988: 217). Cézanne's regionalism was recognized and praised by Gasquet. Cézanne and Gasquet were united in their efforts to revive as well as celebrate Provence's classical tradition but also its folk, peasant culture, in the manner of *ut pictura poesis*: Cézanne through his paintings – not only his classicizing paintings of Provençal bathers, but also his Provençal landscapes, and his paintings of other Provençal customs, such as his series of the cardplayers (Ireson and Wright, 2010: 11); Gasquet through his poetry. Cézanne was to *give* some of his major 'Provençal' works to his young friend (Conisbee, 2006b: 21).

Gasquet became an influential source for Cézanne's thoughts, through his book about the artist, called *Cézanne*, of 1921. According to Theodore Reff, John Rewald, Richard Shiff and others, Gasquet's account of Cézanne is not entirely reliable (Leoussi, 2009). Nevertheless, 'Gasquet's Cézanne' remains valid and particularly illuminating regarding the reception of Cézanne's work by his contemporaries, and especially in nationalist circles, such as the Action Française, which Gasquet also supported (Shiff, 1991: 15–24). Action Française, founded in 1898 by Charles Maurras (1868–1952), another Provençal intellectual, was a monarchist and nationalist ('integralist') movement (Giocanti, 2006). Like other nationalist movements in France at that time, it advocated the restoration in France of the classical spirit (i.e. the civilization of ancient Greece and Rome). It defined the classical spirit as reason, clarity, beauty and discipline. Maurras presented this spirit as a specifically French heritage. This spirit, this cultural tradition, he believed, was lost with the Enlightenment and the 1789 Revolution, and had to be revived for the revitalization of France defeated by Germany (McWilliam, 2005: 269–91). In this vein, Maurras had, already in 1891, founded in Paris, with the Greek-born Jean Moréas, a group of poets who were opposed to the Symbolists as importers of foreign, Anglo-German ideas, and who later became known as the *école romane*.

All the above considerations show the potency of Greek identification in late nineteenth-century France, as a direct result of the Franco-Prussian War. They also give an indication of the proliferation, at that time, as well as overlap, of classicizing cultural and political movements, some of which, such as Action Française, had a darker side, with anti-Semitic, illiberal and fascist implications (Antliff, 2007).

Conclusion

Post-1871 French identification with the ancient Greeks was constructed in the context of French opposition to German nation-cum-state-building, and desire for revenge and the restoration of French national pride. French humiliation in the Franco-Prussian War transformed French public opinion in two important respects: first, it forced French public opinion to accept the importance of care for the body in the regeneration of France after the military defeat; and, second, it caused the aesthetic reconstruction of French identity. The new vision of France recast the modern French nation as a Southern, Mediterranean and Greco-Roman nation rather than a Northern nation moulded by Germanic Franks (Smith, 1989). It thus recast the French nation as a nation embodying, actually and potentially, the ideal beauty of Greek statues. The new focus on the Mediterranean side of French identity made Southern France, '*le Midi*', the centre of French national life. Against this background, I tried to show that:

1   Greek identity was claimed on the basis of: (a) similarity in physical characteristics, which were considered racial, between the modern French and the ancient Greeks; and (b) the construction, with the help of historical, literary and archaeological evidence, of a genealogical history of the mass of the French people that ethnically linked the modern French with the ancient Greeks.
2   Greek identification had practical and institutional implications: it urged the French, not only the elites, but also the mass of the French population, to revive the beautiful, healthy and strong body of the ancient Greeks in their own bodies, through physical exercise and natural life in the open air and sunshine.

The new compulsory schools and voluntary athletic clubs became the main institutional carriers of the Greek physical ideal, adapting it to modern French life. These practices were combined with seasonal visits to the Mediterranean coast.

3   Artists of the avant-garde, such as Paul Cézanne, contributed to Provençal regional and French national identification with the ancient Greeks: (a) by becoming personally involved in nationalist classicising circles; and (b) by showing in their works what physically regenerated France would look like, and how this physical appearance could be achieved. Cézanne's male and female nudes enact the classical and now national ideal of care for the body in the Mediterranean countryside.

In this chapter, I also attempted a critique of Hobsbawm's notion of the 'invention of tradition'. I tried to show that the emergence of classical Greek principles in modern French culture was:

1   A greatly diversified movement. Late nineteenth-century French classicism was not a single ideology about the French nation. Rather, it took many forms, and was combined not only with Catholic revivalism, but also with a variety of scientific (or pseudo-scientific) anthropological theories and political currents – liberal, conservative and proto-fascist. Indeed, there were *many* and even clashing classicisms in France at that time. So much so that the critic Gaston Sauvebois would refer, in 1911, to '*l'équivoque du classicisme*' (Hargrove and McWilliam, 2005: 270). Classical ideals and norms became the means to many different, and even contradictory, ends. Consequently, the idea of deliberate invention by a particular section of French society of a classical myth to mislead the masses, cannot be upheld.

2   Not a creation *ex nihilo* of modernity, an artifice created by the ruling classes and falsely presented as a long-standing French national tradition for the purposes of forging class cohesion and suppressing class conflict. Rather, *fin-de-siècle* French classicism had, in actual fact, deep roots in French culture and history. These roots went back, through the seventeenth century (with Racine, Corneille, Claude, Poussin, etc. as some of the more illustrious carriers of French literary and artistic classicism), and the European Renaissance, in which France had been a major participant, to a historically genuine, Graeco-Roman French past (Hinojosa, 2009: 29–43). This past had been a persistent undercurrent of French collective consciousness, especially among the elites. Re-emerging on its surface as a part of a living and revived tradition, Greek culture, and especially the Greek care for the body was adopted on a national scale to heal the wounds of the trauma of military defeat. Regarding French claims to biological Greek ancestry: although these may be seen as a 'foundation *myth*', they were not inventions *ex nihilo* either. They were grounded in historical and archaeological evidence. Of course, the idea of race was false, but not an 'invention' in Hobsbawm's sense. Finally, the classical Greek body derived its power from the broader, age-old, European attachment to classical Greek civilization, as a 'symbolic centre' – an enduring and common standard

of human excellence (Grosby, 2011a: 78). And it became, like the Hebrew idea of the Messiah, the 'desire of all nations' – a desire not confined to one historical period or community. Its achievement meant a national appropriation of the universal.

3   Innovative and national, involving *all* social strata. The pursuit of the Greek body created new popular and national institutions (e.g. athletic clubs and gymnastics in schools), which cultivated Greek physical characteristics in these new settings. Penetrating avant-garde artistic circles, the Greek physical ideal produced new artistic styles. This apparent return to *l'art des musées* was not a passive imitation of the past as a guide for the present. Rather, it produced radically innovative art, which also showed the relevance and modernity of the past. This art combined the use of classical principles and figural prototypes with the modern, Impressionist concern for translating outdoor light into colourful paint. The Greek revival thus transmuted selected aspects of the 'golden' past into novel creations, adapted to modern problems. We remain, in the twenty-first century, and despite Hobsbawm's claim regarding the inadaptability and short life of 'invented traditions', heirs to this nineteenth-century revival of physical culture, on a national scale, in imitation of ancient Greece. The Olympic Games, which regularly reanimate, and on a global scale, this culture, are probably one of the best testimonies to this.

In ending this chapter, it is worth mentioning, briefly, Hobsbawm's own explanation of the growth of mass physical culture under the Third Republic. In his chapter 'Mass-producing traditions: Europe, 1870–1914', Hobsbawm claimed that 'the invention of tradition played an essential role in maintaining the [Third] Republic . . .', and he examined, in this light, the 'invention' of Bastille Day, but also the invention of 'mass physical exercises', including mass sport (Hobsbawm and Ranger, 1993 [1983]: 300). At the same time, however, Hobsbawm claimed that we know little about the adoption of mass sport in Britain, and 'we know even less about the continent' (ibid.: 290). For Hobsbawm, the function of these invented social practices was to create 'national identification and factitious community' (ibid.: 300). It is hoped that the present chapter will shed more light on both the historical origins and national purposes of physical culture in late nineteenth-century France.

Notes

1   See www.bmlisieux.com/archives/nation04.htm (accessed 18 July 2011).
2   Translation from www.nationalismproject.org/what/renan.htm (accessed 18 July 2011).
3   See www.bmlisieux.com/archives/nation04.htm (accessed 20 July 2011).
4   Translation from www.nationalismproject.org/what/renan.htm (accessed 20 July 2011).
5   Alexis de Tocqueville, www.tocqueville.culture.fr/en/portraits/p_amis-gobineau.html (accessed 28 July 2011).
6   Here Athanassoglou-Kallmyer is quoting Saint-Georges de Bouhélier, originally from 'Un Manifeste', in *La Revue Naturiste* (March 1897).
7   Sénat website, www.senat.fr/evenement/archives/D42/mars1882.pdf (accessed 7 October 2011).

References

Antliff, M. (2007) *Avant-Garde Fascism: The Mobilization of Myth, Art, and Culture in France, 1909–1939*, Durham, NC and London: Duke University Press.

Athanassoglou-Kallmyer, N. M. (2003) *Cézanne and Provence: The Painter in His Culture*, Chicago, IL: University of Chicago Press.

Banton, M. (1990) *Racial Theories*, Cambridge: Cambridge University Press.

Berger, P. and Luckmann, T. (1984 [1966]) *The Social Construction of Reality*, Harmondsworth: Penguin.

Biddiss, M. D. (1970) *Father of Racist Ideology: The Social and Political Thought of Count Gobineau*, London: Weidenfeld & Nicolson.

Breuilly, J. (1992) 'The national idea in modern German history', in J. Breuilly (ed.) *The State of Germany: The National Idea in the Making, Unmaking and Remaking of a Modern Nation-State*, Harlow: Longman, pp. 1–28.

Breuilly, J. (1996) *The Formation of the First German Nation-State, 1800–1871*, Basingstoke: Macmillan.

Brubaker, R. (1992) *Citizenship and Nationhood in France and Germany*, Cambridge, MA: Harvard University Press.

Bulmer, M. and Solomos, J. (eds) (1999) *Racism*, Oxford: Oxford University Press.

Clemenceau, G. (1885) *Journal Officiel*, Chambre des députés, débats du 30 juillet 1885, 1er août 1885: 1677 ff, available at: www.ldh-toulon.net/spip.php?article177 (accessed 24 November 2011).

Conisbee, P. (2006a) 'The Atelier des Lauves', in P. Conisbee and D. Coutagne (eds) *Cézanne in Provence*, exh. cat. National Gallery of Art, Washington, DC; New Haven, CT: Yale University Press, 230–79.

Conisbee, P. (2006b) 'Cézanne's Provence', in P. Conisbee and D. Coutagne (eds) *Cézanne in Provence*, exh. cat. National Gallery of Art, Washington, DC; New Haven, CT: Yale University Press, pp. 1–26.

Durkheim, É. (2008 [1912]) *The Elementary Forms of Religious Life*, trans. C. Cosman, Oxford: Oxford University Press.

Duval, M. and Cuyer, É. (1898) *Histoire de l'Anatomie Plastique: les Maîtres, les Livres et les Écorchés*, Paris: Société Française d'Éditions d'Art (Bibliothèque de l'Enseignement des Beaux-Arts).

Dymond, A. (2003) 'A politicised pastoral: Signac and the cultural geography of Mediterranean France', *Art Bulletin* LXXXV, 2: 353–70.

Garb, T. (1998) *Bodies of Modernity*, London: Thames & Hudson.

Giocanti, S. (2006) *Charles Maurras, le chaos et l'ordre*, Paris: Flammarion.

Gowing, L. (1988) 'The early work of Paul Cézanne', in L. Gowing (ed.) *Cézanne: The Early Years 1859–1872*, exh. cat. London: Royal Academy of Arts.

Grand Palais (1986) *La Sculpture Française au XIXe siècle*, Paris: Réunion des musées nationaux.

Grand Palais (2010) *Renoir au XXe siècle*, Paris: Réunion des musées nationaux.

Grosby, S. (2001) 'Hobsbawm's theory of nationalism', in A. S. Leoussi (ed.) *Encyclopaedia of Nationalism*, New Brunswick, NJ: Transaction, pp. 126–9.

Grosby, S. (2011a) 'Hebraism: the third culture', in J. A. Jacobs (ed.) *Judaic Sources and Western Thought: Jerusalem's Enduring Presence*, Oxford: Oxford University Press, pp. 73–96.

Grosby, S. (2011b) 'Nationalism and social theory: the distinction between community and society', in G. Delanty and S. P. Turner (eds) *Routledge Handbook of Contemporary Social and Political Theory*, London: Routledge, pp. 280–9.

Grosby, S. (2012) 'Review of Caspar Hirschi's *The Origins of Nationalism: An Alternative History from Ancient Rome to Early Modern Germany*, Cambridge, Cambridge University Press, 2011', available at: www.history.ac.uk/reviews/review/1281 (accessed 14 September 2012).

Hargrove, J. and McWilliam, N. (eds) (2005) *Nationalism and French Visual Culture, 1870–1914*, New Haven, CT: Yale University Press.

Harris, R. (2011) *The Man on Devil's Island: Alfred Dreyfus and the Affair that Divided France*, London: Penguin.

Herbert, R. L. (2000) *Nature's Workshop: Renoir's Writings on the Decorative Arts*, New Haven, CT: Yale University Press.

Hinojosa, L. W. (2009) *The Renaissance, English Cultural Nationalism, and Modernism, 1860–1920*, New York: Palgrave Macmillan.

Hobsbawm, E. and Ranger, T. (eds) (1993 [1983]) *The Invention of Tradition*, Cambridge: Cambridge University Press.

Holt, R. (1981) *Sport and Society in Modern France*, London: Macmillan.

House, J. (1985) *Renoir*, exh. cat., London: Hayward Gallery.

House, J. (1998) 'That magical light: impressionists and post-impressionists on the Riviera', in K. Wayne *et al. Impressions of the Riviera: Monet, Renoir, Matisse and their Contemporaries*, Portland, ME: Portland Museum of Art, pp. 10–25.

House, J. (2010) 'Renoir et la tradition, Renoir et le classicisme', in *Renoir au XXe siècle*, Grand Palais, Paris: Réunion des musées nationaux, pp. 28–43.

Hugo, V. (1986) 'L'année terrible', in *Oeuvres Complètes 6 = Poésies 3*, Paris: Laffont.

Hutchinson, J. (1992) 'Moral innovators and the politics of regeneration: the distinctive role of cultural nationalists in nation-building', *International Journal of Comparative Sociology*, XXXIII, 1–2: 101–17.

Hutchinson, J. (2005) *Nations and Zones of Conflict*, London: Sage.

Ireson, N. and Wright, B. (2010) *Cézanne's Card Players*, London: Courtauld Gallery in association with Paul Holberton Publishing.

Kendall, R. (ed.) (1989) *Cézanne by Himself*, London: Folio Society.

Krumrine, M. L. (1988) 'Parisian writers and the early work of Cézanne', in L. Gowing (ed.) *Cézanne: The Early Years 1859–1872*, exh. cat. London: Royal Academy of Arts.

Krumrine, M. L. (2000) *Paul Cézanne: The Bathers*, London: Thames & Hudson.

Lacombe, P. (1909) *Taine, historien et sociologue*, Paris: Giard et Brière Bibliothèque Sociologique Internationale.

Leoussi, A. S. (1998) *Nationalism and Classicism: The Classical Body as National Symbol in Nineteenth-Century England and France*, London: Macmillan.

Leoussi, A. S. (2009) 'From civic to ethnic classicism: the cult of the Greek body in late nineteenth-century French society and art', *International Journal of the Classical Tradition*, Institute for the Classical Tradition, Boston University, 16(3/4): 393–442.

MacAloon, J. J. (2009) *This Great Symbol: Pierre De Coubertin and the Origins of the Modern Olympic Games*, Chicago, IL: University of Chicago Press.

McWilliam, N. (2005) 'Action française, classicism, and the dilemmas of traditionalism in France, 1900–1914', in J. Hargrove and N. McWilliam (eds) *Nationalism and French Visual Culture, 1870–1914*, New Haven, CT: Yale University Press.

New York Times (1879) 'Zola on French Republicans', 4 May, available at: http://query. nytimes.com/gst/abstract.html?res=990CE6DE133EE63BBC4C53DFB36683826 69FDE (accessed 8 July 2013).

Poliakov, L. (1974) *The Aryan Myth*, London: Sussex University Press.

Popper, K. R. (1989) *Conjectures and Refutations: The Growth of Scientific Knowledge*, 5th edn, London: Routledge.

Revel, J. (1995) 'Introduction', in J. Revel and L. Hunt (eds) *Histories: French Constructions of the Past, Vol. 1: Postwar French Thought*, New York: New Press.

Rochet, C. (1886) *Traité d'Anatomie d'Anthropologie et d'Ethnographie appliquées aux Beaux-Arts*, Paris: Librairie Renouard.

Schnapper, D., Bordes-Benayoun, C. and Raphael, F. (2010) *Jewish Citizenship in France*, New Brunswick, NJ: Transaction.

Sénat (n.d.) 'French Senate website', available at: www.senat.fr/evenement/archives/D42/mars1882.pdf (accessed 7 October 2011).

Shiff, R. (1991) 'Introduction', in C. Pemberton (ed.) *Joachim Gasquet's Cézanne: A Memoir with Conversations*, London: Thames & Hudson, pp. 15–24.

Shils, E. (1981) *Tradition*, Chicago, IL: University of Chicago Press.

Shils, E. (1997) *The Virtue of Civility: Selected Essays on Liberalism, Tradition, and Civil Society*, edited by Steven Grosby, Indianapolis: Liberty Fund.

Smith, A. D. (1989) *The Ethnic Origins of Nations*, Oxford: Blackwell.

Smith, A. D. (1991) *National Identity*, London: Penguin.

Smith, A. D. (1995) 'Gastronomy or geology? The role of nationalism in the reconstruction of nations', *Nations and Nationalism*, 1(1): 3–23.

Smith, A. D. (1998) *Nationalism and Modernism*, London: Routledge.

Smith, A. D. (1999) *Myths and Memories of the Nation*, Oxford: Oxford University Press.

Smith, P. (1998) 'Joachim Gasquet, Virgil and Cézanne's landscape "My Beloved Golden Age"', *Apollo*, October: 11–23.

Smith, P. (2006) 'Cézanne's late landscapes', in P. Conisbee and D. Coutagne (eds) *Cézanne in Provence*, exh. cat. National Gallery of Art, Washington, DC; New Haven, CT: Yale University Press.

Taine, H. (1872) *Notes sur l'Angleterre*, Paris: Hachette.

Taine, H. (1905) *Hippolyte Taine: Sa Vie et sa Correspondance*, Paris: Hachette.

Tombs, R. (1992) 'L'Année Terrible, 1870–1871', *The Historical Journal*, 35(3): 713–24.

Weber, E. (1976) *Peasants into Frenchmen*, Palo Alto, CA: Stanford University Press.

Wikipedia (n.d.) 'Escalier monumental de la gare de Marseille-Saint-Charles', available at: http://fr.wikipedia.org/wiki/Escalier_monumental_de_la_gare_de_Marseille-Saint-Charles (accessed 24 November 2011).

Yalouri, E. (2004) 'When the new world meets the ancient: American and Greek experiences of the 1896 "Revival" of the Olympic Games', in C. Koulouri (ed.) *Athens, Olympic City 1896–1906*, Athens: International Olympic Academy, pp. 295–331.

8

'THE NATION'S SHRINE'

Conflict and commemoration at Yasukuni, modern Japan's shrine to the war dead[1]

John Breen

Introduction

Rituals and performances have a vital role to play in the production and repro-duction of nations everywhere. Nations, it seems, need ritual; they demand to be performed. The frequency with which modern nations have staged ritual perform-ances proves the point. The modern Japanese nation is no exception. In Japan, as elsewhere, national ritual has commended itself as a vital technique for intervening in mundane time and space and to engage the people – without whom the nation has no meaning. Participants in national ritual performances go beyond a national 'imagining' to a corporeal, sensory experience of the nation. Rituals are emotional events, after all, and in turn they have a vital ability to generate and articulate the passionate yearning – otherwise known as nationalism – that people have for the nation.

Anthony Smith, in this volume, proposes a useful analytical distinction between two categories of national rite: those that are 'celebratory' and those that are 'commemorative'. The distinction is not always neat, perhaps, but the former typically celebrate the nation's foundation and significant landmarks in national history, while the latter commemorate the sacrifice of those who fell on the nation's behalf (see p. 23 of this volume). But what structural characteristics might qualify either category as 'national', as opposed to 'state' or 'civic' or, in the case of modern Japan, 'imperial' ritual? Handelman suggests a national rite will present the nation to itself in all its conflictual complexity, and all its distinctiveness (Handelman, 1990: 1–83). In pre-war Japan, for example, this meant the ritual engagement of the people – of course – but also the emperor, the state and the military in their relationships of power to one another (Doak, 2007: 33–4). It should be noted at the outset that the modern Japanese nation, born with the Meiji Revolution of 1868, involved the monarchy's restoration to the political centre, and not its removal. The modern

Japanese emperor was sovereign to his subjects, head of state and commander in chief of Japan's armed forces. Imperial symbols left their imprint on all Japan's national ritual performances. It was, moreover, the emperor, unique in his claim of descent from the Sun Goddess, who marked out the Japanese nation as distinct from all others.

A second condition for a national rite concerns its ability to reverberate and resonate (Ben-Amos and Ben-Ari, 1995).[2] National ritual presentations will reverberate far beyond the initial ritual 'beat' struck in the political centre. A sympathetic 'resonance' across the nation – a response, that is, to the beat and the reverberation it generates – is sought. Typically, modern communication technologies, notably the press media, radio, television and film, will be harnessed to maximize the effect. And since national rites are never spontaneous, there is a third condition: namely, a sufficiency of state power and bureaucratic coordination (Alexander, 2005; Ben-Amos and Ben-Ari, 1995).

The existence of Smith's two categories of national rite, 'celebratory' and 'commemorative', is readily confirmed for Japan in the early decades after the 1868 Revolution. The former would include performances to mark the promulgation of the Constitution in 1889 (Kokaze, 2011). In subsequent years, the three 'Great Feasts' of New Year, State Foundation Day and the Emperor's Birthday acquired a national quality, especially in the euphoria following Japan's victory over Russia in 1905. Enthronement rites for emperors Taisho and Showa in 1912 and 1926, respectively, and celebrations in 1940 to mark the 2,600th anniversary of State Foundation are other examples of major celebratory rites that reverberated across Japan and beyond (Breen and Teeuwen, 2010; Ruoff, 2010). In what follows, however, my concern is exclusively with the commemorative category of national rites in Japan. This is partly because they remain little studied, partly also because they present certain difficulties of interpretation. In brief, they appear to confound the expectation that state-sponsored commemorative rites always and everywhere set up a national reverberation and achieve a national resonance.

This chapter's spatial focus is the Yasukuni shrine in Tokyo, dedicated to the Japanese war dead.[3] Founded in the aftermath of the 1868 Meiji Revolution, Yasukuni is not a monument like the Cenotaph in London; nor does it accommodate the remains of the war dead like the national cemetery in Arlington. Yasukuni is, rather, a dynamic ritual site, served by a dedicated community of priests since its foundation. It is the dwelling place for the spirits of the military men and women who fell fighting for Japan in national and international conflicts after 1868.[4] Yasukuni rites, from the shrine's founding to the present day, exhibit an immediately recognizable 'commemorative' quality in Smith's sense, even as they are culturally distinct. They are distinct as Shinto rites, after all, which draw on traditions of great vintage. Yasukuni rites are of two types: (1) enshrinements, which literally enshrine the war dead, so transforming them into gods (*kami*); in Yasukuni discourse, the dead are typically styled 'glorious spirits' (*eirei*); these dynamic rites are, by their nature, occasional and, for obvious reasons, are performed only during, and immediately after, military conflicts; and (2) rites of propitiation, designed to honour, pacify and incur the favour of the glorious spirits; these are regular, seasonal events; from the start of the twentieth century, every spring and autumn great rites of propitiation have been performed at Yasukuni. Enshrinements would typically take place immediately prior to the seasonal rites of propitiation.

Yasukuni's rites of enshrinement were, in time, to become national events, but this transformation was not until 1938, a good half-century after Yasukuni's founding. Moreover, that national quality endured only until 1945. In other words, before 1938 and, indeed, after 1945, Yasukuni's commemorative performances signally failed to engage the nation. Their reverberation was muffled at best. The pre-1938 situation is explained by the fact that the shrine's military masters exhibited no interest in seeing Yasukuni rites engage the nation at large. This position became the cause, as we shall see, of much contestation. The post-1945 situation is more complex: the new constitution, the legacy of war and Japan's Asian diplomacy all contributed to the conflict that has defined the shrine's post-war relationship to the nation. In what follows, I begin with an ethnography of the enshrinement rite of April 1938, and seek to explain what makes it the first genuinely national commemorative rite of modern Japan. The second and third sections then sketch in the complex, fraught and often volatile relationship between Yasukuni and the Japanese nation either side of the period 1938–45.

A national time-space: Yasukuni April 1938

The rites of enshrinement in spring 1938 extended over five days, and it is helpful to approach them analytically as structured about two ritual sequences. The first featured the dynamic act of enshrinement and revolved about the war dead; the second saw the dramatic focus shift from the war dead to the emperor, who arrives

FIGURE 8.1 Priests summon the spirits of the fallen to the altar in Yasukuni's shrine garden.

Source: Yasukuni no inori henshū iinkai ed., 1999. *Yasukuni no inori: me de miru Meiji , Taishō, Shōwa, Heisei*, Sankei Shinbun, p. 111.

FIGURE 8.2 The illuminated palanquin bearing spirits of the fallen from the Shrine Garden to the Main Sanctuary.

Source: Yasukuni no inori henshū iinkai ed., 1999. *Yasukuni no inori: me de miru Meiji, Taishō, Shōwa, Heisei*, Sankei Shinbun, p. 150.

at the shrine to perform an act of veneration. Both sequences involved a procession, which wended its way to the dwelling place of the glorious spirits in the shrine's Main Sanctuary. Together, these two sequences sought to effect transformations on the war dead, on the bereaved and on other ritual observers/participants.[5] The first sequence began on the night of 24 April. Suzuki Takao, Yasukuni chief priest and reserve army general, stood before the altar in the shrine garden, and summoned the spirits of the 4,533 men who had died fighting in Manchuria and China.[6] He did so in the presence of 200 men of the imperial guard, officials of the Army and Navy Ministries and 9,000 of the bereaved, as well as serried ranks of soldiers from the regiments of the fallen. The 'crowd' was, in fact, still larger than it may appear, since the hour-long events in the shrine garden were broadcast live on national AK radio across Japan and beyond to Manchuria.[7]

The spirits descended to the altar and were greeted by the chief priest's declamation of 'Awww!' and the strum of a lute. He feted them with wine, water and produce from land and sea. He invited them on the emperor's behalf to enter the Yasukuni pantheon. He then transferred them to a palanquin, an act involving the physical transfer of a book inscribed with their names. Lanterns in the shrine precinct were extinguished, the darkness relieved only by the illuminations within the palanquin itself. Borne on the shoulders of shrine priests, the palanquin made its stately way across the precinct, past the rows of the seated, silent bereaved to the Main Sanctuary. Co-celebrants led the procession; next came the military band; Army and Navy Ministry officials provided the escort, followed by the Yasukuni Chief priest. Soldiers – comrades of the fallen – brought up the rear. At the Main Sanctuary, the chief priest located the spirits in the innermost recess, restored light to the precinct and, once more, made offerings and intoned prayers. A final act of veneration from the priests brought this first sequence to a close.

It is clear that a dramatic transformation was being worked on the war dead here. They were redeemed from the horrors of the battlefield, summoned from the land of the dead and restored to a realm of peace. Yasukuni, it should be noted, means 'land of peace'. This 'recalling of the dead to life' seems to be common to commemorative rites everywhere (Hutchinson, 2006: 48). At Yasukuni, the dead were recalled, only then to be 'beatified' as glorious spirits through a ritual process of progress, feting and restitution. The bereaved – two family members for each of the dead, transported to Yasukuni at government expense from all corners of the realm – played a vital role here. They were spectators, to be sure, but not merely so. Rather, their presence sanctioned the segregation of the dead into the pantheon to assume a new, heroic and national identity as glorious spirits. Only on the second day, when the dead had been celebrated once more by the state's representatives – shrine priests and military – were the bereaved finally admitted to the Main Sanctuary to pay their own respects. These events were clearly less about mourning, then, than about the production and celebration of national heroes. The celebratory mood was sustained throughout the five days of rites, with the staging of acrobatics, comedy acts, chorus singing, film shows and fireworks in different locations of the shrine precinct.

The climax to the enshrinement rites of April 1938 came, in fact, with the second sequence on day three, 26 April. It featured the emperor's progress to Yasukuni. A crowd estimated at 200,000 gathered in the streets outside Yasukuni to greet the emperor. His motorcade entered the precinct shortly after 10 a.m. The path to the Main Sanctuary was lined with the bereaved, kneeling in disciplined rows under the watchful eye of military guards. Waiting, too, immediately before the shrine's Worship Hall were Prime Minister Konoe Fumimaro and his cabinet, senior officials from all government ministries, lords and dukes, prefectural governors, the leaders of the upper and lower houses of the Diet, assorted Diet members and recipients of various imperial honours. The emperor, wearing the uniform of the Supreme Commander of the Armed Forces, alighted from his car and was escorted into the Main Sanctuary. There he knelt before the spirits of the war dead, offered

FIGURE 8.3 The bereaved await the emperor, 26 April 1938.

Source: *Shōwa 13nen 4gatsu Yasukuni jinja rinji taisai kinen shashin chō*, Yasukuni Kaiko bunko shitsu shozō.

FIGURE 8.4 Emperor Hirohito arrives at Yasukuni, 26 April 1938.

Source: *Shōwa 13nen 4gatsu Yasukuni jinja rinji taisai kinen shashin chō*, Yasukuni Kaiko bunko shitsu shozō.

them a branch of the *sakaki* tree and, as a siren sounded, bowed and observed a minute's silence. The emperor was later followed into the Main Sanctuary by the empress, and then by Prime Minister Konoe, his cabinet and all of the nation's great and good. After their departure, the bereaved were once more admitted. The vast crowds who had gathered outside the shrine to witness the emperor's coming formed the final, seething segment of the procession that led into the presence of the glorious spirits.

What sense are we to make of the emperor's ritual actions at Yasukuni on this day? A *Yomiuri* newspaper journalist put it like this:

> The loyal spirits who sleep under the ground, and the 90 million people of the Japanese nation, weep together as one, overcome with emotion [at the emperor's presence]. It is now [with his act of veneration] that this glorious event, solemn beyond compare, reaches its climax.
>
> (*Yomiuri shinbun*, 26 April 1938)

The journalist conveyed to his readers the striking but unmistakable impression that the dead and the living were gathered at Yasukuni to celebrate the emperor. The emperor alone made sense of the soldiers' deaths; it was for his sake that they had made the ultimate sacrifice. This emperor, moreover, was no longer an ordinary man. By the late 1930s, he was cast as a living god. Alternative views of the emperor as a Western-style constitutional monarch had been banned from the public realm in 1937, and their proponents silenced. *Izoku no shiori*, a guidebook distributed to the bereaved at Yasukuni, assured them that the emperor 'augustly' conferred status on the dead as national gods, before he, 'with his most precious body, *itself a living god*, deigned to venerate them' (Kamo, 1932: 6, emphasis added). The crucial point was that it was the emperor – no longer the war dead – who now struck the ritual beat. The beat reverberated through the minute's silence the length and breadth of Japan. Silence and its imposition constituted a new technique, employed at Yasukuni now for the first time. Its purpose was to stop the nation in its tracks at the very moment the emperor venerated the war dead.

The emperor was a transformative presence. His personal veneration rendered the war dead incomparably glorious, completing the process that had begun with the act of enshrinement three days before. Their glory now took its place in Yasukuni's narrative of Japan's past. A vital transformation was worked on the bereaved, too. First, they prostrated themselves as the emperor's motorcade approached, and then, just before his car passed by, they raised their heads as one to gaze on his 'dragon face'. They ceased now to be mourning mothers and fathers, sons and daughters. The emperor's presence rendered mourning and sorrow obsolete. The aforementioned guidebook for the bereaved made this quite clear: 'While there is bound to be sorrow at the loss, the more pressing need is to rejoice and praise [the war dead] for their loyalty to the emperor and their service to the imperial realm' (Kamo, 1932: 2). The immense 'honour' attached to being bereaved was accompanied by new social obligations. The families of the dead were themselves to become 'models of loyal subject-hood for their local community' (ibid.: 46).

As Jon Fox intimates in this volume, there are real dangers in assuming national events such as these are ever consumed as they are produced. Still, there are suggestions that the emperor's presence effected a transformation – however fleeting – upon some at least of those comprising the ritual audience. The bestselling woman's weekly *Shufu no tomo* marked this 1938 enshrinement by interviewing some of the mothers of the fallen. How had they experienced the event? Mrs Takai responded: 'My boy was my gift to our great emperor. Who was I to hold him back? The emperor made use of our boys, boys of inconsequential people like us . . .' 'For people like us to have borne children whom the emperor could use: what an honour!' responded Mrs Nakamura. Mrs Saitō: 'Our great emperor, too, turned up to venerate them all! What an honour for us then to venerate him in turn! If I were to die today, I would die a happy woman. I could die with a smile on my face.' Mrs Nakamura spoke of the sorrow of her son's loss, but 'when I reflect on how he died for his country, and how he was honoured by the emperor, I am so happy I can forget everything else. It gives me strength' (*Shufu no tomo*, June 1938: 101–4).[8]

The nation's shrine

What made Yasukuni's enshrinement rites of April 1938 national was that, for the first time, they represented the nation to itself in all its complexity: emperor, nobility, prime minister, military and, above all, the people participated at Yasukuni together for the first time. And, for the first time, the state implemented techniques – most notably the minute's silence – designed to ensure the ritual beat reverberated across Japan. The people were engaged now in numbers previously unimaginable: 9,000 bereaved had privileged access to the shrine precinct; 200,000 Tokyo citizens were gathered outside the shrine and, beyond them, the radio and the minute's silence remotely engaged millions more. The coordinated efforts of the Army and Navy Ministries, the Finance and Home Ministries, and the Ministries of Communication and Education made it happen. Yasukuni had never before hosted an event such as this, and this fact raises fundamental questions about the connection between Yasukuni and its rites, on the one hand, and the Japanese nation, on the other, before April 1938. What sort of site was it, and how were its enshrinement rites transformed into national events?

From its founding by imperial fiat in 1869, Yasukuni was an unmistakably imperial site. Its buildings were adorned with the imperial chrysanthemum; an imperial emissary was typically dispatched to celebrate the great rites of propitiation, and very occasionally – just seven times in his 44-year reign (1868–1912) – the Meiji emperor himself had attended enshrinement rites. Yasukuni was, at the same time, a military shrine through and through. It was built to enshrine the military dead, and was administered jointly by the Army and Navy Ministries. Its priests were appointed by the military, and military men organized its ritual performances and served as co-celebrants. No other shrine in modern Japan – they numbered around 100,000 – had a similar relationship to the military, since all others answered to the Home Ministry. Only one other shrine in Japan had a comparable relationship to the emperor: the shrine in Ise dedicated to his great ancestor, the Sun Goddess. Yasukuni rites, from their beginnings, celebrated the privileged connection between the military, the war dead and the emperor.

Somewhat incongruously, perhaps, this same Yasukuni shrine quickly became one of Tokyo's top tourist attractions. Tourist guides in the 1870s and 1880s duly noted Yasukuni's function as a sacred site for the fallen, but commended it for its entertainment value. It had a Western style park with all manner of shrubs and plants, and water fountains; a lighthouse (Yasukuni overlooked Tokyo bay); illuminations by gas and, later, electric light; a race track surrounded by cherry trees. This was the Yasukuni that featured in countless nineteenth-century colour prints, a symbol of modern Japanese life. Architecturally, Yasukuni was by no means egregious as a shrine, but its huge wooden *torii* gate, its towering bronze statue of Ōmura Masujirō, founder of the modern Japanese military, and its war museum designed by an Italian architect, enhanced the shrine's popular appeal. Sizable crowds of Tokyo citizens gathered at Yasukuni as early as the 1870s, giving its rites a genuinely festive quality, even if it was the horse racing, the acrobatics and the fireworks that exercised the real pull (Kobori, 1996: 72–9).

Yasukuni's character began to change in the early twentieth century. The unprecedented losses suffered by the military in the Russo-Japanese War of 1904–5 help account for this. Ninety thousand soldiers and sailors was the price Japan paid for its astonishing victory over Russia. The rites of enshrinement held in spring 1906 and 1907 were duly staged with unprecedented grandeur. Government bureaucrats and Tokyo-resident soldiers and recruits were given the day off. The bereaved who were able to attend were offered not only the usual entertainments in the shrine precinct, but also access to Tokyo's imperial sites: imperial residences on the city outskirts, imperial parks and the imperial museum. Vast crowds gathered to witness the emperor's arrival for the mass enshrinements held in spring 1906 and 1907. Kamo Momoki, chief priest at Yasukuni from 1909, wrote retrospectively of the magnificence of these two events (Kamo, 1911: 89–90). He attributed that magnificence partly at least to the presence of the prime minister and his cabinet. In doing so, he makes what is, in fact, the first ever reference to a prime minister setting foot in Yasukuni. It is, however, a puzzling one. For no corroboratory evidence exists. The print media makes no comment on the prime minister's attendance; nor, indeed, do either of the two official Yasukuni chronologies (Moriya, 1972; Yasukuni jinja, 1987). The mystery remains. As we shall see, the first independently verifiable instance of a prime minister attending Yasukuni is not until a generation later in spring 1932.

The point is that pre-1938 Yasukuni, civilian prime ministers appear not to have been welcome. Yasukuni was an imperial shrine, a military shrine, but not a shrine for civilians. This became a major point of contention following Kamo Momoki's appointment as chief priest in 1909. Kamo had been a leading voice in the national Shinto community, and so an obvious choice perhaps for the job of Yasukuni chief priest. In fact, however, he was an egregious one. For, unlike his predecessors and his successors – at least until 1945 – Kamo was himself not a military man, but a civilian. Kamo worked daily with bureaucrats of the Army Ministry, and the numerous transformations the shrine underwent in the first decades of the early twentieth century can only be understood as the result of close coopera-tion between them. For example, Yasukuni's spaces were transformed during Kamo's tenure by the construction of an imposing wooden thatched portal across the central pathway, and then the erection of a massive bronze *torii* gate at the start of that pathway. Kamo's tenure saw the construction of new buildings in the precinct: a reception hall for visiting dignitaries, an exhibition hall to accommodate military hardware, and a sword-smith's atelier. There was also a redesigned, relocated and much-expanded 'sacred garden'; it was here that the 1938 rite of enshrinement began (Yasukuni no inori, 1999: 102–3).

All of this attests to close cooperation between the civilian and the military, but what came to define his tenure was conflict, and the conflict concerned ritual performance. Kamo came to question the military's overwhelming influence on Yasukuni rites, which he believed compromised their 'national' potential; the military begged to differ (Fujita, 2007: 209–10). Ritual-centred conflict first reared its head in the years after the First World War. Japan was now an elite member of the international community, one of four permanent members on the council of the League of Nations. It is not surprising that Yasukuni's chief priest showed a keen interest in how Japan's allies in Europe and the US commemorated their dead. Kamo had himself begun to speak of Yasukuni as an 'international shrine', and he played host to numerous foreign dignitaries at Yasukuni, including European royalty (Moriya, 1972: 96, 98). It becomes clear that his new knowledge of Western practice informed his antagonism towards his military masters. In September 1924, Kamo composed a carefully worded position paper, proposing Yasukuni be removed from military control and transferred to the Home Ministry. He granted the powerful spiritual effect of having military men venerate the military dead, and conceded the military should retain a ritual function. However, the time had now come for the Home Ministry to assume charge of Yasukuni. 'The control of Yasukuni by the Army and Navy Ministries may enhance military morale, but [the shrine] fails in the edification of the nation at large' (Yasukuni jinja, 1983: 154).

Western influence was explicit in a second Kamo petition, one he submitted to Prime Minister Katō Takaaki early in 1925. Here, Kamo cited the examples of Arlington cemetery in the US, the Cenotaph in London, and French and Italian practices before painting a woeful picture of Yasukuni's failure to engage with all Japanese. Yasukuni, he insisted, failed as a shrine for the nation. Kamo proposed a series of measures to effect its transformation. The key was the government declaring Yasukuni's great spring and autumn rites of propitiation to be national holidays. It was essential the prime minister and his cabinet participate at Yasukuni on these days 'and so provide a model for the nation in its entirety'. He lamented that prime ministers' attendance at these events was unheard of till now. On these new feast days, all Japanese – their homes decorated with the national flag – should pause at 9 a.m., the very moment the imperial emissary offers up prayers to the war dead on the emperor's behalf. All school children should assemble at school, and there turn to face Yasukuni and perform 'remote' acts of veneration. Children may have learned of Yasukuni shrine in their school textbooks, but they remained quite ignorant of Yasukuni's great rites of propitiation. Of course, the military might retain a presence at Yasukuni rites, but unless they relinquished control of the shrine, fundamental change was impossible (Fujita, 2009: 225–6; Yasukuni jinja, 1983: 154–5).

Government ministers were persuaded by Kamo's arguments, and launched a deliberative committee to plan for Yasukuni's transfer to Home Ministry control. The committee's view was precisely that of Kamo: 'Yasukuni is not to be seen as a shrine with exclusive connections to the Army and Navy. Rendering [Yasukuni] a shrine for the nation is, indeed, essential to stirring the national spirit' (Fujita, 2007: 213–15). The Army and Navy, however, thwarted this challenge to their authority, and their ability to do so was testament to their influence in the politics of 1920s Japan. But Kamo was undeterred, and he continued to insist on the need for Yasukuni's rites to reverberate throughout the nation. This he did most boldly in a radio broadcast in April 1932 (Fujita, 2007: 228). Perhaps this broadcast exerted a measure of influence on the concession that the military offered later that month. They allowed Prime Minister Inukai Tsuyoshi to attend a Yasukuni rite of enshrinement. The rites were performed for the men who had died in the occupation of Manchuria, and Inukai was there to greet the emperor (Yasukuni jinja, 1987: 310). Inukai was the first premier, whose attendance at Yasukuni can be verified.

Yasukuni was never, in fact, wrested from military control, but substantial change in the character of shrine rites began to surface in the summer of 1937, after the Marco Polo Bridge incident. Japan was now at war. The aim of the new government under Konoe Fumimaro – a civilian – was no longer simply consolidating Manchuria as an independent state, but annihilating the nationalist Chinese. The imperial army, with some 500,000 troops deployed in China, had begun its long march south to Nanking. Meanwhile, at home, Konoe launched his 'National Spiritual Mobilization Movement' the better to unite 'state and people' and so overcome 'the difficulties of the moment and promote imperial fortunes' (Kaigunshō, 1972: 1061). In December, the army took Nanking, wreaking untold havoc in the process. Konoe celebrated by declaring an end to all negotiations with the Chinese, and it was now, in the total-war situation of January 1938, that new life was breathed into Kamo's national vision for Yasukuni. In the Diet that month, politician Tsutsumi Kōjirō argued – just like Kamo Momoki before him – that Yasukuni and its rites must now assume a central role in national life. He put it to Home Minister Suetsugu Nobumasa that Yasukuni must learn from the Cenotaph in London so that what he called Yasukuni's 'lonely' rites of propitiation might become rites for the entire nation.

> [In Britain] the sovereign represents the state, and pays his respects on 11 November at the Cenotaph; the prime minster and his entire cabinet, as well as the military, are all present. For two minutes, trains and motorcars and all forms of transport come to a halt, and silence is observed. Military men shoulder arms in expression of their sorrow.
>
> (Yasukuni jinja, 1983: 409–10)

Tsutsumi conceded that enshrinement rites – as opposed to those of propitiation – were always splendid whenever the emperor attended but, with Japan now engaged in total war, it was vital to seek other opportunities to 'move' the people. Those other opportunities should involve invigorating the rites of propitiation. The government should emulate British practice, and start by adding the spring and autumn propitiation rites to the calendar as national holidays. Home Minister Suetsugu parried Tsutsumi's proposal, insisting Yasukuni was a matter for the military. But the very next day Diet member Takechi Yūki pursued the matter at a cross-party meeting. There, he distributed a discussion document that was almost an exact copy of Kamo's 1925 proposal discussed above. It demanded Yasukuni's spring and autumn rites of propitiation be declared national holidays; it called for the presence at Yasukuni on those days of the prime minister, his cabinet and diet members; for the observation of a minute's silence as the imperial emissary offered up prayers to the war dead; for the flying of the flag at homes across Japan; and for children in every school to face Yasukuni and venerate the war dead (*Yomiuri shinbun*, 25 January 1938). Takechi's document differed only in that it no longer insisted Yasukuni be removed from military control. In Japan of 1938, this was no longer a realistic hope.

These cross-party discussions generated a momentum that finally bore fruit in the unprecedented national events of April 1938. In some important ways, these events departed from the Kamo–Tsutsumi–Takechi proposals. Most obviously, the government's interest was not in rites of propitiation, but the inherently more dynamic rites of enshrinement. It chose now to supercharge these with a new national quality. The emperor, till now an irregular presence at Yasukuni, would attend all enshrinement rites. The innovative presence of the prime minster and his cabinet, and the new technique of a minute's silence imposed across Japan, would serve to present the nation to itself and ensure the ritual reverberated across Japan. These rites were never declared national holidays, although banks and many businesses did in fact close, and bureaucrats and service personnel were given time off to attend Yasukuni. It was the combination of emperor, prime minister and the minute's silence that was essential to the new national quality of the events that began in April 1938.

The minute's silence, the technique intended to secure mass participation, was approved at a Vice Ministers council meeting on 7 April. The press announced it the next day, and published reminders repeatedly thereafter up until 26 April. Notice was also carried later in April in *Shūhō*, the government gazette. Silence would commence with siren blasts across Japan and announcements on the radio. Silence would be observed from 10.15 a.m. on 26 April, the precise moment when the emperor venerated the war dead (Kaigunshō, 1972: 1077–8). The influence on this innovation of Cenotaph practice seems clear enough, but it also formed a perfect fit with strategies already deployed by Prime Minister Konoe in his 'National Spiritual Mobilization Movement'. The movement's organizing committee had, from the outset, exhibited an unprecedented preoccupation with 'simultaneity'. The committee's very first move in October 1937 had been to introduce 'morning worship' on national radio, inviting listeners across Japan to face the imperial palace at precisely 8 a.m. and venerate the emperor. The same committee then took charge of New Year celebrations in January 1938, directing all Japanese to venerate the emperor at precisely 10 a.m. on 1 January. Similarly calibrated practices were implemented for State Foundation in February and later too for the emperor's birthday (Hara, 2004; Kaigunshō, 1972: 1070–1, 1073). Like these other techniques, the minute's silence at Yasukuni in April 1938 was always intended to focus the nation's attention on the divine presence of the emperor.

Post-war Yasukuni and the resumption of conflict

The new national rites of enshrinement that began at Yasukuni in April 1938 established a precedent that held, more or less, until 1945. There were adjustments to the *mise-en-scène*, but few changes of substance. In 1939, for example, the acrobatics, comedy sketches, fireworks and the several hundred stalls intended to entertain the bereaved were swept away and 'solemnity was restored to Yasukuni's sacred spaces'. The bereaved were now confronted with a new war panorama, featuring weapons seized from the Chinese enemy (Yasukuni jinja, 1987: 356). The ever-greater number of war dead meant that, by autumn 1941, the rites of enshrinement occupied an extra three days (Moriya, 1972: 141). Then, from autumn 1944, fears of American bombing prompted a change to the shrine crowd. Only the Tokyo-resident bereaved were invited to attend; those from outside the capital were encouraged to gather at local government offices across Japan, listen to the rites of enshrinement on national radio and 'worship the war dead from afar' (Yasukuni jinja, 1987: 402). In 1945, US bomber raids made it too dangerous to invite any of the bereaved to the enshrinements, although the emperor attended as he had done for the previous seven years.

Before Japan's surrender and the start of the occupation, the US government had made up its collective mind about Yasukuni and its ritual performances. In March 1944, it produced a memorandum styled 'Japan: Freedom of Worship', which defined Yasukuni and other sites 'not [as] places of worship as we understand the term, but [as] nationalist shrines dedicated to the veneration of nationalist, militarist heroes and to the fostering of a militant national spirit' (Nishida, 1986: 226–9). In December 1945, three months into the occupation, the US military issued the 'Shinto Directive', which dislocated Yasukuni – and all other Shinto shrines – from the state (Breen and Teeuwen, 2010: 1–24). Religious freedom and a rigorous separation of religion and state were then enshrined into the Constitution of 1946. Yasukuni survived the upheaval as a 'religious juridical person', which it remains to this day (Mullins, 2010). There are still great rites in spring and autumn. It is now served by a full-time Shinto priesthood, who perform daily rites of propitiation for the glorious spirits still venerated there.

The first point to make about Yasukuni and the post-war Japanese nation is that, while the shrine is a fully functioning ritual site, it is no longer a 'national' ritual site. Its rites are private rites; they are not the state-sponsored, nation-producing events they were between 1938 and 1945. Post-war Japan's 'national' site of mourning is the Chidorigafuchi National Cemetery, constructed about a tomb for the unknown war dead (military and civilian) elsewhere in Tokyo. Japan's 'National Rite of Mourning' takes place in the Tokyo Budōkan Hall on 15 August every year. The emperor presides, the prime minister and his cabinet attend along with the bereaved, and the event is broadcast live on national TV and radio. It features a minute's silence, which the national press invite all Japanese to observe (Breen, 2012: 286–9). In this situation, what connection, if any, can there be between Yasukuni and its rites, on the one hand, and the post-war nation, on the other? We might usefully address this question by reflecting on the relationship to the shrine of those different, conflictual components of the nation that gave its rites meaning from 1938: the military, the imperial institution, the government (in the person of the prime minister) and, of course, the people.

Japan today has no army, air force or navy; they are banned under Article 9 of the Constitution. Rather, Japan has a Self-Defence Force, but Yasukuni, as a private juridical person, has no organic links to the SDF, and does not enshrine SDF personnel who die on duty. A Defence Agency memorandum in 1974 warned commanding officers and personnel not to attend religious rites such as those at Yasukuni in an official capacity; and that warning remains in force (Nishida, 1986: 403–4). Nonetheless, Yasukuni every year invites the Chiefs of Staff of the Air, Sea and Land SDF to attend its spring and autumn rites of propitiation. Although they decline, the SDF is regularly represented by the chairman of the Staff Officers'

Committee in civilian dress. Of course, there survives at post-war Yasukuni an unmistakable martial quality. After all, priests in their daily ritual activity propitiate Japan's fallen soldiers and sailors. The shrine's martial quality is also nurtured in the war museum that stands adjacent to the Main Sanctuary (Breen, 2012: 291–2; Nelson, 2003; Tōgō, 2008: 48–53). Yasukuni once enjoyed an intimacy with the Imperial Japanese Army and Navy that transcended the boundaries between life and death; but the Imperial Army and Navy are no more.

Yet Yasukuni today retains an important imperial quality. The present emperor, like his father before him, dispatches an emissary to participate in Yasukuni's spring and autumn propitiation rites. Imperial princes also often attend. However the imperial institution's relationship with Yasukuni today is one of tension. The present emperor, Akihito, has never participated in Yasukuni rites; his father, Hirohito, who attended so assiduously from 1938 till 1945, visited just eight times in the 45 years between Japan's defeat and his death in 1989; he was last there in 1975. The tensions between emperor and shrine date back to the 1970s. In 1978, Yasukuni enshrined the spirits of fourteen Class A war criminals, men condemned by the Tokyo war crimes tribunal who were subsequently executed or died in prison. Their enshrinement took place probably without the emperor's foreknowledge, certainly without his approval. The emperor objected to their enshrinement. Revelations published in 2006 and 2007 by two of his closest aides leave no room for doubt (Breen, 2012: 296–8). The question that now taxes Yasukuni priests and satellite organizations, like the Japan Society for the War Bereaved (JSWB), is how to dissolve these tensions and secure the reigning emperor's participation in Yasukuni rites once more. The answer proposed most recently by the JSWB is the ritual transfer of the Class As to some other site. Shrine priests, however, bitterly oppose such 'interference'.

Keener still is the conflict between the post-war state and the shrine. For all that successive post-war prime ministers have wished to honour the war dead at Yasukuni rites, and despite priests' insistence that they do so, the relationship between state and shrine is one of discord. The war criminal presence is, indeed, part of the problem. They accounted for the boycotting of Yasukuni rites by the Democratic Party of Japan when it held power between 2009 and 2011. To be sure, the war criminals posed no problem for Liberal Democratic Party prime ministerss such as Nakasone, Hashimoto, and Koizumi, all of whom patronized Yasukuni after 1978. Prime Ministers Abe, Fukuda and Asō had no personal objections to the war criminal presence, but they stayed away for fear of antagonizing the Chinese (Breen, 2012: 285–6). Tensions between state and shrine are intimately related also to the constitutional separation of state and religion. For prime ministers' attendance at Yasukuni breach Article 20 of the constitution – or so it is argued (ibid.: 281–4). Yasukuni priests, however, find quite unacceptable the solution to the problem proposed by successive LDP administrations: namely, the stripping away of Yasukuni's 'religiosity' to render its rites 'non-religious', and so sidestepping the constitutional problem (Breen, 2010).[9]

Finally, any consideration of post-war Yasukuni and the nation must take account of the people's presence at Yasukuni rites. What place for the people? Yasukuni claims to attract 6 million visitors annually. Shrine statistics are not independently verifiable, but Yasukuni certainly seems to thrive at the start of the twenty-first century. An explanation for this demands more space than is permitted here. Suffice it to say that today's crowds are drawn typically from Tokyo, and they come not for the spring and autumn rites of propitiation, which are once more the 'lonely' affairs they were before 1938. Rather, it is New Year, the July *mitama* festival and, to a lesser extent, end-of-war commemoration on 15 August that attracts them. Over a quarter of a million Tokyo citizens celebrated New Year at Yasukuni in 2010, and 300,000 ensured the success of the 2011 *mitama* festival; this latter is a post-war creation similar to the Buddhist *bon* festival for the spirits of the dead. Some 160,000 marked the end of the war at Yasukuni on 15 August 2011. The composition of the Yasukuni crowds has changed radically over the two post-war generations. The parents and wives and, increasingly too, the sons and daughters of the fallen have passed on; and so have the veterans. For New Year, and the summer *mitama* festival, the Yasukuni clientele is local, but on 15 August the shrine is a magnet to paramilitary ultranationalists who hail from all over Japan. They arrive in military-style trucks emblazoned with pro-emperor, anti-foreign, anti-government slogans. Their loudspeakers blast out patriotic songs, and they shriek insults at the riot police awaiting them. Clad in paramilitary style uniforms, or heavy black suits, they strut through the shrine precinct bringing a real sense of menace to Yasukuni. Yasukuni, on such days, is a place of (often violent) conflict.

Yasukuni attracts extreme nationalists because, like nowhere else in Japan, it affords an intense experience of the imperial past, in which such groups find meaning. In Yasukuni rites, the war dead are indiscriminately celebrated and honoured. Yasukuni renders them all paragons of self-sacrifice, loyalty and patriotism. To the paramilitaries – and also to the many ultraconservative intellectuals who hover about Yasukuni – the fallen embody an imperial ideal to be emulated by society at large. One could perhaps sum up post-war Yasukuni by saying that while 'nationalism' is alive and kicking there today, the nation is conspicuous by its absence. The organic linkage between the shrine, its rites and nationalism on the one hand, and the Japanese nation on the other, is no more.

Conclusion

Every year between 1938 until 1945, Yasukuni held spring and autumn rites of enshrinement for the military war dead. These performances presented the nation to itself in all its conflictual complexity: emperor, prime minister, military – and the people in vast numbers. First the war dead, in the drama of their enshrinement, and then the emperor, in his act of veneration, struck powerful ritual beats that reverberated the length and breadth of Japan. Yasukuni only now became the sort of 'national shrine' for which Kamo Momoki especially had campaigned. Kamo's petitions shaped the national character of the shrine and its rites during this brief period. But that new character was only acquired in the context of Japan's all-out war with China.[10] The military never loosened its grip on Yasukuni. The war obviated that need, and it was the war that ensured that enshrinement rites reverberated far and wide. In any discussion of national rites, the related question of resonance – the extent to which the nation picked up the ritual beat – merits consideration. How many people actually tuned into the radio or observed the minute's silence, and what did they make of what they heard and what they did? Were the bereaved moved to become models of ethical behaviour in their local communities? What can we read into the sentiments voiced by the mothers featured in the magazine *Shufu no tomo*? These questions are impossible to answer, but Japan was at total war from 1938 to 1945 – first with China and then with the Western world – and, in such profound national crises, the gap between elite intentions and the common people's engagement is inevitably narrowed.[11]

Yasukuni was created by imperial fiat in the 1860s; it was funded thereafter by the civilian government but entrusted to the care of the military to enshrine and propitiate the nation's war dead. And yet Yasukuni's ritual performances did not, for most of the shrine's pre-war existence, achieve a national reverberation. This demonstrates not that modern Japan had no need for national rites; such an assertion might be disproven easily with a study of the many celebratory rites the state sponsored from the late nineteenth century through to the twentiethth century. Rather, it was that Yasukuni's national potential was hamstrung by the grip of the military on the shrine's ritual performances, until the unprecedented national crisis of 1938. As for post-war Japan, Yasukuni rites lost all national potential when the shrine became a (private) religious juridical person in law. Today, its links to the SDF are tenuous in the extreme; its relationships both to government and imperial institution are defined by conflict and tension. Occasional post-war enshrinements, as well as the seasonal rites of propitiation, have thus been very subdued affairs, whose appeal to the commfon man and woman appears non-existent. Yasukuni, it is true, hosts many visitors today, but the vast majority are citizens of the capital, and it is not the shrine's traditional great rites that draw them. Visitors who perform any act of veneration – and many do not – do so typically as individuals. Finally, what of the nationalism that does survive and, on occasions, thrive at Yasukuni? Post-war Japanese nationalism is, as Yoshino Kosaku reminds us, of a highly 'fragmentary' nature (Yoshino, 1992: 148, 223). Yasukuni's brand of 'nationalism' is therefore best understood as one fragment among many.

Notes

1 The author wishes to thank Mr Noda Anpei of Yasukuni shrine for his generosity and his friendship, and Kevin Doak for many insights into Japanese nationalism.
2 The auditory metaphor deployed here is borrowed and adapted from the fine article by Ben-Amos and Ben-Ari (1995).
3 There is a growing body of literature on Yasukuni in English. See especially Nelson (2003) and the essays in Breen (2008) and Breen (2012). However, all of this work focuses on Yasukuni in its problematic post-war manifestation. Of pre-war Yasukuni, there are no studies in English and, apart from Fujita (2007), only passing references in Japanese.

4 It is important to note that Yasukuni was never the *only* site in modern Japan where commemorative rites for the war dead were held. By the end of the nineteenth century, most prefectures had 'spirit-summoning shrines' for the local war dead, as well as a variety of Buddhist and Shinto stone monuments (Imai, 2008: 382). Local commemorative rites are still performed at the shrines and several of the monuments to this day.

5 I have drawn on two principal sources to recreate the events of April 1938: (1) the *Yomiuri shinbun* newspaper; and (2) *Shōwa 13nen 4gatu Yasukuni jinja rinji taisai kinen shashin chō*, a photographic collection kept in the Kaiko bunko archive at Yasukuni shrine.

6 These enshrinements brought the total number in the national pantheon at Yasukuni to some 140,000 spirits in all. The vast majority were the fallen from the Russo-Japanese War (1904–5).

7 The broadcast from 1938 has not been preserved, but that of the 1940 enshrinement can be heard to this day at the Yasukuni war museum, the Yūshūkan.

8 Hashikawa (1974) cites from these interviews, although he mistakenly dates them 1939. Takahashi (2005) also cites them, repeating the error of the date.

9 The latest advocate of this position was Foreign Minister Asō Tarō in 2006. His views can be read online at www.aso-taro.jp/lecture/talk/060808.html (accessed 30 March 2012).

10 Kamo Momoki mysteriously departed from Yasukuni shrine just three days before the April enshrinement took place. He was replaced as chief priest by General Suzuki.

11 On the gap between elites and ordinary people, see the chapters by Anthony Smith and Jon Fox in this volume.

References

Alexander, J. (2005) 'Performance and power', *Culture*, 20: 1–5.

Ben-Amos, A. and Ben-Ari, E. (1995) 'Resonance and reverberation: ritual and bureaucracy in the state funerals of the French Third Republic', *Theory and Society*, 24: 163–91.

Breen, J. (2008) 'Yasukuni and the loss of historical memory', in J. Breen (ed.) *Yasukuni, the War Dead and the Struggle for Japan's Past*, New York: Columbia University Press, pp. 143–62.

Breen, J. (2010) 'Popes, bishops and war criminals: reflections on Catholics and Yasukuni in post-war Japan', *The Asia-Pacific Journal*, 9: 3-10.

Breen, J. (2012) '"Voices of rage": six paths to the problem of Yasukuni', in R. Starrs (ed.) *Red Sun, White Lotus: Politics and Religion in Japan*, Basingstoke: Palgrave Macmillan, pp. 278–304.

Breen, J. and Teeuwen, M. (2010) *A New History of Shinto*, Hoboken, NJ: Wiley-Blackwell.

Doak, K. (2007) *A History of Nationalism in Modern Japan: Placing the People*, Leiden: Brill.

Fujita Hiromasa (2007) 'Kokka Shintō to Yasukuni jinja ni kansuru ichi kōsatsu: jinja gyōsei tōitsu no zasetsu to Kamo Momoki no gensetsu o megutte', *Kokugakuin daigaku kenkyū kaihatsu suishin senta- kenkyū kiyō*, 1: 199–254.

Handelman, D. (1990) *Models and Mirrors: Towards an Anthropology of Public Events*, New York: Berghahn Books.

Hara Takeshi (2004) 'Senchūki no jikan shihai', *Misuzu*, 52: 28–44.

Hashikawa Bunzō (1974) 'Yasukuni shisō no seiritsu to henyō', in Hashikawa Bunzō, *Hashikawa Bunzō Chosakushū*, 2, Chikuma Shobō, pp. 194–225.

Hutchinson, J. (2006) 'Warfare, remembrance and national identity', in A. Leoussi and S. Grosby (eds) *Nationalism and Ethnosymbolism: History, Culture and Ethnicity in the Formation of Nations*, Edinburgh: Edinburgh University Press, pp. 42–54.

Imai Akihiko (2008) 'Chūreitō kensetsu ni kansuru kōsatsu', *Kokuritsu rekishi minzoku hakubutsukan kenkyū hōkoku*, 147: 375–411.

Kaigunshō (ed.) (1972) *Meiji hyakuknenshi sōsho 192: Kaigun seido enkaku*, Hara Shobō.

Kamo Momoki (1911) *Yasukuni jinja shi*, Yasukuni jinja.

Kamo Momoki (1932) *Yasukuni jinja gosaijin: izoku no shiori*, Yasukuni jinja.

Kobori Keiichirō (1996) *Yasukuni jinja to Nihonjin*, PHP Shinsho.

Kokaze Hidemasa (2011) 'The political space of Meiji 22 (1898): the promulgation of the constitution and the birth of the nation', *Japan Review*, 23: 119–41.

Moriya Hidesuke (ed.) (1972) *Yasukuni jinja ryaku nenpyō*, Yasukuni Jinja Shamusho.

Mullins, M. (2010) 'How Yasukuni survived the occupation: a critical examination of popular claims', *Monumenta Nipponica*, 65(1): 89–136.

Nelson, J. (2003) 'Social memory as ritual practice: commemorating spirits of the military dead at Yasukuni Shinto shrine', *Journal of Asian Studies*, 62(2): 443–67.

Nishida Kōgi (ed.) (1986) *Zōho kaitei kindai jinja Shintō shi*, Jinja Shinpōsha.

Ruoff, K. (2010) *Imperial Japan at its Zenith: The Wartime Celebration of the Empire's 2600th Anniversary*, Ithaca, NY: Cornell University Press.

Takahashi Tetsuya (2005) *Yasukuni mondai*, Chikuma Shobō.

Tōgō Kazuhiko (2008) *Rekishi to gaikō: Yasukuni, Ajia, Tōkyō saiban*, Kōdansha.

Yasukuni jinja (ed.) (1983) *Yasukuni jinja hyakunen shishiryō hen jō*, Hara Shobō.

Yasukuni jinja (ed.) (1987) *Yasukuni jinja hyakunen shi jireki nenpyō*, Hara Shobō.

Yasukuni no inori (ed.) (1999) *Yasukuni no inori: me de miru Meiji, Taishō, Shōwa, Heisei*, Sankei Shinbun.

Yoshino Kosaku (1992) *Cultural Nationalism in Contemporary Japan: A Sociological Inquiry*, London: Routledge.

9

COLLECTIVE ACTION AND NATIONAL IDENTITY

The rally to restore sanity

Rachel D. Hutchins

The 'culture wars' took root in the United States in the 1960s, and have been expanding since the 1980s, opposing (very broadly speaking) progressive secularism and conservative evangelicalism. This deep conflict over the country's ideological core has taken place against the backdrop of the 'browning' of America (as the proportion of 'whites' in the population declines and is projected to decline further in coming years), the growth of secularism (particularly among cultural elites) and the decline of the hegemony of evangelical Protestantism (Hunter, 2009; Kaufmann, 2004). At issue has been the prominence of orthodox religious morality in the public sphere, as reflected in such diverse touchstone domains as gender roles, homosexuality, abortion, the artistic canon and production, public history and education (Hunter, 2009). This ongoing series of cultural and political conflicts has significant implications for the study of nationalism, given that the nation state is a contested political arena, and that nationalist discourse has largely been the medium through which ideological clashes have taken place as competitors advance rival claims to speak for the nation's true best interests. As James Hunter has argued, these debates have been dominated by elites on both sides, leading to increased polarization, an exaggerated dichotomy between competing worldviews, and a 'semi-permanent legitimation crisis' in which each side rejects outright the exercise of power by the other (ibid.: 1321). Nevertheless, these culture wars are not fought merely in the media by elites, but are also waged on the ground by various grassroots organizations.

In order to examine the ways in which national identity is thus negotiated and employed as a political strategy — and the nation, in this manner, reproduced — aspects of these ongoing ideological clashes offer opportunities to view the interplay of action and practice by elites and by ordinary citizens, as well as the dissemination and reception of discourse. A few studies (notably, Jill Lepore's 2010 book) have emerged examining (explicitly or not) performative aspects of recent right-wing nationalist advocacy, and, regarding left-wing activism, studies on the Occupy movement have begun to appear. However, the vast majority of literature on the culture wars has focused on discourse rather than performance. This state of affairs is hardly surprising, given that much of the impetus behind multiculturalism and progressivism comes from within the academy, and therefore takes written form, and the conservative media opposition is so visible that it can be easy to overlook what is happening on the ground.

Many of the chapters in this volume focus on national holidays and rituals – celebrations and commemorations of the nation that are held annually – considering, for the most part, top-down traditions that mark the national calendar. The focus of this chapter is different: I look not at an official national day of commemoration, but at an instance of extraordinary collective action (though still organized by elites), born of the culture wars, which was framed in national terms and which, I will argue, sought to re-appropriate nationalist discourse and symbols in a manner that illustrates the simultaneous use of nationalism as a political strategy to advance an ideological agenda and an attempt to renegotiate the vision of national identity.

This event, Jon Stewart and Stephen Colbert's Rally to Restore Sanity, which I shall present in its context below, combines elements that many nationalism scholars believe merit greater study. Organized, as it was, by media elites, attended by ordinary citizens, promoted via the internet and television, widely covered in the news media, this gathering in Washington DC incorporated national symbols, rituals and practices, as well as entertainment, comedy, music and more serious discourse. It thus offers a rich complex of potential emotional reactions of the public, which might lead to varied, multilayered experiences of this collective event.

This chapter will thus examine a combination of performative aspects of the rally, as well as audience reception and resonance of the organizers' discourse (focusing particularly on their constructions of national identity). In order to provide as complete a picture of national reproduction as possible, I employ a variety of disciplinary and theoretical approaches. In terms of nationalism scholarship, this chapter draws, for instance, on work by Michael Billig (1995), Craig Calhoun (1997) and Umut Özkirimli (2003), who focus on nationalism as a discursive formation, calling for examinations of the ways in which rhetorical strategies reproduce nationhood. The present study is further informed by John Breuilly's focus on nationalism as a political strategy (Breuilly, 1993 [1985]), as well as by Anthony Smith's theories on competing visions of national identity (Smith, 1999).

Regarding performance and collective action, I mainly draw on Randall Collins's work on interaction ritual. Collins has defined ritual as: 'a mechanism of mutually focused emotion and attention producing a momentarily shared reality, which thereby generates solidarity and symbols of group membership' (Collins, 2004: 7). Collins has posited the importance of face-to-face interaction for generating emotion, a sense of belonging and identity, and he has stressed the importance of the emotion thus generated, particularly Durkheimian 'collective effervescence', in spurring groups of people to action (Collins, 2004, 2011). Furthermore, Collins emphasizes how entertainment venues, musical performance, political rallies and shared laughter can form powerful interaction rituals that bind groups of people together, on both micro and macro levels (Collins, 2004: 59–60). The Rally to Restore Sanity combined all of these elements. In addition, it was framed within an ensemble of national symbolic resources (Zimmer, 2003), thus making it the type of event conducive to fostering the 'heightened national cohesion' to which Jonathan Fox and Cynthia Miller-Idriss have referred:

> Nationhood is also given symbolic meaning in the ritual performances of everyday (and not-so-everyday) life. Symbols are the cultural ciphers through which meanings are assigned to phenomena and attachments made between people and things (Geertz, 1973: 216). National symbols – flags, anthems, statues and landmarks – are neatly packaged distillations of the nation: they are the linchpins that connect people to the nation (Cerulo, 1995; Smith, 1986). Rituals provide occasions for the visual and audible realization of these symbolic attachments. Through the choreographed exhibition and collective performance of national symbols, those in attendance are united in the transitory awareness of heightened national cohesion. The electricity of the crowd, momentarily subsuming the individual to the collective, generates the experience of 'collective effervescence'.
>
> (Fox and Miller-Idriss, 2008: 545)

Furthermore, because the rally was organized and broadcast nationally, drawing its audience from all over the USA (including satellite rallies in other cities), it also provides the sort of simultaneity of celebration and a sense of community across space, throughout the national territory, that Benedict Anderson contends contributes to constituting the imagined community (Anderson, 2006: 6–7, 145).

This chapter will begin with an overview of the context in which the Rally to Restore Sanity was held. It will then examine the use of national symbols and rituals by the rally organizers, followed by an analysis of their nationalist discourse. The final section of the chapter studies the salience and resonance for the rally audience of these conceptions and constructions of national sentiment and identity through a study of crowd reactions, as visible on television coverage of the event, and through written interviews that I conducted of rally attendees (the methodology of which is discussed with the presentation of the findings). Due to the limitations of sample size and self-selection, these interviews are illustrative rather than statistically definitive. Nevertheless, they propose a simple framework for comparing the prevalence of nationalist themes and goals as proposed by elites in participants' reported experience.

Indeed, I wish to preface this chapter with a caveat. As Jon Fox notes (in this volume) and as Gordana Uzelac has also argued (Uzelac, 2010), nationalism scholars tend to focus on supply (top-down) manifestations and promotions of nationalism. This trend is, of course, partly due to the fact that measuring reception from the bottom up poses a certain number of methodological difficulties. There are the practical problems of the sample (and researcher's resources), and perhaps even more difficult to overcome are the obstacles to measuring emotion and accounting for the dynamic nature of people's sentiments. (As both Collins, 2004 and Uzelac, 2010 emphasize, even the emotional reaction of a successful performance fades as people return to their daily routines.)

I thus look primarily at supply, specifically focusing on how nationalist messages are now being used by elites of the centre-left in an attempt to regain ideological ground from the right, which has traditionally been more likely to appropriate these symbols and discourse. My small interview sample represents an initial step in examining the potential interaction (though we cannot infer a causal relationship) between the rally organizers' discourse (supply), as promoted by this performance, and the audience's reported experience (demand). In this way, this study aims to explore the extent to which events of this type may (re)generate a sense of nationhood, and thereby to offer some insight into ways in which interdisciplinary studies of performance may inform the field of nationalism scholarship.

Ideological/political context of the rally

Conservative organizations, notably including the 'Christian Right', have led ongoing campaigns to make their voices heard and elect their candidates on local, state and national levels, as well as to influence a broad range of policy issues. If evangelical activism reached a high point with 2004 electoral victories in the reelection of George W. Bush and the securing of Republican majorities in both houses of Congress, the 2006 congressional mid-term electoral gains by Democrats and the 2008 election of Barack Obama marked a sharp progressive swing. As a result, the latest conservative movement emerged: the Tea Party.

The Tea Party is an elite-driven movement (as Williamson *et al.*, 2011 have shown) that has attracted substantial grass-roots support among 'debranded' Republicans or conservative independents. While it is not a monolithic bloc, broadly speaking, the Tea Party is to the right of the Republican mainstream; it advocates limited government, based on a narrative regarding the American founding that sees anything more than minimal taxation as illegitimate and regards wealth redistribution as antithetical to American values (Ashbee, 2011; Lepore, 2010; Williamson *et al.*, 2011). The Tea Party held considerable sway in and leading up to the November 2010 mid-term elections, succeeding in nominating its more conservative candidates over more mainstream (and, in some cases, well-established) Republicans in several states' primaries, and contributing to conservatives' electoral gains nationwide, including retaking a majority in the House of Representatives. As Williamson, Skocpol and Coggin argue regarding the Tea Party's prominence: 'The most likely near-term dynamic . . . is that the presence of newly-elected Tea Party representatives will only reinforce the 2009–10 Republican strategy of total opposition to the Obama agenda' (Williamson *et al.*, 2011: 37). The growth of conservatism in the United States, reflected by the Tea Party's success, is thus part of the reason for increased polarization and congressional gridlock.

The nature of American social and political culture is at the heart of Tea Party discourse. Many scholars have argued that undergirding both Tea Party opposition to President Obama and their discourse against redistribution of wealth are racialized beliefs directed against Latino immigrants and the stereotype of African-American beneficiaries of welfare, though often not expressed in explicitly racist terms (Ashbee, 2011; Lepore, 2010; Williamson *et al.*, 2011). Tea Party focus on Obama's 'otherness', for instance, has taken the form of questioning his status as an American-born citizen (and therefore eligibility to be president), and repeated charges that he is a socialist, and, as such, opposed to core American capitalist values. Tea Party discourse on the essence of American political culture and values employs nationalist techniques of historicism. Consistent with ongoing efforts by conservative movements to define national identity through the promotion of their vision of US history (as in schoolbook and curricula controversies, cf. Hutchins, 2011), the Tea Party has focused heavily on history, justifying their vision of national culture and how government should work based on their (historically inaccurate) interpretations of the USA's founding (see Lepore, 2010). This historicist approach has largely been driven by Glenn Beck, a talk show host whose now defunct programme ran on Fox News and began the day before President Obama's 2009 inauguration. Beck, along with other Fox News commentators, as Williamson *et al.* (2011) have argued, did not simply raise the public profile of the Tea Party, but in fact largely orchestrated and promoted the movement. Beck organized two of the largest Tea Party demonstrations, the first on 12 September 2009, the second – the Restoring Honour Rally – on 28 August 2010 (which NBC News estimated to have drawn a crowd of 300,000 to Washington DC; Zernike *et al.*, 2010).

It was in response to Beck's rally of August 2010, and to the growing polarization of American politics and news media that, on 30 October 2010, Jon Stewart, host of *The Daily Show*, and Stephen Colbert, host of *The Colbert Report*, sister news parody programmes produced by the cable television network Comedy Central (owned by Viacom), held the Rally to Restore Sanity and/or Fear[1] in Washington DC. The rally drew more than 200,000 people to the National Mall and garnered much media attention. Stewart and Colbert have become powerful media voices and shapers of public opinion on the centre-left, and particularly among audiences under age 50, as has been demonstrated by a great many academic studies (for a review of the early literature, see Ross and York, 2007: 351–5; Kakutani, 2008), as well as studies such as the 2007 poll by the Pew Research Center for the People and the Press, which found that Americans ranked Stewart on equal footing as most admired journalist with network news anchors (cf. Kakutani, 2008).

This event was initially billed as a sort of counter-protest against Beck's Restoring Honor Rally; however, Stewart and Colbert quickly stopped emphasizing this aspect of their rally, presenting it instead as an uncontroversial gathering of moderates who oppose the extremism and polarizing discourse that the comedians contend has come to dominate much of the news media and government activity.

The rally, like *The Daily Show* itself, led various media outlets and commentators to struggle to define its meaning. Some see it as primarily satirical, others as political (whether or not they approve), still others as a publicity stunt for what is, after all, a commercial venture (and one run by part of a media conglomerate – Viacom – whose co-owner, Sumner Redstone, is known for his opposition to Fox News's proprietor Rupert Murdoch). Stewart and Colbert, however, have repeatedly insisted that the rally was not political in its aims, that they are comedians above all. The event was, indeed, not a typical political rally. It was organized as an open-air variety show, mostly featuring music and comedy sketches. While it is true that the rally was not narrowly political – in that it made no mention of the mid-term elections to be held three days later and did not advocate any particular policy agendas – in a broader sense, this was satire with serious intentions, as it sought to influence political discourse on a much more fundamental level. In arguments grounded in appeals to nationalism and claims to speak for the nation, Stewart and Colbert attempted nothing less than to negotiate the definition of American national identity.

National symbolic resources

From the beginning of the publicity campaign announcing it, the Rally to Restore Sanity and/or Fear was framed in national discourse. The banner, which was somewhat ironically unfurled behind Stewart on his show when he first announced the rally to advocate more civil and less sensationalistic dialogue, stated 'Take it down a notch, for America' (Stewart, 2010b). The rally itself employed a wealth of national symbolic resources, and like much of *The Daily Show* and *The Colbert Report* discourse, the flagging of American national identity, national belonging and national sentiment combines sincerity and irony. Stewart and Colbert offer both a satirical parody of the patriotic rhetoric so common in the American media and a deliberate, more or less self-conscious effort to reclaim and redefine the discourse of patriotism.[2]

The rally's very location was the first such instance. It was held in Washington, DC, on the National Mall, in front of the Capitol building. This choice appears to be an answer to Glenn Beck of Fox News, whose rally was held on a different section of the Mall, on the steps of Lincoln Memorial (on the anniversary of Martin Luther King's famous 'I Have a Dream' speech, which, incidentally, might be interpreted as a right-wing attempt to appropriate the discourse of inclusion). The choice of the Capitol in itself is also rich in symbolic importance. Through their mass pilgrimages to these types of sites, Americans demonstrate their attachment for national monuments, which hold quasi-sacred status (Wallace, 1996: 5). As Wilbur Zelinsky argues:

> By their very nature public monuments, of whatever description, verge close to sacredness, not unlike the temples, shrines, and historic landmarks with which they are often associated. Indeed, as Marvin Trachtenberg has so tellingly characterized them, monuments 'function as social magnets, crystal-lizations of social energy, one of the means civilization has devised to reinforce its cohesiveness and to give meaning and structure to life. Monuments

are a way men transmit communal emotions, a medium of continuity and interaction between generations, not only in space but across time, for to be monumental is to be permanent'.

(Zelinsky, 1988: 181)

National monuments thus serve as a rallying point for national sentiment and temporal transcendence, notions that characterize all nationalist symbols and allow them to forge links between citizens and the nation state.

As the meeting place of Congress – the direct representatives of the people – the Capitol represents democracy and the American government. Though it is not, strictly speaking, purely a monument, it functions in a similar manner, as it has acquired the status of a 'transcendent national icon', whose image is reproduced, like that of the Statue of Liberty or the Washington Monument, on all sorts of objects, from publicity logos to tourist souvenirs (Zelinsky, 1988: 211). In addition, as we shall see, this location provided Stewart with the opportunity to illustrate his criticisms of government. The rally's location thus situates the event very much on the national political stage, framed as a citizens' address to their national leaders, evoking themes of rights and responsibilities in a republic and of civic community. Furthermore, it appears as a more symbolically responsible response to Beck's Tea Partiers and their attempt to appropriate (illegitimately, Stewart had previously indicated on his programme; Stewart, 2010a) the legacy of the Civil Rights Movement.

The rally also made abundant use of American flags and flag motifs. The symbolic importance and omnipresence of the American flag in the United States has been the object of ample study. Billig, for instance, has remarked, 'Of all countries, the United States is arguably today the home of what Renan called "the cult of the flag"' (Billig, 1995: 39). Wilbur Zelinsky, in his extensive study of American nationalism, stated: 'The modern nation-state has made its flag into a literally holy object, the equivalent of the cross or communion wafer, and nowhere is the observation more apt than in the United States' (Zelinsky, 1988: 243). As flags represent national unity but are generally devoid of specific content (cf. Elgenius, 2011: 15; Eriksen and Jenkins, 2007: 3–5), they can effectively be appropriated by different groups in different contexts to confer patriotic associations upon a variety of objects, people and ideas. It is thus, perhaps, not surprising that the American flag should constitute one of the primary symbolic domains where satire and sincerity coexist and complement each other to convey Stewart's message.

Flag motif graphics and backdrops were used on television and online to introduce the rally as well as after the event on the website with links to video footage. Most spectacularly, the stage itself was lined at the back with 12 flags. In his faux-arch-conservative persona, Colbert makes abundant and prominent use of flags and flag motifs on his programme and website, which are clearly designed to mimic and mock the conservative tendency to wave the flag. However, while the abundance of flags at the Rally to Restore Sanity is partly meant to ridicule conservatives, there is no question of hinting at disrespect for the symbol itself.

On the contrary, overwhelmingly, the rally's use of the flag is clearly intended to be interpreted as sincere. This is notably true in its association with the performing of the national anthem.

The USA's national anthem, which focuses on love of country and devotion to the American flag, reinforces the sacred character of the banner for which it is named. And, of course, the national anthem in itself plays an important role in affirming and almost certainly in constructing affective ties to the nation. Scholars of nationalism compare the anthem not infrequently to a religious hymn. However, I would argue that this analogy does not go far enough. After all, religions have many songs and/or chants to choose from. While there are other patriotic songs in the USA, none is performed in the same capacity and with the same protocol protecting its sacred status. Like the flag, the anthem is a uniquely sacred symbolic resource, not to be treated lightly; those who perform it in unorthodox manners (such as Jimi Hendrix's rock version or comedian Roseanne Barr's irreverent 1990 rendition) are subject to criticism as unpatriotic provocateurs.

The anthem also harnesses particular performative power through the ability of music to affect emotion (cf. Juslin and Sloboda, 2010): 'Of all the modes of human expression, perhaps none has greater immediate emotional power, and thus the potential for quickening nationalist passion, than does music' (Zelinsky, 1988: 171). As Anderson says, language itself, but also poetry and music, link communities across time and space:

> . . . there is a special kind of contemporaneous community which language alone suggests – above all in the form of poetry and songs. Take national anthems, for example, sung on national holidays. No matter how banal the words and mediocre the tunes, there is in this singing an experience of simultaneity. At precisely such moments, people wholly unknown to each other utter the same verses to the same melody. The image: unisonance. Singing the Marseillaise, Waltzing Matilda, and Indonesia Raya provide occasions for unisonality, for the echoed physical realization of the imagined community
> (Anderson, 2006: 145)

The rally organizers made skilful use of this unisonance coupled with presentations of the flag to frame their event and its audience as representative of the nation. The rally began (as did Beck's) with a rendition of the national anthem. Here, it was sung a cappella by a vocal quartet called 4Troops, who were, indeed, four soldiers in uniform. Throughout the singing of the anthem, images of the American flag were displayed on a large screen on the stage, and the television coverage interspersed shots of the singers with images of flags flying from the Capitol and held by audience members at the rally (4Troops, 2010). This completely sincere, humourless, traditional display of martial patriotism reflects both the sacred nature of these symbols and also serves to allow Stewart and Colbert to claim symbols often used and appropriated by the right as their own, as if in answer to challenges of their (or, more generally, the left's) love of country.

Similarly, another patriotic song, 'America, the Beautiful', closed the rally, so that the event both began and ended with nationalist music. This piece was sung a cappella by aging superstar Tony Bennett, and in a moment of Durkheimian collective effervescence, at the end of the song, the crowd – seemingly spontaneously – erupted into (apparently not ironic) chants of 'USA! USA! . . .' (Bennett, 2010). Billig has commented on the significance of this song, when arguing that in the attachment to the national territory, it is essential that the homeland be seen as extending to the borders – including not just the metropolitan areas, but also peripheral districts (Billig, 1995: 75), and 'America, the Beautiful', Billig asserts, proclaims the beauty of the whole country. In choosing this song, the rally planners therefore emphasize territorial attachment, typical of a voluntarist conception of the nation that is inclusive of the whole population within the national territory.

The singing of both the anthem and 'America, the Beautiful' constitute powerful moments of national belonging, thus supporting the impression that the rally planners sought to reclaim patriotism and thereby the right to define national character and values. This sincere use of national symbols is significant and powerful, but perhaps Stewart and Colbert's particular strength as satirists lies in the fact that they use humour to mock and undermine conservatives' displays of symbols to support their own claims to speak for the nation. At the same time, by employing the same symbols in even greater abundance with a combination of irony and sincerity, the comedians both challenge their opponents' use of these symbols and re-appropriate them, precisely as they do with nationalist discourse more generally.

Nationalism and political discourse

The ways in which Stewart and Colbert engage in patriotic discourse illustrate theories such as those of John Breuilly (1993 [1985]) or Michael Billig (1995), which maintain that the ideology of nationalism serves as a vehicle for political goals, and not only for those on the right. Conservative parties are not alone in playing the 'patriotic card' (cf. Billig, 1995: 100).

> Populist patriots may be found predominantly on the political right, but, because the nation-state is the forum for electoral politics, the left, too, aspires to represent the nation. Left-wingers often appeal to what Antonio Gramsci's called 'the national-popular collective will'.
>
> (Billig, 1995: 104)

Billig has also argued:

> If flagging is the general condition of contemporary, democratic politics, then, as Nigel Harris has written, 'nationalism provides the framework and language for almost all political discussion' (1990, p. 269). On this reckoning, nationalism is not a particular political strategy, but is the condition for conventional strategies, whatever the particular politics.
>
> (Billig, 1995: 99)

Jon Stewart, though not seeking electoral office, does seek to affect political discourse in general, and he does claim to speak for the 'national-popular collective will', which he defines as the moderate, 'reasonable' majority. As Stewart re-appropriates techniques more frequently used by conservatives in his use of national symbols, he also attempts to take back the populist mantle, which the right wing has made the centre of its claims to speak for the nation (cf. Cunningham, 2010: 5–6). However, in Stewart's vision, the dangerous elites who go against the silenced majority's interests are not overeducated progressives, but divisive seekers of the media and political spotlight, who spread polarization at the expense of national unity and responsible governance.

Like his mixed approach to national symbolic resources, Stewart's overall vision of national identity is also vehicled through a combination of satire and sincerity, which come together perhaps most explicitly (combined, significantly, with music) in an original song sung by both Jon Stewart and Stephen Colbert, entitled 'No One More American than Me'. In this song, Stephen Colbert takes on the faux arch-conservative persona in which he generally hosts his show, and Stewart accentuates the values of the centre-left. The men pretend to argue over who is more American, both mimicking and mocking accusations, especially by those on the right (notably the Tea Party) that they are the 'real Americans' and that liberals (in American parlance) are unpatriotic. Colbert, as rabid conservative, starts out challenging Stewart in this way. They appear onstage wearing identical American flag motif jackets, and Colbert demands that Stewart remove his, saying, 'I'm wearing [the sweater]; you're desecrating it! . . . Take it off! . . . Jon, you cannot wear a flag unless you love America'. Jon counters, as the sincere liberal, that he also loves America, and then literally sings the praises of tolerance as an American virtue and value.

Though both men have humorous lines gently mocking the extremes of high- and low-brow American culture, the song has a definite and clear message, which appears to resonate with the crowd. For instance, here are the lyrics from the first refrain, sung by Colbert, followed by Stewart's first verse:

> [Colbert:] It's the greatest, strongest country in the world.
> It's the greatest, strongest country in the world.
> From North to South, East to West and diagonally,
> There's no one more American than me.
> [Stewart:] I agree!
> But I've got just as much right to wear this sweater.
> I'm a tolerant American and that's why I'm better.
> I embody the spirit of the founders, I know
> 'Cause I watched John Adams on the HBO.
>
> (Stewart and Colbert, 2010)

(We should note that these last lines may be seen as reclaiming historical interpretation of the founders' intentions, which has been a recurring argument and focus of the Tea Party – and conservatives more generally – though otherwise the rally focused on the present and the future, rather than discussing history. We shall return to this point below.)

Towards the end of the song, the comedians invite audience members to add the name of their home towns in place of the original, more general 'from North to South', etc. We then see video of the crowd singing along (the lyrics were put up on the jumbo screens) and, in the final line, instead of singing 'there's no one more American than me' as they have done to that point, Stewart and Colbert sing 'there's no one more American than we', with a joint gesture in which both men sweep an arm across the crowd, to include everyone in this definition, at which the audience applauds and cheers enthusiastically. This does appear to have been a successful interaction ritual in which the performers' nationalist discourse seems to have found resonance with the public. (We shall return to this question below.) Furthermore, the song's emphasis on territory as the basis for national inclusion and belonging reinforces the same voluntarist message conveyed by 'America, the Beautiful', as mentioned above. This voluntarism, which represents a projected ideal of an inclusive nation, is both an aspiration and a symbol of the centre-left, positioning them in opposition to a more exclusionist vision of the right.

The definition of American national identity as built around values of tolerance, diversity and moderation is repeated and emphasized perhaps even more explicitly in Stewart's closing address, where he also calls for unity and cooperation in public life, chastising the media and politicians for what he portrays as crippling polarization and partisanship.

> We hear every damned day about how fragile our country is, on the brink of catastrophe, torn by polarizing hate, and how it's a shame that we can't work together to get things done, but the truth is, we do! We work together to get things done every damned day! The only place we don't is here [he gestures toward the Capitol] or on cable TV!
>
> But Americans don't live here [again indicating the Capitol], or on cable TV. Where we live, our values and principles form the foundation that sustains us while we get things done – not the barriers that prevent us from getting things done.
>
> Most Americans don't live their lives solely as Democrats, Republicans, liberals or conservatives. Americans live their lives more as people that are just a little bit late for something they have to do. Often something they do not want to do! But they do it. Impossible things, every day, that are only made possible through the little, reasonable compromises we all make. [. . .]
>
> Because we know, instinctively, as a people, that if we are to get through the darkness and back into the light, we have to work together. And the

truth is there will always be darkness, and sometimes the light at the end of the tunnel isn't the promised land.

Sometimes, it's just New Jersey

(Stewart, 2010c)

Stewart's message is one of hope and optimism, on the condition that Americans reassert their unity. He thus posits moderate progressivism as the positive alternative to what he presents as the irresponsible divisiveness of the media (especially right-wing Fox News, regular viewers of his programme would assume) and the putative fear-mongering of both the media and conservatives more generally (as represented – and mocked – by Colbert's persona). Stewart shows this divisive discourse to be a threat to national identity (as well as to the democratic process and the country's security).

As the right demonizes the left as unpatriotic, a charge that the obvious nationalist imagery and discourse of the rally specifically challenges, Stewart's more left-leaning claims to represent the centre demonize extremists on both ends of the political spectrum (though he focuses more heavily on the right). He thus appropriates not only the positive symbols of nationalism and the right to speak for and define the nation, but also the negative approach of designating enemies within the nation who threaten its well-being.

Generally, Stewart and Colbert engage in the counter and reframing strategies that characterize many social movements (Snow, 2004), and which the right has used deliberately and successfully for decades (Lakoff, 2002 [1996]). The satirists' use of these techniques is not limited to the rally, as they have built their television programmes around denouncing distortions, inaccuracies and ideological slant in the media and politicians' discourse. Colbert popularized the phrase 'truthiness' in 2005 to counteract what he identifies as hypocrisy and fear-mongering (notably of the Christian right), defined as 'the quality of preferring concepts or facts one wishes to be true, rather than concepts or facts known to be true' (American Dialect Society, 2006). The very name of Rally to Restore Sanity and the surrounding discourse of reasonableness and rationality posit its supporters as guardians of the truth – the veritable American values – against the delusional or hypocritical extremists.

It is noteworthy that (with the small exception mentioned above) one major type of symbolic resource is conspicuously absent: that of history. Right-wing movements tend to focus more on the past (which is in keeping with a greater emphasis on organic construction of the nation and traditionalism), as they advocate guarding or reviving the historical glory of the nation. The (centre-)left, on the other hand, tends to focus more on the future, on the projection and construction of the community, which is more in line with a voluntarist conception of national identity that seeks to incorporate all those present on the national territory – along with at least certain aspects of their cultural diversity – into the community. While the American right wing also embraces a certain amount of voluntarism – which is, indeed, seen as one of the historically established elements of the American ethos – they see the heart of American identity as being rooted in a pre-modern past, defined by Anglo-Saxon Protestant culture. Stewart's rally reflects the typical centre-left focus on the present and the future.

The salience of questions of national identity, defining the national character and national political discourse, which are central in the organizers' rhetoric, is also reflected in attendees' comments in online open-answer questionnaires.

National character

Regarding the methodology of these interviews, I administered questionnaires online to rally attendees one month after the rally, sending the URL link to the questions via email and using the rally's official page on Facebook. I chose to use the rally's Facebook page as it had been a major mode of organization for the rally planners and, as the most popular social media site in the US at the time, it permitted distribution of the survey to a fairly broad range of rally attendees. Twenty-eight people completed the questionnaires. The questions were phrased in a way to allow examination of the salience of national identity issues: I avoided framing the open-answer questions in national terms, in order to see whether interviewees themselves were thinking within a national(ist) framework. Attendees were asked their reasons for attending the rally; whether they felt that they shared these reasons with other attendees; what they felt were the organizers' goals in holding the rally; and what, if anything, they felt that the rally had achieved. As with any self-selecting survey, and particularly one distributed via social media, the data collected are not intended to be viewed as a representative sample; rather, it is suggestive of trends in the rally-goers' perceptions. Nevertheless, respondents do represent demographic variety. Most, but not all, respondents indicated that they are 'regular' *The Daily Show* and/or *The Colbert Report* viewers (nine out of the 28 are not). Half travelled more than 200 miles to attend the rally. The respondents also represent a wide range of ages, though unequally distributed across the spectrum. (Ten respondents were aged 20–34, two 35–44, five 45–54, eight 55–64 and three 65 and up.) All indicated that they are 'liberal' to some degree in their politics (which is to be understood, in the American sense of the word, as a synonym of 'progressive'). Specifically, half (14) identify themselves as 'liberal', nine as 'extremely liberal' and five as 'slightly liberal'. Twenty-four out of 28 say they are 'very interested' in politics (with two identifying themselves as 'somewhat' interested and two as 'slightly' interested). Due to a lack of official demographic data on the rally attendance, I cannot measure the degree to which the small sampling represented here reflects the broader audience. Further, more systematic research would be required for a more statistically complete picture. In addition, as mentioned previously, there are broader difficulties with measuring resonance, including the fact that simply participating in a performance does not necessarily mean that one is connected to it, nor (even when participants report sentiments parallel to those advocated by organizers) can we conclude that there is a causal relationship between supply and demand. This study, then, aims only to show, in keeping with Jon Fox (Fox and Miller-Idriss, 2008; see also Chapter 3 of this volume) and Gordana Uzelac's (2010) calls that there may be covariation between – in this case – rally organizers' and attendees' experiences of the event and its meaning. With these caveats in mind, the survey answers presented below are sufficiently consistent to point, at least, to trends that merit attention.

When asked to give their reasons for attending the rally, not surprisingly, nearly all (25 out of 28) respondents mention goals similar to those most heavily publicized by the organizers: defending 'reason' and 'rationality' against the polarization of politics and political discourse and 'fear-mongering' in the press. Nine respondents cite opposition to Republicans, the Tea Party and/or Glenn Beck among their reasons for attending the rally. While the attendees' comments do, therefore, tend to support media reports that accentuate the politicization of the rally, in that many participants did see it as a political event (at least in a broad sense of the word), respondents still overwhelmingly adopted similar rhetoric to that of Jon Stewart in advocating and defining national identity based on ideological moderation and unity.

Three quarters of respondents (21 out of 28) use explicitly national language, referring to the national community ('the country', 'our country', 'the nation', 'America', 'Americans', 'the US'; in addition, the expected deictical expressions that also flag the national context are common: 'our news media', etc.). Nearly half (13 out of 28) explicitly comment on national character and define national values (other references to the national community focus on problems the country faces). Comments on both national identity and problems echo the rhetoric of the rally hosts. For instance, when asked about her reasons for attending the rally, one respondent combined messages of patriotism and the populism of a core group of reasonable Americans: 'To know there is and to be part of a larger group of like minded people who are appalled at the half truths and lies being used in politics and see it as ultimately destructive to the country we love . . .'.[3] Similarly, another stated:

> A desire for reasonableness between citizens, in government, and in the media. Cooperation and rational debate based on fact are needed rather than partisan politicking and fear-mongering. American citizens have more in common with each other than not, but lately efforts have been to emphasize differences and go to extremes, a trend which needs to be stopped. In addition to political reasons, I wanted to see Stewart and Colbert for the entertainment value and because I have a great deal of respect for both of them.

This post also alludes to the entertainment value of the event, which is not to be discounted, given the importance of successful interaction rituals for creating a sense of community.

Similarly, when commenting on what they believed to be the organizers' goals, respondents again demonstrate being attuned to the implications for national identity, as well as concerns over the country's political situation, as reflected in official pronouncements of the rally's intentions to fight polarization, though the respondents focus more specifically on opposing right-wing claims to speak for the nation. For instance, the same respondent who referred to 'the country we love' above continued here explicitly to evoke definitions of the American people and to frame her discussion in nationalist terms: 'To have a tangible demonstration that there are many Americans not part of "the american people" that Beck, O'Reilly, Hannity McConnell or Beohnner claim, to represent'. Another respondent indicated simply that the organizers aimed: 'To show that the tea party doesn't really represent the vast majority of US.'

Responses regarding what the rally achieved point even more directly to a heightened sense of national awareness through a feeling of belonging to a national community, which the rally helped participants to see as sharing a similar conception of American identity. While nine respondents referred to what the rally achieved on the national political scene in terms of election outcomes or media coverage, the other 19 respondents gave more personal replies, all of which referred to a feeling of community. They wrote that they and others present had gained a 'sense of camaraderie' and seen that they 'were not alone'. The phrase 'like-minded people' was used by five of the respondents, and, perhaps not surprisingly, all of the respondents reached through the rally's Facebook page indicated that they had maintained contact after the rally with this newly found community.

Although we cannot determine cause and effect (i.e. to what extent respondents were influenced by Stewart's rhetoric), and further research with a greater sample size would be required in order to draw more definitive conclusions, these responses certainly point to the resonance of the rally planners' concern with and conception of national identity among rally attendees. In addition, when considering the evident enthusiasm of the crowd (cheering, laughter, applause, singing, chanting, etc.), there does appear to have been a sense of Durkheimian 'collective effervescence' (i.e. essential to a successful interaction ritual) that was, at times, set within a framework of the negotiation of national identity.

Conclusion

It therefore appears that the Rally to Restore Sanity, and events of this type, could contribute to regeneration of national attachment through appropriating national symbolic resources, including the discourse of nationalism itself, and enacting them in collective performance. That is, as the renegotiation of national identity advances political agendas, it also revives the feeling of belonging to the national community through a renewed sense that the groups to which one belongs that may be more salient in everyday life (such as '*The Daily Show* viewer', 'progressive', 'reasonable citizen') are an integral part of the nation.

The long-term effects of the rally and the extent to which Stewart and Colbert may be successful in reframing national political discourse remain to be seen, and will, no doubt, be difficult, if not impossible, to measure. Measuring the 'success' of the rally depends on what we define as the goals. Many participants and observers felt that the rally was not successful in achieving what they felt was (or should have been) its goal of promoting a progressive policy agenda and candidates on the eve of mid-term elections. This, though, was not the organizers' stated goal, nor is it our focus here. If we look at the rally as an attempt to reframe debate and political discourse and action more broadly, and if we consider defining national identity and claiming to speak for the nation and in its best interests to be both a tool by which this transformation can be accomplished and a desired outcome in itself for those involved, we then view the rally's success differently. One rally (organized by entertainers) does not a social movement make, and any collective effervescence achieved that day would need continued action to take root. Furthermore, in addition to the many variables in play that complicate evaluating the rally's success, the pace of change may be too slow for easy observation, and would, in any case, defy inference of causality. Yet the apparent salience of national discourse, rituals and symbols, the resonance of these themes, the unisonance perhaps achieved in this collective action, the displayed and reported senses of shared emotion as reflected, notably, in the recurrence of rhetoric similar to that of the organizers in the majority of questionnaire responses, all show how the seeds of regeneration of national identity might be sown. Indeed, as Randall Collins has argued, an interaction ritual is successful when it imparts to its participants a sense of shared purpose and experience (Collins, 2004). Once again, further research and more data would be required to expand upon my tentative conclusions. However, the present small survey has at least shown a degree of covariation between the organizers' stated goals and the participants' perceptions. Rally attendees' responses to the questionnaire demonstrate that many gained a sense of community from the rally and that they extrapolated the vision of this community to a broader segment of the national population. All of this points to the power of nationalism as a discursive framework to legitimize particular ideological stances and the power of performance to embody and thereby promote competing visions of the nation.

Concerning the rally's political and ideological aims, as mentioned previously, Stewart himself has argued repeatedly that he is not a politician, but a comedian. His reasons for abstaining from electoral politics are understandable. However, generally speaking, Democrats are more likely to favour compromise than are Republicans (Jones, 2010), but as congressional Republicans have become more conservative since the 1994 'conservative capture' of Congress (with the Christian right, neo-cons, and now the Tea Party holding ever more power within the GOP) (Smith, 2010), one can see why more progressive citizens might be wary of Democrats being too focused on compromise. Mainstream Republicans have forged coalitions with more right-wing conservatives, including the Tea Party, thereby advancing a more traditionalist conception of American identity. While members of the Tea Party, for instance, argue that they are the true defenders of a colour-blind, unified nation, their vision is based on a fundamentalist, organic view of the United States. As previously mentioned, though they reject explicit racism, their opposition to Obama's leadership clearly has frequent undertones of discomfort with an African-American president (Lepore, 2010: 95). Perhaps more importantly, they focus obsessively on returning to the ideals of the founders, as they understand them, a decidedly ahistorical vision that erases diversity – both racial and ideological – from the country's past, leaving only the illusion of unity behind conservative laissez-faire capitalism and the dismantling of the welfare state. In the tradition of many a right-wing movement before it, their rhetoric is based on fear of national decline and designation of their political enemies as enemies of the nation.

The rally, like the television programmes of its hosts, was a challenge to the Tea Party and its 'fear-mongering'. Perhaps if others on the centre-left emulate Stewart and Colbert and successfully reframe the issues in order to demonize purveyors of polarization, while also re-appropriating national symbolic resources and visibly regenerating national belonging among progressives – turning progressivism itself into a symbol of attachment to the nation – they might successfully contribute to redefining the national political agenda. This argument coincides with Randall Collins's assertion that group sentiment and impetus to action for social change only gain longevity when they are embodied by symbols:

> Now we come to the results of ritual. Collective effervescence is a momentary state, but it carries over into more prolonged effects when it becomes embodied in sentiments of group solidarity, symbols or sacred objects, and individual emotional energy. The experience of heightened mutual awareness and emotional arousal gives rise to group emblems, markers of group identity . . . Sentiments can only be prolonged by symbols.
>
> (Collins, 2004: 36–7)

It remains to be seen whether Stewart's conciliatory rhetoric at the rally, most of which reflected a consensual vision of multiculturalism grounded in a modernist belief in progress, was a modest, measured step in this direction, aiming to begin reframing the debate with seemingly neutral ideology, or whether he lost potential momentum by taking the cautious approach that characterizes so much multiculturalist discourse, weakening a commitment to social welfare in exchange for largely symbolic gains.

Stewart and Colbert's rally (like their television programmes more generally) does appear to be a sort of progressive counter-backlash against the neo-conservative movement that has played a major role in American politics since the late 1960s. As we have seen, both men effectively employ a range of techniques more frequently used by the right to renegotiate national identity and thereby reframe political discourse. This instance supports Billig's contentions (quoting Shotter) that argument is constructive of the national community:

> John Shotter (1993a), in a perceptive insight, describes nationalism 'as a tradition of argumentation' (p. 200). By this, Shotter means that nations have traditions of arguing about who 'we' are. Rival politicians and opposing factions present their different visions of the nation to their national

electorates. In order for the political argument to take place within the nation, there must be elements which are beyond argument. Different factions may argue about how 'we' should think of 'ourselves' and what is to be 'our' national destiny. In so doing they will take for granted the reality of 'us', the people in its national place; In classical rhetorical theory, the topos, or rhetorical place, referred to the topic of argument. In the rhetoric of established nationalism, there is a topos homeland – and the process of argumentation itself rhetorically reaffirms this national topos.

(Billig, 1995: 95–6)

Clearly, Stewart and Colbert's use of national symbolic resources and nationalist discourse demonstrate these processes of arguing about national character all the while taking for granted the existence of a national 'us' for whom they claim to speak. Their message takes its strength from equating divisiveness with enemies of the nation and positing unity and cooperation as key American values. However, the rally's use of these symbols and this rhetoric in itself, while perhaps serving to advocate a more tolerant national community, is nonetheless conservative, in that it still focuses on the national community and national pride, rather than fostering a sense of transnational solidarity and belonging.

The rally is thus representative of a trend that characterizes the 'culture wars' that have raged in the media since the 1980s, in which neo-conservatives and progressive multiculturalists have battled over policy, school curricula, museum exhibits, and other instances of public history and memory (cf. Gitlin, 1995; Guerlain, 1998; Hunter, 1991, 2009). As Americans have fought over national identity and values in the past three decades, what has emerged is a more visible commitment to nationalism across the political spectrum.

Notes

1 While Stewart hosts his programme in his own persona – as a left-of-centre, critical and sometimes simply humorous commentator – Colbert has created a faux arch-conservative character through which he lampoons right-wing positions. He thus portrays many conservatives as fear-mongers (or, at least, overly fearful) by playing up a series of imaginary (and largely irrational) fears. When Stewart announced his rally in favour of moderation and reasonable discourse, Colbert – in character – countered, 'Shame on you Jon Stewart. America cannot afford a rally to restore sanity in the middle of a recession. Did you even consider how many panic-related jobs that might cost us in the fear-industrial complex?' (Colbert, 2010). He then announced his own 'counter rally', the March to Keep Fear Alive. Eventually, the two comedians merged the rallies into the Rally to Restore Sanity and/or Fear.

2 Please note that I am adhering to Billig's affirmation that patriotism is not distinct from nationalism (Billig, 1995: 55), and also am relying on a similar understanding to his of the definition of nationalism according to which it is 'the ideology that creates and maintains nation-states' (ibid.: 19).

3 Please note that I have chosen not to correct survey replies for grammar, spelling or punctuation, and, because they were written hastily and contain many errors, I have also omitted indicating '[sic]', as it would be overly prevalent.

References

4Troops (2010) 'National anthem', Rally to Restore Sanity, 30 October, available at: www.comedycentral.com/videos/index.jhtml?videoId=363845&title=4troops-national-anthem (accessed 11 May 2011).

American Dialect Society (2006) '*Truthiness* voted 2005 Word of the Year by American Dialect Society', available at: www.americandialect.org/Words_of_the_Year_2005.pdf (accessed 31 May 2011).

Anderson, B. (2006) *Imagined Communities*, rev. edn, London: Verso.

Ashbee, E. (2011) 'Bewitched – the Tea Party movement: ideas, interests and institutions', *The Political Quarterly*, 82(2): 157–64.

Bennett, T. (2010) 'America, the beautiful', Rally to Restore Sanity, 30 October, available at: www.comedycentral.com/shows/rally_to_restore_sanity_and_or_fear/index.jhtml (accessed 11 May 2011).

Billig, M. (1995) *Banal Nationalism*, London: Sage.

Breuilly, J. (1993 [1985]) *Nationalism and the State*, 2nd edn, Manchester: Manchester University Press.

Calhoun, C. (1997) *Nationalism*, Minneapolis, MN: University of Minnesota Press.

Cerulo, K. (1995) *Identity Designs: The Sights and Sounds of a Nation*, New Brunswick, NJ: Rutgers University Press.

Colbert, S. (2010) 'March to keep fear alive announcement', *The Colbert Report*, 16 September, available at: www.colbertnation.com/the-colbert-report-videos/359382/september-16-2010/march-to-keep-fear-alive-announcement (accessed 12 May 2011).

Collins, R. (2004) *Interaction Ritual Chains*, Princeton, NJ: Princeton University Press.

Collins, R. (2011) 'Interaction rituals and the new electronic media', *The Sociological Eye*, available at: http://sociological-eye.blogspot.com/ (accessed 30 March 2011).

Cunningham, S. P. (2010) *Cowboy Conservatism: Texas and the Rise of the Modern Right*, Lexington, KY: University Press of Kentucky.

Elgenius, G. (2011) *Symbols of Nations and Nationalism: Celebrating Nationhood*, London: Palgrave Macmillan.

Eriksen, T. H. and Jenkins, R. (eds) (2007) *Flag, Nation and Symbolism in Europe and America*, London and New York: Routledge.

Fox, J. E. and Miller-Idriss, C. (2008) 'Everyday nationhood', *Ethnicities*, 8(4): 536–76.

Geertz, C. (1973) *The Interpretation of Cultures: Selected Essays*, New York: Basic Books.

Gitlin, T. (1995) *The Twilight of Common Dreams: Why America is Wracked by Culture Wars*, New York: Metropolitan Books.

Guerlain, P. (1998) 'Les Guerres culturelles américaines: un psychodrame médiatique', *Revue française d'études américaines*, 75: 88–114.

Harris, N. (1990) *National Liberation*, New York: St Martin's Press.

Hunter, J. D. (1991) *Culture Wars: The Struggle to Define America*, New York: Basic Books.

Hunter, J. D. (2009) 'The culture war and the sacred/secular divide: the problem of pluralism and weak hegemony', *Social Research*, 76(4): 1307–22.

Hutchins, R. D. (2011) 'Traditional heroes and the renegotiation of national identity in United States history textbooks: representations of George Washington and Abraham Lincoln, 1982–2003', *Nations and Nationalism*, 17(3): 649–68.

Jones, J. M. (2010) 'Democrats, Republicans differ in views of compromise in D.C.', Gallup Poll Briefing, 10 November, available at Business Source Complete Database (accessed 12 May 2011).

Juslin, P. N. and Sloboda, J. (eds) (2010) *Handbook of Music and Emotion: Theory, Research, Applications*, Oxford: Oxford University Press.

Kakutani, M. (2008) 'Is Jon Stewart the most trusted man in America?', *New York Times*, 17 August, available at: www.nytimes.com/2008/08/17/arts/television/17kaku.html?ref=jonstewart (accessed 12 May 2011).

Kaufmann, E. P. (2004) *The Rise and Fall of Anglo-America*, Cambridge, MA and London: Harvard University Press.

Lakoff, G. (2002 [1996]) *Moral Politics: How Liberals and Conservatives Think*, 2nd edn, Chicago, IL and London: University of Chicago Press.

Lepore, J. (2010) *The Whites of Their Eyes: The Tea Party's Revolution and the Battle over American History*, Princeton, NJ: Princeton University Press.

Özkirimli, U. (2003) 'The nation as an artichoke? A critique of ethnosymbolist interpretations of nationalism', *Nations and Nationalism*, 9(3): 339–55.

Ross, M. L. and York, L. (2007) ' "First, they're Foreigners": *The Daily Show* with Jon Stewart and the limits of dissident laughter', *Canadian Review of American Studies*, 37(3): 351–70.

Shotter, J. (1993) *Cultural Politics of Everyday Life*, Toronto: University of Toronto Press.

Smith, A. D. (1986) *The Ethnic Origins of Nations*. London: Wiley-Blackwell.

Smith, A. D. (1999) *Myths and Memories of the Nation*, Oxford and New York: Oxford University Press.

Smith, A. T. T. (2010) 'Faith, science and the political imagination: moderate Republicans and the politics of embryonic stem cell research', *The Sociological Review*, 58(4): 623–37.

Snow, D. A. (2004) 'Framing processes, ideology, and discursive fields', in D. A. Snow, S. A. Soule and H. Kriesi (eds) *The Blackwell Companion to Social Movements*, Malden, MA, Oxford and Victoria: Blackwell, pp. 380–412.

Stewart, J. (2010a) 'I have a scheme', *The Daily Show*, 26 August, available at: www.thedailyshow.com/watch/thu-august-26–2010/i-have-a-scheme (accessed 11 May 2011).

Stewart, J. (2010b) 'Rally to Restore Sanity announcement', *The Daily Show*, 16 September, available at: www.thedailyshow.com/watch/thu-september-16–2010/rally-to-restore-sanity (accessed 11 May 2011).

Stewart, J. (2010c) 'Moment of sincerity', Rally to Restore Sanity, 30 October, available at: www.comedycentral.com/videos/index.jhtml?videoId=363864&title=jon-stewart-moment-of-sincerity (accessed 11 May 2011).

Stewart, J. and Colbert, S. (2010) 'I'm more American than you', Rally to Restore Sanity, 30 October, available at: www.comedycentral.com/videos/index.jhtml?videoId=363859&title=jon-and-stephen-im-more (accessed 11 May 2011).

Uzelac, G. (2010) 'National ceremonies: the pursuit of authenticity', *Ethnic and Racial Studies*, 33(10): 1718–36.

Wallace, M. (1996) *Mickey Mouse History and Other Essays on American Memory*, Philadelphia, PA: Temple University Press.

Williamson, V., Skocpol, T. and Coggin, J. (2011) 'The Tea Party and the remaking of Republican conservatism', *Perspectives on Politics*, 9(1): 25–43.

Zelinsky, W. (1988) *Nation into State: The Shifting Symbolic Foundations of American Nationalism*, Chapel Hill, NC and London: University of North Carolina Press.

Zernike, Kate, Hulse, C. and Knowlton, B. (2010) 'At Lincoln Memorial, a call for religious rebirth', *New York Times*, 28 August, available at: www.nytimes.com/2010/08/29/us/politics/29beck.html (accessed 12 May 2011).

Zimmer, O. (2003) 'Boundary mechanisms and symbolic resources: towards a process-oriented approach to national identity', *Nations and Nationalism*, 9(2): 173–93.

10

BRITONS IN MAORILAND

Narratives of identity during the 1901 royal visit to New Zealand

Christopher McDonald

On first reading, the 1901 royal tour was an imperial mission designed to strengthen ties between the motherland and the far-flung settler societies of 'Greater Britain'. Wherever the Duke and Duchess of Cornwall and York travelled, the welcomes had a single dominant theme: loyalty to the Crown and affection for the royal family. However, in New Zealand, careful examination of royal visit ephemera reveals a second narrative about separation between the metropolitan centre and the self-styled 'Britain of the South'. Ceremonial venues and performances demonstrate that New Zealand colonists were alert to their own distinctiveness and set themselves apart from their fellow Britons. The 1901 royal visit shows that, while most New Zealand colonists perceived themselves as British, theirs was a nuanced identity that incorporated ambivalence and conscious difference.

The 1901 tour also suggests that distinctions between New Zealand and other parts of the Empire altered the conventional opposition of European settler and indigenous inhabitant. *Pakeha* New Zealanders referred to Maori when defining their own distinctiveness, but they did not engage in a conventional 'Othering' of the indigenous culture. Instead, the European settlers imagined themselves as a 'new breed' of colonist inhabiting a fictitious bicultural state sometimes called 'Maoriland'. These claims depended on the colonists' favourable depictions of Maori, and on seemingly enlightened approaches to 'Native' welfare and development. The colonists' determination to be seen as more progressive and fair minded than that of other Britons helps to explain how *pakeha* New Zealanders could portray themselves as inhabiting two strikingly different imaginary settings: the Britain of the South and Maoriland.

Against the clamour of British patriotic slogans, it is easy to overlook the second less strident message in royal visit discourse. However, applying Victor Turner's concept of multivocal symbols (Turner, 1974: 28), this chapter attempts to read key performances associated with the 1901 royal visit *both* as demonstrations of imperial unity *and* as declarations of New Zealand's unique character and growing independence. Following Catherine Bell's more recent work on the inherent ambiguity of ritual practices (Bell, 1992: 113,183–4), the chapter attempts to show how two ceremonies confirmed New Zealand's orientation towards the metropolitan centre but also forecast an assertive role for the future dominion among Britain's Pacific territories. Guided by Lyn Spillman's study of commemoration and national identity, the research places Maori imagery within a loose-fit collection of imprecise symbols and associations, which Spillman calls a 'symbolic repertoire' (Spillman, 1997: 7–8). The flexible and, at times, unstable meanings of these images are linked to recessive yet recurring narratives about New Zealand's distinctiveness.

Like the centennials that feature in Spillman's work, the 1901 royal visit was experienced as an amalgam of constructions and demonstrations, costumes and decorations, illustrations and text. Usually, each element amplifies a simple message about unity or loyalty, ensuring that a redundancy of communication occurs around these core themes. However, some of the visit's more complex meanings only become apparent in the convergence of different media. Consequently, the analysis of royal receptions combines rhetoric, setting and event, treating these as a single 'ritual complex' in which symbols are often mutually constitutive. This idea is borrowed from Eric Hobsbawn's introduction to *The Invention of Tradition*, in which he uses the phrase 'ritual and symbolic complexes' to describe the rich composite images that accompanied celebrations of Swiss nationalism (Hobsbawm, 1983: 4, 6). Whereas Hobsbawm focuses on ephemera, 'Britons in Maoriland' broadens the scope of 'ritual complex' to include architecture, sculpture and other permanent components of the urban landscape, as well as the representations made of key ceremonial events. In this regard, the research is influenced by H. V. Nelles's detailed account of Quebec's tercentenary (Nelles, 1999), Victoria Smith's work on the construction and dissemination of Queen Victoria's image (Smith, 1998) and Brian Osborne's sustained inquiry into the role of symbolic places and performances in the development of Canadian national identity (Osborne, 1988, 1998, 2001).

These scholars perceive advantages in the inherent ambiguity of symbols and in the fine shades of meaning carried by composite images. Because a single ceremonial event will support different interpretations, a wide variety of participants can become involved in a centenary, a royal jubilee or the dedication of a war memorial. Any potential for dysfunction, such as the appropriation of Queen Victoria's image by Indian dissidents, is outweighed by the inclusive appeal of effective symbols and their ability to create the appearance of unity among loosely allied groups. Indeed, for Victor Turner, Catherine Bell and Lyn Spillman, one of the powers of ritual is its capacity to cut across political or ethnic boundaries, thereby enabling elites to attract support from the margins of society.

While this argument may be applied to aspects of New Zealand's 1901 royal visit – for example, the need to include Irish Catholics in public displays of loyalty – 'Britons in Maoriland' searches for a different kind of functionality in the bewildering array of symbols that welcomed the Duke and Duchess. Specifically, the research attempts to show how Maori imagery contributed to a multivocal ritual complex that could accommodate the problematic issue of colonial identity. To operate in this manner, the royal visit's symbolic repertoire had to conceal the suppressed conflicts and unresolved ambiguities of life in a settler society. A central concern was the place of Maori within a 'Greater Britain' defined by 'race' as well as politics and geography. The status of European settlers was no more secure. Like the product of any diaspora, *pakeha* New Zealanders occupied an ambiguous position in relation to their putative Homeland. Arguably, when the colonists depicted themselves for their royal guests, finding a satisfactory articulation of these relationships was just as important an outcome as co-opting support from social peripheries or rival interests.

The European 'Other' and the construction of colonial identity

Few environments are more contingent or uncertain than a new colony. Ambiguity stems from the unsettled relationship that exists between colonizer and colonized. Terms such as 'contestation', 'resistance' and 'transgression' draw attention to the provisional nature of many social and spatial boundaries (Hall, 2002; Raychaudhuri, 2001; Scott, 2004). In this setting, the construction of an ethnically defined 'Other' provided an important mechanism for protecting European identity from the dangers of cross-cultural contact (Popke, 2003: 264). Unfamiliar physical environments also challenged European agency. For this reason, colonizers attempted to classify, separate and create effective boundaries until the landscape they occupied was 'readable like a book' (Mitchell, 1988: 33). When these 'enframing' strategies succeeded, the resulting order strengthened colonial identity and authority (ibid.: 44). More often, the effect was incomplete or illusory. Commenting on the spatial compromises made by the eighteenth-century British in Patna, Rebecca Brown suggests that the familiar colonial dualism of European and 'Native' enclaves was so elusive it should be understood not as a 'pattern on the ground', but as a conceptual device employed discursively by the colonizers to situate themselves more securely in an unfamiliar land (Brown, 2003: 157).

Within this wider postcolonial discourse, some scholars have further destabilized colonial identity by detaching the colonists from their European roots. Lindsay Proudfoot refers to the 'ephemeral localism of settler identities'. These identities are provisional and incomplete because they rely on 'unstable semiotic landscapes' derived partly from metropolitan sources and partly from the less familiar 'here and now' of the colony (Proudfoot, 2005). Extending this idea, Proudfoot writes:

> Thus framed, the individual [settler's] experience of Empire was both inchoate and conditional: inchoate because it was always developing, always in a state of 'becoming'; conditional, because the trajectory of individual experience necessarily invoked the 'Other' of hegemonic and subaltern difference against which to measure the Self.
>
> (Proudfoot, 2005: 63)

Proudfoot's 'Other' is not the indigenous population that so often provides the antithesis to European colonial society. It is either metropolitan culture as remembered – Proudfoot repeatedly refers to collective 'cultural memory' – or it is a distanced alienated colonial culture that the newly arrived settler cannot fully identify with. Or it is both.

These fractures or displacements allow Lindsay Proudfoot and his collaborator Michael Roche to adapt Homi Bhabha's concept of 'hybridity' and apply it to European colonial society. In Bhabha's usage, the term describes the effects of cross-cultural contact in 'colonies of exploitation' with clear racial divides. In this context, hybridity refers to the manner in which colonized indigenes adopt European characteristics such as dress or behaviour. When these changes are initiated by the colonized peoples, they become a form of 'mimicry' that challenges the racial and cultural stereotypes underpinning European claims to authority (Bhabha, 1984).

Proudfoot and Roche (2005: 203–4) use the term differently and apply it to the colonists themselves. In this sense, it describes divisions among the colonists and the accompanying dislocation of colonial culture from its metropolitan roots. In their book *(Dis)Placing Empire*, the two authors argue that 'cultural hybridity' is 'fundamental to the spatial inscription of specifically settler identities'. Accordingly, the concept of hybridity includes not just Bhabha's 'third space' between European and 'Native', but also the cultural 'ambivalence' experienced by Europeans in a colonial setting. Proudfoot and Roche link their interpretation of cultural hybridity to the concept of 'diaspora'. Diasporic communities share a common origin but, with each successive generation, they become 'increasingly estranged from their original identity'.

Anita Callaway (2000) explores these possibilities at greater length in her book *Visual Ephemera: Theatrical Art in Nineteenth-Century Australia*. Introducing a chapter on colonial fascination with 'tableaux vivants' (live performers imitating famous European art works), Callaway writes: 'Bhabha's terminology, although devised to describe a deliberate cultural stratagem of indigenous colonised peoples, can be ascribed to the unintentional cultural ambivalence of non-indigenous peoples' (ibid.: 199, note 2). Just as Proudfoot and Roche have done, Callaway transposes the concepts of 'ambivalence', 'mimicry' and 'Otherness' from one side of the 'colonising equation' to the other:

> Any attempt to recreate a half-forgotten European culture results in the colonial mimicry (and inevitable burlesque) that Homi Bhabha characterises as behaviour that is 'almost the same, but not quite'.
>
> (Callaway, 2000: 60)

Callaway concludes that early Australian attempts to recreate European culture resulted in 'unconscious parody'. As a result: 'Australian settler culture is not quite the same as its European counterpart; rather it seems to have passed through a distorting lens, like Western tradition lampooned in a pantomime' (Callaway, 2000:

viii, 169). Callaway also argues that colonial society in Australia was self-consciously and sometimes willingly different from its metropolitan parent. Although Australian colonists sought to maintain or emulate some aspects of metropolitan life, they benefited from the 'sharp focus' provided by distance. Consequently, metropolitan influences were regarded critically and adopted selectively in a process that Callaway calls 'filtering' (ibid.: 36).

Callaway suggests that this critical faculty increased over time, at least in the field of visual art. At first, colonial mimicry resulted in 'unconscious parody'. Eventually, it produced a deliberate caricature and finally 'successful hybridisation'. Like all hybrids, Australian art could appear 'exaggerated', 'distorted' and even 'ludicrous'. However, it could also be 'robust' and 'liberating'. Callaway concludes: 'The naturalised product was not necessarily a corrupted art form, but perhaps even an improved one'. Later, Callaway restates this finding using Bhabha's terminology. By the early twentieth century, Australian visual culture 'reveals neither the precision of mimesis nor the slippage of mimicry, but the reverse power of a mutation' (Callaway, 2000: 124, 169, 189).

Following the work of Callaway, Proudfoot and Roche, this chapter argues that New Zealand colonists were aware of their own difference and referred to this when constructing nuanced versions of imperial and national identities. In particular, this chapter examines the 1901 visit of the Duke and Duchess of Cornwall and York, treating their tour as a conscious attempt at nation-building. Many events in the tour itinerary were examples of Callaway's 'parodies': clumsy approximations of royal ceremonies in England that confirmed metropolitan prejudices about the shallowness of colonial society. However, along with the mimicry, colonists engaged in deliberate demonstrations of their own perceived distinctiveness. Searching for evidence of these displays, the research compares two major performances in the tour: the 'Native Demonstration' at Rotorua and the Duke and Duchess's arrival in Wellington.

The research draws upon an extensive archive of photographs and other images recorded during the visit. Analysis focuses on decorations and performances, examining how these support claims about identity. Postcolonial theory provides the main analytical perspective for the work. However, the research is also informed by the concepts and methods of urban history and design. Particular emphasis is given to the use of space and the embellishment of streets, buildings and places of assembly. Government records and newspaper articles provide a text-based account of events, which assists the interpretation of visual ephemera. This commentary is augmented by three books that were published in the wake of the 1901 tour: Maxwell's *With the 'Ophir' Round the Empire*, McKenzie Wallace's *Web of Empire* and Loughnan's *Royalty in New Zealand*. These offer popular impressions or officially sanctioned readings of the various spectacles and receptions.

The 1901 royal visit to New Zealand was not a single event, but a collection of celebrations interspersed with solemn commemorations of the colony's sacrifices in the South African War. Some performances were repetitive and predictable, being based on well-established royal traditions in Britain. The state entry of the

Duke and Duchess into major cities is one example. Other practices, such as the 'Native Demonstration' at Rotorua, were experimental and involved a degree of uncertainty and risk. Itineraries were meticulously planned by a small group of senior government officials who sought guidance from London and from other British dominions with recent experience in hosting royal tourists. The less important details of street decorations and civic welcomes were decided by local reception committees, which were also dominated by social and political elites. To be successful, most events also required the active participation of large enthusiastic crowds. Organizers facilitated this involvement by declaring holidays and subsidizing travel to the receptions. Officials also sought to direct popular interpretations of the visit by publishing souvenir programmes and other promotional material. School children, the military and other easily co-opted groups were assigned prominent roles in the performances. Occasionally embarrassing unscripted moments did occur, but these were either ignored in the official record or written into the narrative as evidence of the spontaneity and intensity of the colonists' welcome. Outright opposition to the visit was rare, and was largely confined to muted protests about expense and satirical comments on the fawning behaviour of senior politicians.

Because the research for this chapter is based mainly on government archives and mainstream publications, it necessarily presents a 'top-down' view of the royal visit. This bias is difficult to avoid when examining an event that occurred more than a century ago, especially when there exist few scholarly accounts of this episode in New Zealand's history. The exceptional nature of the Duke and Duchess's tour also encourages a 'top-down' perspective: the visit was perceived as a 'once-in-a-lifetime' celebration that prompted meticulous planning by officials but presented ordinary New Zealanders with an unprecedented series of experiences. Under these circumstances, few benchmarks are available for gauging the public's response. Most importantly, the chapter foregrounds official records because the research assigns a peripheral and provisional status to colonial society *as a whole*. According to this construction, members of Wellington's social and political elite were themselves marginalized in relation to their royal guests and their metropolitan counterparts. For this reason, the inquiry does not focus on contested relations between social centres and their peripheries inside the colony. Instead, the work searches for ambiguities and competing claims in discursive treatment of the visit by leading New Zealanders.

Resuscitation of ancient history: the 'native demonstration' at Rotorua

Five thousand Maori converged on Rotorua from all parts of the North Island, and as many as 2,000 took part in the performance at the town's racecourse (*EP*, 25 April 1901: 5). Official guests occupied a specially built pavilion. Two thousand spectators paid to sit in stands, while thousands more watched from the perimeter of the track (*EP*, 10 May 1901: 5). To the crowd's delight, the Duchess arrived at the ground wearing a kiwi feather cloak around her shoulders and three huia feathers in her hat. During the demonstration, the Duke donned a dog-skin cloak and accepted other emblems of chiefly status (*EP*, 17 June 1901: 2).

The demonstration began with a mock attack. Visiting tribes sprang from concealed positions and advanced menacingly towards their hosts. The local Arawa people were assembled in the centre of the field, and met the challenge with a vigorous *haka* or war dance (Figure 10.1). This contrived scene was intended to recall the pre-contact period of inter-tribal warfare. Once the 'hostilities' were over, all the performers joined in a mass display suggesting peaceful coexistence under the *Pax Britannica*. Reinforcing the theme of unity, the Minister of Native Affairs welcomed the Duke and Duchess on behalf of the combined tribes (*EP*, 25 April 1901: 5). Chiefs from each *iwi* (tribe) came forward to lay gifts before the royal pavilion and, in return, they received souvenir gold medals from the Duke. These were the only moments of formal ceremony. The remainder of the two-and-a-half-hour programme had the character of entertainment: 'grotesque' *haka*, 'graceful' *poi* dances and poignant *waiata* (songs) lamenting the death of Queen Victoria (*EP*, 10 May 1901: 5).

Members of the royal party were aware that the demonstration was a form of theatre rather than a strict observance of Maori customs (McKenzie Wallace, 1902: 251–60). Participants took to the field wearing fanciful versions of traditional dress, which one observer called 'semi-native costume'. These included coloured sashes and 'kilts' designed to identify the various tribes and enhance the synchronized movements of the dances. Some performances involved the 'artificial resuscitation of ancient history'. Others included a contemporary flourish. One *haka* even featured a 'comical bit of pantomime' depicting the capture of Boers as they ran from the field of battle in South Africa.

FIGURE 10.1 Te Arawa warriors performing a *haka* at Rotorua during the visit of the Duke and Duchess of Cornwall.

Source: Alexander Turnbull Library, Wellington, NZ: Ref. F-32633-1/2. Photographer unknown. Reproduced with kind permission from Alexander Turnbull Library, New Zealand.

FIGURE 10.2 In Maoriland: an old chief and his tribesmen offering gifts to their royal highnesses.

Source: Sir Donald McKenzie Wallace. 1902. *The Web of Empire etc.* Plate 30. Photo by C. McDonald. Illustrator: S. P. Hall.

There were also skilful displays of dancing and touches of authenticity. Honours for the best performances were shared between the Ngatituwharetoa from the central North Island and the East Coast tribes from Gisborne and Hawkes Bay. Some participants dressed in 'traditional native-made costume'. The older chiefs wore valuable cloaks and carried ancient greenstone or whalebone weapons. During the course of the morning, many of these heirlooms were spontaneously presented to the Duke and Duchess, thus adding to the collection of gifts already heaped before the royal pavilion.

The Rotorua reception delighted the visitors. The Duke's Chief of Staff, Lord Wenlock (1901), wrote to his wife: 'we saw the most wonderful collection of Maoris . . . each tribe went through the most fascinating and weird dances – most dramatic in effect – and though fantastic most extremely attractive . . . Never have I seen a native dance which gave any pleasure before – but these were quite delightful.' The colonists were equally enamoured with the event. The demonstration was applauded as the highlight of the North Island tour comparable, in terms of spectacle, to a vast military review later staged at Christchurch. Wellington's *Evening Post* newspaper reported: 'It has been a unique ceremonial in the Royal tour. In no other country of the world could such a demonstration be made' (*EP*, 17 June 1901: 2). Weeks later, after the royal visit was over, New Zealand's governor told parliament that the demonstration at Rotorua had been 'magnificent' (*EP*, 2 July 1901: 6).

A 'great storm of loyalty': the entry procession at Wellington

The Duke and Duchess had their next encounter with Maori culture in Wellington. Here, the setting was far from unique. Indeed, it must have been all too familiar to members of the royal party. At each port of call, they were greeted with the same tedious rituals: a public landing at the wharf, an address from the local mayor and a protracted journey through what one commentator described as a 'great storm of loyalty' (Loughnan, 1902: 150).

As they surveyed Wellington's streets from their open carriage, the Duke and Duchess might have searched for details that distinguished the latest reception from those in Melbourne, Brisbane, Sydney and Auckland. If so, they could not have travelled far before noticing the Maori greetings and imagery inscribed along the path of the procession. Before the royal landau had left the wharf, the Duke and Duchess were confronted with bold slogans on the Central Post Office (Figure 10.3). 'Welcome to *Te Aotearoa*' (The Land of the Long White Cloud), these announced. '*Nau mai e te kotuku rerengatahi*' (Welcome to the white crane that is seen once in a lifetime). These mottos were woven into a larger decorative scheme that included references to British military and naval victories (*NZM*, 20 June 1901: 44).

Displays on other public buildings incorporated similar motifs. In every case, ephemeral references to indigenous culture were placed alongside emblems of British patriotism. On the municipality's Civic Arch, faux classicism framed a welcome 'from *Pakeha*' and 'from Maori'. The government's main contribution to the decorations was a castellated Tudor arch supposedly based on Balmoral Castle. One side proclaimed: '*Ma Te Atua Korua e Atawhai*'. The opposite face carried the translation: 'God bless the Duke and Duchess' (Loughnan, 1902: 157). The symmetry of these messages confirmed a prediction about New Zealand's welcome to the Duke and Duchess: 'Maori words and English words of greeting will be their equal offering' (*NZM*, 1 June 1901: 655).

FIGURE 10.3 Royal visit illuminations on the central post office, Wellington.

Source: Alexander Turnbull Library, Wellington, NZ: Ref. PA-Coll-0526-1. E. M. Roberts collection. Photo by J. Spiller. Reproduced with kind permission from Alexander Turnbull Library, New Zealand.

Maori words and imagery also featured prominently on business premises. In Cuba Street, one commercial frontage announced: 'Welcome to Maoriland' (*EP*, 17 June 1901: 6). Further along the processional route, the Bank of New Zealand displayed a large transparency depicting a Maori warrior holding both rifle and *mere* (short club). On one side of the image were the words: 'For King and Empire'. On the opposite side was the translation: '*Mo te Kingi me te Empaea*'. Wellington's *Evening Post* newspaper published a detailed description of the decorations on its Willis Street building. The central picture showed a Maori chief standing in the bow of a war canoe escorting the royal yacht HMS 'Ophir' into Wellington Harbour. Above this scene there were portraits of the Duke and Duchess and the words: 'For Unity of Empire'. Below, the caption read: '*Haere Mai ki Poneke*' (Welcome to Port Nicholson). The newspaper explained that the decorations depict 'the most striking feature of the present ceremonies – the linking of the old *Rangitira* [chief] to the Prince of the modern Empire'.

Two of Wellington's 11 welcome arches were styled entirely as Maori constructions. The first of these was a relatively modest affair in Cuba Street, built by Te Aro House, a well-known firm of drapers. Unlike other arches with commercial sponsors, it did not promote merchandise but created a crudely decorated *whaharoa* (gateway) across the street. The government built a 'Maori Arch' in Charlotte Street, and this was a more elaborate structure (Figure 10.4). Uniquely, it inserted a 'Maori' place into the otherwise European landscape of Wellington's government precinct. As if to enhance this effect, the depth of the arch was exaggerated, creating the impression of an elevated *pataka* (food store) or *whare* (house) (*EP*, 5 June 1901: 6; *NZM*, 20 June 1901: 36). As a result, the royal carriage did not simply pass through the structure, it entered a building and was momentarily

FIGURE 10.4 The Duke and Duchess of Cornwall and York passing the Government Maori Arch in Charlotte Street, Wellington.

Source: Alexander Turnbull Library, Wellington, NZ: Ref. PA-Coll-4558-3-03. Photo by Sarony Studio, Wellington. Reproduced with kind permission from Alexander Turnbull Library, New Zealand.

enclosed by walls decorated with carved panels and woven mats. As if to emphasize the possibility of inhabitation, groups of traditionally dressed *wahine* (women) and *tamariki* (children) formed picturesque human tableaux beneath the gables (*EP*, 18 June 1901: 5). Fleetingly, and in simulated form, the Duke and Duchess visited a Maori space as their carriage neared Government House (McDonald, 2010: 268).

Apart from the performers at the Maori Arch in Charlotte Street, the royal visitors would have seen few Maori faces among the crowds. The Maori imagery on the capital's streets was the work of *pakeha* architects, engineers and draftsmen. It was limited to clichéd phrases and familiar motifs chosen because they were easily accessible to a European audience. Significantly, Wellington's turn-of-the-century architecture carried no permanent trace of the Maori inscriptions and motifs that featured so insistently in the city's decorations. Nevertheless, by the time they arrived at the governor's residence, the Duke and Duchess must have felt that they had indeed entered the capital of 'Maoriland', a bicultural state where two races lived in equality and harmony. After the enthusiastic welcome in Rotorua, Wellington's ephemera offered further proof of Premier Richard Seddon's confident assertion to the Duke: 'Both races are living in amity together' (*AJHR*, 1902 vol.1: 1).

A Maori 'Zealandia': convergence between New Zealand's two 'races'

Seddon's remark underscored one of the central claims in royal visit discourse. Maori were full participants in the political life of the colony, and were united with *pakeha* by their common loyalty to the Crown. Supporting this argument was the notion of an emerging pan-tribal identity for Maori. In this construction of a new Maori polity, joint agency became possible because ancient inter-tribal rivalries had been quelled by the stabilizing British presence. Quick to learn European ways, Maori were at once partners in the emerging state and willing recipients of a civilizing modernizing culture that was beneficial but inimical to their own ancient traditions. In this way, New Zealand was characterized as having two 'races' but increasingly a single British way of life.

For the most part, these characterizations bore little resemblance to reality. Few *pakeha* had any day-to-day contact with Maori, and physical evidence of indigenous inhabitation had almost vanished from New Zealand's main cities. The 1901 census showed the first increase in Maori population since the start of systematic European settlement. However, Maori were omitted from many surveys and statistics, and this fact helped to disguise poverty, poor health and inadequate housing (King, 2003: 325; Mein Smith, 2005: 111). Meanwhile, the economic welfare of Maori was being further undermined by the government's vigorously applied land policy. In the North Island, the best tribal land was acquired cheaply by the state for redistribution to *pakeha* farmers equipped with subsidized loans (Mein Smith, 2005: 109).

Although ephemera concealed the true condition of Maori, royal visit discourse did not attempt the complete 'Othering' of New Zealand's indigenous people.

Distinguished Maori were admired for being conversant in ancient protocols yet accepted at the highest levels of colonial society. During the Rotorua Demonstration, a Maori barrister of the Supreme Court 'doffed his European clothes' to perform a *haka*. One prominent chief wore 'war paint' when he appeared as a 'wild warrior' with his tribe, but later 'transformed himself' into a 'sedate and courtly gentleman'. Maori leaders even seemed to possess a natural affinity with the royal tourists and their aristocratic courtiers. A conspicuous figure at the demonstration was Mrs Donnelly, 'high chieftainess of the East Coast tribes' and a 'princess of the bluest blood'. In the Duchess's company, Donnelly did not exhibit 'nervousness or awkwardness', but behaved with 'the ease and grace of [a] born [gentlewoman]'. Collectively, Maori were seen to exhibit similar dignity and restraint. When the Duke and Duchess walked among the ranks of performers at Rotorua, there was 'no pressing of the parvenu' as sometimes occurred among the crowds of fawning or overenthusiastic colonists in Auckland and Wellington (*EP*, 17 June 1901: 2, 14 June 1901: 5).

British journalists were alert to these messages, and penned flattering portraits of Maori for a metropolitan audience. Sir William Maxwell, special correspondent for the *London Standard*, described how Maori men had adopted 'the dress and habits of Britons . . . without loss of dignity'. Furthermore, Maori were 'the only coloured race out of India with whom the Briton will associate on terms of seeming equality'. With surprising frankness and equanimity, Maxwell even raised the prospect of New Zealand's two races becoming one: 'The "*pakeha*", or white man, readily mates with the dusky [*wahine*]' (Maxwell, 1902: 170–1).

Other royal visit ephemera made vigorous efforts to write Maori into New Zealand's foundation myths. Parallels were drawn between Polynesian seafarers, Captain Cook and the first British settlers sent out by the New Zealand Company. Like 'Wakefield's valiant colonisers', Maori were the 'descendants' of 'voyagers', and the two peoples were united by the transforming experience of landfall upon a distant shore (*NZIM*, 1 June 1901: 655). Maori warriors also entered royal visit narratives about colonial military prowess. They appeared either as loyal allies or as worthy opponents during the New Zealand Wars of the 1860s. Veterans of this conflict were old men by 1901, but they featured prominently at the Rotorua reception. Imperial policy prevented Maori from joining the New Zealand contingents in South Africa (King, 2003: 287–8). However, some Maori with European names managed to enlist and, when these men received their war medals from the Duke, commentators noted that Maori 'battle skills and bravery' could make a valuable contribution to future imperial military campaigns (Mein Smith, 2005: 118–19; *RR*, 20 July 1901: 22–3). To emphasize this point, the North Wairarapa Mounted Rifles, New Zealand's only all-Maori company of soldiers, provided a military escort for the Duke and Duchess during their say in Rotorua (*EP*, 31 May 1901: 5).

In the most complete attempt to achieve cultural convergence, Maori were even characterized as a lost 'Aryan' race (Mein Smith, 2005: 111–12). This theory gained little popular acceptance, and certainly attracted no scientific support. Nor was it an explicit theme in royal visit ephemera. However, the notion of an estranged northern tribe inhabiting the 'Southern Isles' resonates with the emblematic figure of a Maori 'Zealandia' portrayed in verse in the official tour programme (*Royal Visit to New Zealand, etc.*, 1901) (Figure 10.5). With 'ruddy cheeks', 'raven hair' and 'soft brown eyes', this young woman is only just discernible as indigenous (McDonald, 2010: 270). Like Maxwell's reference to intermarriage, this example of cross-identification between *pakeha* and Maori appears to transgress racial boundaries. It is difficult to reconcile with conventional accounts of colonization, which place colonizer and colonized in an oppositional relationship. However, as part of a wider discourse on New Zealand identity, images such as 'Zealandia' served the settlers' claims about good government and social progress. In simple terms, *pakeha* were better colonists because Maori were a superior native race (Mein Smith, 2005: 112).

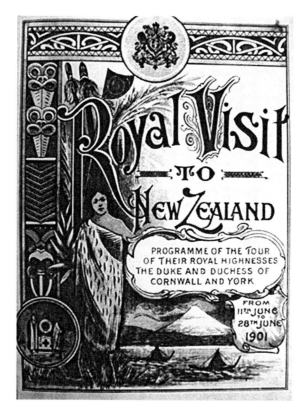

FIGURE 10.5 Official programme for the 1901 royal visit to New Zealand. (Cover illustration.)

Source: Alexander Turnbull Library, Wellington NZ: Ref. PBox q394.4 ROY 1901. Photo by C. McDonald. Reproduced with kind permission from Alexander Turnbull Library, New Zealand.

The 'race question' in Australia and New Zealand's Pacific future

Two events gave this message particular currency during the 1901 royal visit. These were Australian Federation and the extension of New Zealand's boundaries to include Pacific territories. When New Zealand rejected membership in the new Commonwealth of Australian States, colonists were forced to imagine an alternative future. In large part, this consisted of closer ties within the British Empire. Indeed, unification of the Australian colonies was widely interpreted as a forerunner to Imperial Federation. At the same time, Seddon's government was intent on projecting New Zealand's influence across a vast area of the South Pacific (King, 2003: 292–3; Mein Smith, 2005: 116; Salesa, 2009: 153, 156). In political and strategic terms, New Zealand's annexation of the Cook Islands could not be compared with Federation in Australia. Nevertheless, the proclamation of New Zealand's new boundaries helped to set the colony on a different trajectory from its nearest neighbour (McDonald, 2010: 267).

New Zealand's 'Pacific' future was closely linked to the status of Maori. Seddon bolstered the colony's claim for greater regional influence by arguing that Polynesians were culturally and ethnically similar to Maori (Salesa, 2009: 156). Equally, New Zealand's mandate to govern Pacific territories relied on the successful handling of 'Native' issues within the colony itself. Favourable treatment of Maori also had broader implications for settler society. It allowed *pakeha* New Zealanders to characterize themselves as fit empire builders who epitomized the supposedly British traits of tolerance and inclusion. A special editorial in the *New Zealand Mail* described this quality with evident smugness:

> [The key to] Great Britain's pre-eminent success in colonisation [and to] the prosperous development of her colonies [is] the practice of that toleration whereby peoples widely diverse in race, creeds and morals find free exercise for all their physical and intellectual energies.
>
> (*NZM*, 20 June 1901: 24)

By placing themselves in the vanguard of enlightened colonization initiatives, New Zealanders also differentiated themselves from their fellow colonists in Australia. This distinction was particularly evident in 1901 when New Zealand's Federation Commission had named 'the race question' as one of the chief impediments to unity with Australia. The finding referred to the contentious 'White Australia' policy, which was a reaction to the use of Asian and Melanesian labourers on Queensland's sugar plantations (Mein Smith, 2005: 112). New Zealand could claim to be free of such problems and the challenges they posed to British concepts of justice and fair play.[1] The royal visit helped to carry this message to a metropolitan audience. Based on what he had seen travelling with the Duke and Duchess, Sir William Maxwell confidently informed his readers: 'New Zealand has no native question' and Maori 'have been accepted without reserve, and placed on exactly the same footing as white men'. For Maxwell, this was one of several features that set the New Zealanders apart from their Australian cousins (Maxwell, 1902: 147).

Seddon's address of welcome and the Duke's reply emphasized the importance of these arguments in royal visit discourse. The two short speeches were far more than an exchange of pleasantries. Occurring on-board the 'Ophir' at the start of the visit, the address and reply provided a lexicon for interpreting ensuing public ceremonies. The condition of Maori and the prospect of Pacific annexation were both prominent themes. Having claimed that Maori and *pakeha* lived in complete harmony, Seddon assured the Duke that the imminent extension of New Zealand's boundaries gave 'satisfaction' to all. The Duke echoed these remarks in his response. Referring to annexation, he noted: 'with the same wise and sympathetic system of government which has secured the contentment and happiness of the Maoris, I have no doubt [the extension of the colony's boundaries will] be of lasting advantage to the people' (*AJHR*, 1902: vol. 1).

Seddon placed great emphasis on the annexation ceremony. Early in the planning stages of the tour, he hoped the Duke himself would put the colony's new boundaries into effect (*EP*, 11 May 1901: 5). When it became clear that only the governor could perform this act, the premier considered appointing the Duke temporarily to the vice-regal office. Officials in London soon dismissed this idea, but the proclamation ceremony remained the very first item on the royal tour itinerary. Barely had the royal party landed in Auckland before the Duke mounted a platform and asked Governor Ranfurly to carry out the historic task (*EP*, 12 May 1901: 5). Seddon described the moment as the most interesting and important of the whole royal visit (Seddon, 1901). Following so closely after Australian Federation, the proclamation ceremony can be seen as an attempt to imagine New Zealand as the centre of a constellation of Pacific territories and cultures rather than an appendage to the Australian Commonwealth.[2]

In this way, royal visit rhetoric about Maori was part of a wider attempt to discursively define New Zealand's relationship with Britain and Australia. Writing in *A Concise History of New Zealand*, Philippa Mein Smith describes how *pakeha* settlers fashioned an identity by comparing themselves to Australians:

> Ever since the propaganda of the New Zealand Company settlements, New Zealand had absorbed the myth that New Zealand's 'Better Britons' were superior to the Australian Britons. New Zealanders lacked the taint of convictism, they were moulded by a vigorous, cooler climate, and they enjoyed relations with a superior type of 'native'. Thus elevating Maori to honorary whites was a further way to render *Pakeha* superior to white Australians, as well as affirming the long-held belief in a hierarchy of races in which Maori were superior to Aboriginal Australians.
>
> (Mein Smith, 2005: 112)

'A volcano of action': Maori imagery and New Zealand's natural context

Maori imagery was closely associated with depictions of New Zealand's natural environment, and this relationship also drew attention to the colony's unique character (Figure 10.6). Gifts, programmes, invitations and souvenirs all contained images of iconic landscapes such as Fiordland's Mitre Peak, the Southern Alps and the North Island's Lakes District. It might even be said that the Duke and Duchess were taken on a virtual tour of the colony's scenery while official duties confined them to the major cities. These emblematic landscapes often appear framed by Maori figures. A *waka* or a rustic *whare* frequently provides the only sign of human inhabitation. Likewise, ornamental *kowhaiwhai* patterns perform the same decorative function as floral motifs based on the native clematis and pohutukawa.

Superficially, these images were a novelty for metropolitan consumption. On a symbolic level, the interwoven motifs reinforced the distinct identity being constructed by *pakeha* New Zealanders. The terms 'Native' and 'Nature' often possess equivalence in accounts of colonial life. If not tamed or eliminated, both conditions have the potential to alienate the settler from his or her adopted home. However, in the case of New Zealand, this discourse is more complex and more nuanced. New Zealand's geography and climate were central to claims that the colony was the Britain of the South. Like Britain, New Zealand was composed of islands and possessed a temperate climate. In physical extent, New Zealand's landmass was comparable with that of the British Isles. In character, the colony's scenery was more varied and dramatic than England's but satisfied a European taste

FIGURE 10.6 Invitation to parliamentary reception for the Duke and Duchess of Cornwall and York.

Source: Alexander Turnbull Library, Wellington NZ: Ref. PA-Coll-4558-3-03. Keiller Album. Photo by C. McDonald. Reproduced with kind permission from Alexander Turnbull Library, New Zealand.

for the sublime. Most importantly, the positions of Britain and New Zealand were roughly antipodal on the globe. This polarity established a conceptual as well as physical relationship between the two entities. Significantly, the connection was a flexible one, which suggested opposition and equivalence rather than complete equality.

These attributes singled New Zealand out. No other British colony could claim to possess the same favourable combination of climate, landform and situation. In particular, New Zealand's physical environment was starkly different from that of its larger neighbour. Australia's hot summers and continental scale meant that similarities between New Zealand and the British Isles implicitly distanced the New Zealand colonists from their counterparts across the Tasman Sea. In 1901, this distinction formed an important part of the New Zealand colonists' emerging identity. For the *Standard*'s correspondent, contrasts in climate and geography were so great that they reduced the prospect of unification for the two countries. To illustrate his point, Maxwell (1902: 148) compared Sydney's harbour with that of Auckland. In Sydney, the landscape resembled a painting by Birket Foster. In Auckland, the 'mist rolled away' to reveal 'a land full of light and colour' in a scene reminiscent of Turner's works. Referring to Auckland's mild but humid weather, Maxwell continued: 'The atmosphere, too, is English – at any rate in winter – cold and damp, and the people have the clear rosy complexion that a moist and temperate climate gives to their brothers and sisters at home' (Maxwell, 1902: 149). When Maxwell distinguished between Australia and New Zealand, he relied heavily on physical differences that affected the colonists' ability to maintain a British way of life.

These remarks would have delighted the royal party's hosts. The assessment would have confirmed a belief that Britain's most distant dominion provided ideal conditions for nurturing Anglo-Saxon stock (Maxwell, 1902: 149; Mein Smith, 2005: 115). Yet, this claim also presented the colonists with a paradox. There was no denying that Maoriland and the Britain of the South occupied the same benign geography. Aryan or not, Maori had evolved physically and culturally in a world with distinct similarities to the British Isles. Under these circumstances, it is not surprising to find Maori occasionally compared with Scottish Highlanders (McKenzie Wallace, 1902: 256–7).

The full significance of this analogy is clear when Mein Smith's comments about 'Better Britons' are recalled. The New Zealanders' claim to be superior colonists rested partly on geography and partly on association with a noble indigenous race. Just as New Zealand's physical environment was likened to that of 'Home' but distinguished from that of its nearest neighbour, Maori were contrasted with Aboriginal Australians but compared with one of the sub-national groups that comprised Great Britain. In the colonist's mind, these similarities and differences were causally connected. According to this discourse, Maori motifs and natural elements were both positively valued and contributed to a single symbolic repertoire. As a result, published ephemera for the 1901 tour was able to combine the two sources of imagery in a single visual narrative about identity.

In similar fashion, the 'Native Demonstration' and New Zealand's famed volcanic wonderland were co-located within the spatial footprint of the 1901 royal visit. The New Zealand government initiated the idea of a single Maori reception for the Duke and Duchess, and made an early decision to locate the event at Rotorua (Ranfurly, 15 February 1901). This choice was made despite invitations from more historic locations and more powerful tribal groups.[3] The government justified its preference for Rotorua as a way to avoid inter-tribal jealously. However, another compelling motive was the desire to place the Native Demonstration in an exotic natural setting that could not be matched elsewhere in the Empire (*EP*, 16 March 1901: 5). The district was a well-known tourist destination, famous for its lakes and thermal activity. Indeed, the Rotorua visit was first presented to the Duke and Duchess as an opportunity for sightseeing rather than official duties. Significantly, the Duke and Duchess spent their first full day in Rotorua visiting celebrated tourist spots, including the picturesque Maori village at Ohinemutu and the geothermal fields at Whakarewarewa and Tikitere (*EP*, 15 June 1901: 5; *Programme of Celebrations*, 1901: 11).

Visiting journalists also played up the association between the 'strange, weird scenery of Rotorua' and displays by Maori that seemed equally exotic and bizarre (McDonald, 2010: 268–9). One magazine article compared the performers with their natural setting, referring to a 'human landscape' that was 'more picturesque and suggestive than even the natural scenery' (*RR*, 20 July 1901: 22–3). Just as the indigenous performers became merged with the landscape, so the landscape became a performer in the Native Demonstration. Commenting on the display, Maxwell metaphorically removed all distinction between Maori and their environment:

> Finally, came the dance of all the natives. I am told that while it was in progress there was an earthquake . . . It may have been inexperience, or the thunderous tramp of four thousand savages, that made me oblivious of the tremulous earth. All I am conscious of is a brown mass of twisting and writhing human flesh – a volcano of action, out of which rose strange and terrible cries that ended in a shout of welcome.
>
> (Maxwell, 1902: 177)

These accounts from Rotorua invite a similar reading of Maori themes in ephemera at Wellington. The government's Maori Arch stood within the curtilage of Government House and the Colonial Parliament, yet it was visually removed from the main cluster of government buildings on Lambton Quay. Compared with other streets that the Duke and Duchess had travelled, Charlotte Street was a much narrower thoroughfare. Trees pressed in on the site from either side, and this effect was enhanced by the deliberate placement of decorative foliage. In contrast to the garlands of greenery that lined the rest of the processional route, entire *harakeke*, *nikau* and flax plants were dug into the street edge, creating the impression of thick living bush.

The effect was quite deliberate. The Colonial Government's official historian described the arch's contrived surroundings as a 'forest' (Loughnan, 1902: 159). A newspaper report referred to the scene as 'a bit of "old" New Zealand' that was 'robed in all the glory of its magnificent natural covering' (*EP*, 18 June 1901: 5). Significantly, the Maori Arch occupied the first 'natural' setting encountered by the Duke and Duchess after their arrival in Wellington. The verdant surroundings ensured that, when the Duke and Duchess visited a 'Maori' space, they also entered a 'natural' context. As occurred at Rotorua, the conflation of 'Native' with 'Nature' underscored New Zealand's unique position in the empire, and reminded onlookers that neither the colony's noble indigenous race nor its benign physical environment threatened the colonists' cultural identity (McDonald, 2010: 268).

'Simulated till it was all but real': protecting colonial identity from indigenous culture

If New Zealand's royal visit discourse avoided stark contrasts between colonizer and colonized, it also inoculated colonial culture against corrupting influences. Settler society happily identified as *pakeha* and comfortably inhabited either Maoriland or the Britain of the South. However, complete transgression across racially defined boundaries was never countenanced. In text, image and performance, royal visit ephemera carefully distanced the colonists' version of Britishness from a living, thriving Maori culture.

The single 'national' welcome in Rotorua supported rhetoric about New Zealand's distinctiveness, but it also removed Maori from any prominent role in receptions at the main centres.[4] Attempts to include real Maori in the urban ceremonies failed. The government rejected calls for an 'immense' Maori welcome in the capital (*EP*, 1 May 1901: 5). The premier himself blocked efforts by Auckland's Reception Committee to have a fleet of *waka* escort the royal yacht into Auckland Harbour and to stage an impressive welcome from the powerful Waikato tribe. Backed by his Minister for Native Affairs, Seddon argued that such an event would offend Maori gathered at Rotorua and would endanger the official reception (Ranfurly, 4 July 1901).[5] Containing Maori in this manner did not produce the uncontaminated 'white city' that frequently features in models of colonial urbanism. On the contrary, in both Auckland and Wellington, New Zealand's indigenous culture was placed on display. However, as Wellington's entry procession shows, Maori culture took the form of simulacra and ephemera: themed decorations authored entirely by *pakeha* for a European audience.

The fiction of a dying Maori culture provided further guarantees about the persistent Britishness of colonial identity. During the last quarter of the nineteenth century, Maori were expected to disappear from New Zealand: victims of a form of social Darwinism that forecast the extinction of all primitive races once they had contact with a more advanced culture. By the first decade of the twentieth century, this expectation had to be modified. Maori were becoming more numerous, and the narrative about a dying race gave way to a conviction that Maori *traditions* would disappear, at least as part of a lived culture (King, 2003: 325; Mein Smith, 2005: 111). The latter message featured prominently in royal visit ephemera. The Native Demonstration was presented as a more or less accurate reconstruction of once thriving cultural practices. As one magazine reported: 'The whole ancient and perished ritual of the great fighting race of the Pacific, the Maori nation, seemed, for the moment, to be revived to do honor to the British throne' *(RR,* 20 July: 23–33*)*. Maxwell (1902: 178) wrote: 'We shall not look upon its like again'. Even members of the royal party were aware of the anachronistic character of the great Maori welcome. The spectacle brought them 'face to face with the last remnant on earth of primeval man in the ecstasy and frenzy of passion simulated till it was all but real' *(RR,* 20 July: 22–3).

The government's Maori Arch and its 'inhabitants' were not quite real either. Like Rotorua, where the performance was 'more fascinating' because it had 'ceased to be dangerous', Charlotte Street was a convincing but unthreatening simulation separated spatially and temporally from the rest of the entry ritual (Maxwell, 1902: 178). This fact was not lost on the visitors. The Duke's Assistant Private Secretary, Sir Donald McKenzie Wallace (1902: 265), referred to the Maori Arch together with its occupants and surroundings as 'representing the New Zealand of olden time'. Unlike the 'gesticulating' warriors and 'chanting' women in Charlotte Street, 'real' Maori had either disappeared from Wellington or obligingly adopted European ways. Regardless of its veracity, this was the message the government sought to project for the royal tourists. If local *iwi* gathered to watch the procession pass through the capital's pre-eminent 'Maori' space, they conspicuously did not resemble the cloaked and painted figures beneath the '*whare*'. Instead, they merged invisibly with the crowds of *pakeha* onlookers, and their very anonymity was evidence of the 'triumph' of 'British civilization' *(RR,* 20 July 1901: 22–3). The obvious historicity of the arch and actors drew attention to this transformation (McDonald, 2010: 269).

Like the theatrical performance staged at Rotorua, the government's Maori Arch was a reconstruction. There was no pretence that Maori in Charlotte Street represented local tribes or contemporary indigenous culture. Instead, costumed actors delivered a scripted welcome that was no less contrived than the arch itself:

> As the Royal carriage and its accompanying cheers came to the Maori Arch a party of *wahines* and *tamarikis* in the recess of the house, under the carvings, gave the Royal visitors a graceful *waiata* of welcome, and a body of tattooed warriors in mat and feathers danced a *peruperu* (war dance) in the roadway below.
>
> (Loughnan, 1902: 159)

For all its novelty, this performance cast Maori in historical roles that differed from those of other participants in the procession. Just as the arch was displaced from an urban setting to a 'natural' one, the performers were situated in a lost past rather than a lived present.

Conclusion: distinctiveness with a double comparison

The 1901 royal visit shows that New Zealand's colonists did not distinguish themselves by assuming Maori characteristics, as a literal application of the term 'hybrid' might imply. As scholars, collectors and tourists, the settlers instead became critics, custodians and even carriers of traditional Maori culture. While they might happily identify as *pakeha*, they could not adopt indigenous ways without placing their own Britishness in question. Rather, the colonists styled for themselves a particular variant of British culture based partly on their relationship with Maori. For this reason, royal visit ephemera presented New Zealand's indigenous culture in a favourable light. Far from creating an opposition between Maori and European, text, image and performance stressed equivalence and even convergence between the two 'races'. The resulting discourse helped to construct an imagined identity not just for Maori, but for the colonists themselves.

Distinctiveness involved a double comparison: first with Britons 'at Home' and, second, with British colonists elsewhere. Both references called attention to differences as well as similarities. In a process not unlike Callaway's 'filtering', comparisons with Home were made selectively. They were based on abstract qualities presumed to exist in the metropolitan population but perceived to have been nurtured by the particular demands of colonial life. According to this claim, *pakeha* attitudes towards Maori epitomized the British virtues of tolerance and fair mindedness. The second comparison invoked specific practices, and this was directed at New Zealand's nearest neighbour, Australia. Contrasting their own enlightened treatment of Maori to the vexing 'native question' in the new Commonwealth, *pakeha* New Zealanders identified themselves as a new breed of colonist ideally suited for a central role in the Pacific.

This study has attempted to show how the colonists' portrayals of Maori defy a conventional reading but can be explained as part of a strategy of differentiation for one group of British settlers. By constructing this argument, this chapter supports the view that colonists forged 'new societies' rather than straightforward copies of metropolitan culture. Moreover, the research contends that colonial identity was defined *relatively* within a broader interconnected 'British' world. In establishing their unique traits, *pakeha* New Zealanders did not focus exclusively on the relationship between colonizer and colonized. Nor did they refer solely to the imperial centre and its periphery. The colonists' sense of self and sense of place combined *both* these references with *inter-colonial* comparisons such as the one with Australia. If New Zealand's colonists perceived themselves to be a healthy offshoot of metropolitan culture, then they measured the extent of their distinctiveness and assessed its value partly by comparing themselves to fellow colonists across the Tasman Sea. Consequently, when *pakeha* settlers imagined a partnership with Maori, they were also clarifying their relationship with other Britons.

This characterization suggests there is value in bringing an inter-colonial or pan-colonial perspective to the study of settler identity. Proudfoot and Roche open the way for this type of analysis by recognising the existence of 'Others' *within* the

European society of a single colony. This account of the 1901 royal visit carries the construction of a European 'Other' one step further by suggesting that *pakeha* New Zealanders sought to define their identity in relation to British colonists elsewhere. In taking this approach, the research adds further 'cross-cutting' divisions to the already fragmented picture that forms of colonial life (Hall, 2002: 16). However, this chapter consciously focuses on positive distinctions to which the colonists themselves drew attention. If the 1901 royal visit raised a mirror to New Zealand's unique colonial identity, the image portrayed was intentionally a flattering one: more like Callaway's robust hybrid than the rootless transplant that occupies Proudfoot's narrative.

There are several limitations to these findings. The first is the singular relationship that exists between Australia and New Zealand. In 1901, the different attitudes towards 'race' in the two countries took on greater significance because New Zealand and Australia were alike in so many other ways. While early twentieth-century New Zealanders actively differentiated themselves from their nearest neighbours, it is questionable whether similar distinctions can be drawn between other settler colonies. A second limitation in the work is the residual uncertainty that exists about the veracity and effectiveness of royal visit rhetoric. The 1901 tour was a carefully scripted performance, and it is difficult to know whether the visitors or their hosts believed the strident messages projected at public spectacles. Ephemera flared briefly before a large domestic audience, but interest waned as soon as the Duke and Duchess had departed. Also, although the visit was promoted as an international event, the New Zealand sector of the tour attracted little attention abroad, even in England and Australia. As for Maori, having almost no direct voice in royal visit discourse, they could neither agree nor disagree with representations of their relationship with *pakeha*.

Despite these limitations and uncertainties, the 1901 royal visit provides a revealing lens through which to examine New Zealanders' emerging sense of difference. The picture formed is largely an illusion in which people and places are briefly enhanced by the transformative power of ephemera. Thus, Rotorua becomes a kind of 'Maori capital' while Wellington's 'dingy' streets (*EP*, 12 April 1901: 5) are reinvented as a glittering processional way through an 'Empire City' (*EP*, 13 April 1901: 5). Indeed, magic provides a recurring metaphor for these effects. In an article entitled 'The Spell of Beauty', the *New Zealand Mail* describes Melbourne's royal visit illuminations as 'heavenly' and 'enchanted' (*NZM*, 30 May 1901: 22). Meanwhile, along Wellington's waterfront, specially installed electric lights produce a 'dream-like glimpse of fairyland' (*EP*, 19 June 1901: 5). In a more serious vein, the 1901 tour was heralded as a tribute to the colony's recent sacrifices in South Africa. In New Zealand, as in British dominions elsewhere, the 'first imperial war' was perceived as a rite of passage leading to a greater role in imperial affairs (*NZFL*, 22 June 1901: 8). These expectations added to the liminal character of the receptions, and allowed the whole visit to be seen as a coming-of-age ritual for a new state.

Continuing the theme of metamorphosis, an *Evening Post* editorial suggests that the royal visit had caused a 'general awakening' among Wellington's citizens. Remarking on 'The End of the Festival', the newspaper's leader describes how the visit 'lifted' people out of the routines of everyday life and brought them in touch with 'very large ideas' (*EP*, 22 June 1901: 4). One of these ideas was the growing distinctiveness of New Zealand society. Emblems of a unique 'national' identity had not yet been permanently embodied in the colony's architecture or urban landscape. However, during this period of intense symbolic activity, the early rhetoric of nationhood was rehearsed using the helpfully ambiguous language of street decorations and public spectacles. Indigenous culture provided essential imagery for this new symbolic repertoire. Activated by demonstrations and receptions, public spaces in Wellington and Rotorua presented a flattering portrait of Maori in order to portray *pakeha* New Zealanders as 'better Britons'.

Abbreviations

AJHR	*Appendix to the Journal of the House of Representatives*
Archives NZ	Archives New Zealand (Wellington)
ATL	Alexander Turnbull Library
EP	*Evening Post* (newspaper)
NZFL	*New Zealand Free Lance* (newspaper)
NZIM	*New Zealand Illustrated Magazine*
NZM	*New Zealand Mail* (newspaper)
RR	*Review of Reviews (Australasian Edition)*

Notes

1 By 1901, New Zealand's electoral system treated Maori and *pakeha* equally. Conversely, in 1902, new legislation removed voting rights from indigenous Australians. This disparity created another impediment to the unification of the two countries (Mein Smith, 2005: 103,112).

2 Seddon's determination to increase the strategic importance of the royal visit is evident from the fact that he invited the prime ministers of Australia and Canada and the premiers of New South Wales, South Australia and Victoria to New Zealand for the event. These statesmen declined, as did all but a handful of senior officials in the new Commonwealth (*NZM*, 9 May 1901: 30).

3 Northern Maori sought to host the royal tourists at the Bay of Islands where the Treaty of Waitangi was signed (Ranfurly, 21 March 1901). Waikato tribes asked for the itinerary to include Ngauruawhahia, seat of the influential pan-tribal *Kingitanga* movement (*EP*, 18 January 1901: 5). Both these proposals were rejected.

4 The government's decision also constrained *pakeha* participation in the Rotorua visit. There was no 'civic' reception when the Duke and Duchess arrived. The town's European mayor was required to present his welcome address in Auckland together with civic leaders from the upper half of the North Island. As the premier himself made clear, the visit to Rotorua was to be an entirely Maori affair combined with 'private' sightseeing for the royal party (Ranfurly, 3 March 1901).

5 Seddon's decision was unpopular with the Aucklanders, who hoped a Maori welcome would distinguish their reception from others in the colony. Public feeling on this subject was so strong that the premier was openly jeered when he appeared with the Duke and Duchess in the city (Ranfurly, 4 July 1901).

References

Books and journals

Bell, C. (1992) *Ritual Theory, Ritual Practice*, Oxford: Oxford University Press.

Bhabha, H. (1984) 'Of mimicry and man: the ambivalence of colonial discourse', *October*, 28: 125–33.

Brown, R. M. (2003) 'The cemeteries and the suburbs: Patna's challenge to the colonial city in South Asia', *Journal of Urban History*, 29(2): 151–72.

Callaway, A. (2000) *Visual Ephemera: Theatrical Art in Nineteenth-Century Australia*, Sydney: University of New South Wales.

Hall, C. (2002) *Civilising Subjects: Metropole and Colony in the English Imagination, 1830–1867*, Oxford: Polity.

Henry, W. A. (2001) 'Royal representation, ceremony, and cultural identity in the building of the Canadian nation, 1860–1911', PhD thesis, University of British Columbia, Department of History.

Hobsbawm, E. (1983) 'Introduction: inventing traditions', in E. Hobsbawm and T. Ranger (eds) *The Invention of Tradition*, Cambridge: Cambridge University Press, pp. 1–14.

King, M. (2003) *The Penguin History of New Zealand*, Auckland: Penguin.

Loughnan, R. A. (1902) *Royalty in New Zealand: The Visit of Their Royal Highnesses the Duke and Duchess of Cornwall and York etc.*, Wellington: Government Printer.

McDonald, C. (2010) 'Ephemeral presence: Maori imagery during the 1901 royal visit to New Zealand', in M. Chapman and M. Ostwald (eds) *Imagining . . . Proceedings of the 27th International SAHANZ Conference*, Newcastle, NSW, Australia, Society of Architectural Historian, Australia and New Zealand (SAHANZ), pp. 265–70.

McKenzie Wallace, Sir D. (1902) *The Web of Empire etc.*, London: Macmillan.

Maxwell, Sir W. (1902) *With the 'Ophir' Round the Empire*, London: Cassel & Company.

Mein Smith, P. (2005) *A Concise History of New Zealand*, Melbourne: Cambridge University Press.

Mitchell, T. (1988) *Colonising Egypt*, Berkeley, CA: University of California Press.

Nelles, H. V. (1999) *The Art of Nation-Building: Pageantry and Spectacle at Quebec's Tercentenary*, Toronto: University of Toronto Press.

Osborne, B. S. (1988) 'The iconography of nationhood in Canadian art', in D. Cosgrove and S. Daniels (eds) *The Iconography of Landscape*, Cambridge: Cambridge University Press, pp. 162–78.

Osborne, B. S. (1998) 'Constructing landscapes of power: the George Etienne Cartier monument, Montreal', *Journal of Historical Geography*, 24(4): 431–58.

Osborne, B. S. (2001) 'Landscapes, memory, monuments, and communication: putting identity in its place', *Canadian Ethnic Studies Journal*, 33(3): 39–77.

Popke, E. J. (2003) 'Managing colonial alterity: narratives of race, space and labor in Durban, 1870–1920', *Journal of Historical Geography*, 29(2): 248–67.

Proudfoot, L. (2005) 'Place and presbyterian discourse in colonial Australia', in L. Proudfoot and M. Roche (eds) *(Dis)Placing Empire*, Aldershot: Ashgate, pp. 61–79.

Proudfoot, L. and Roche, M. (2005) 'Displacement', in L. Proudfoot and M. Roche (eds) *(Dis)Placing Empire*, Aldershot: Ashgate, pp. 201–6.

Raychaudhuri, S. (2001) 'Colonialism, indigenous elites and the transformation of cities in the non-Western world: Ahmedabad (Western India), 1890–1947', *Modern Asian Studies*, 35(3): 677–726.

Salesa, D. (2009) 'New Zealand's Pacific', in G. Byrnes (ed.) *The New Oxford History of New Zealand*, Melbourne: Oxford University Press, pp. 149–72.

Scott, H. V. (2004) 'A mirage of colonial consensus: resettlement schemes in early Spanish Peru', *Environment and Planning D, Society & Space*, 22(6): 885–99.

Smith, V. (1998) 'Constructing Victoria: the representation of Queen Victoria in England, India, and Canada, 1897–1914', PhD dissertation, New Brunswick, NJ: Rutgers, State University of New Jersey.

Spillman, L. (1997) *Nation and Commemoration: Creating National Identities in the United States and Australia*, Cambridge: Cambridge University Press.

Turner, V. (1974) *Dramas, Fields, and Metaphors: Symbolic Action in Human Society*, Ithaca, NY: Cornell University Press.

Newspapers

Evening Post *(1901)*

'What the Maoris Propose', 18 January: 5.
'More Suggestions from the Premier', 16 March: 5.
'The Coming Royal Visit. Wellington's Arrangements', 13 April: 5.
'The Coming Royal Visit', 20 April: 5.
'The Native Reception', 25 April: 5.
'The Coming Royal Visit', 1 May: 5.
'The Great Maori Meeting', 10 May: 5.
'The Auckland Programme', 11 May: 5.
'New Zealand's Share in the Royal Visit', 31 May: 5.
'Brief Ceremonies', 12 June: 5.
'An Interesting Description', 14 June: 5.
'The Duke in Rotorua', 14 June: 5.
'The Duke in Geyserland', 17 June: 2.
'Splendid Chants of Welcome', 17 June: 2.
'Progress of the Arches', 17 June: 6.
'Progress of Preparations', 17 June: 6.
'A Bit of Old New Zealand', 18 June: 5.
'The End of the Festival', 22 June: 4.
'Other Particulars', 24 June: 2.
'Parliament. The Governor's Speech', 2 July: 6.

New Zealand Free Lance *(1901)*

'The Royal Visit. Well Done Wellington!', 22 June: 8.

New Zealand Illustrated Magazine *(1901)*

'Our Sailor Prince and Princess May', 1 June: 655.

New Zealand Mail *(1901)*

'A Loyal Welcome', 20 June: 24.
'The Street Decorations', 20 June: 36.
'Illuminations – General Post Office', 20 June: 44.

Review of Reviews *(Australasian Edition) (1901)*

'The Prince Among the Maoris', 20 July: 22–3.

Archives, ephemera and manuscripts

Alexandra, Queen. Letter to (writer unknown), dated 'Ophir' 26 June 1901, RA GEO V/O/2548: 60.

Programme of Celebrations, etc. ATL Pam 1901 NZR 2496.

Ranfurly, Lord. Telegram to Lord Chamberlain, 15 February 1901, in *Telegrams to/from Secretary of State etc.* Archives NZ Governor Series ACHK 16561 G5 5.

Ranfurly, Lord. Telegram to Richard Seddon, 3 March 1901, in *Miscellaneous Inwards Telegrams etc. – 11 March 1900–24 March 1901.* Archives NZ Governor Series ACHK 16571 G15 3.

Ranfurly, Lord. Telegram to Carroll, 21 March 1901, in *Miscellaneous Inwards Telegrams etc. – 25 March 1901–30 December 1901.* Archives NZ Governor Series ACHK 16571 G15 4.

Ranfurly, Lord. 'Sixteenth Quarterly Report July 4th 1901', in *Drafts or Copies of Dispatches to Secretary of State.* ATL MS-Papers-6357–03 (MS-Copy-Micro-0734–1).

Royal Visit to New Zealand: Programme etc. ATL Ephemera P Box q394.4 ROY 1901: 35.

Seddon, Richard. Telegram to Lord Ranfurly, 5 June 1901, in *Miscellaneous Inwards Telegrams etc. – 25 March 1901–30 December 1901.* Archives NZ Governor Series ACHK 16571 G15 4.

Wenlock, Lord. Letter to Lady Constance Wenlock, 16 June 1901, in *Lady Constance Wenlock – Papers.* ATL MS-Coll-20–2654.

INDEX

CPSIA information can be obtained at www.ICGtesting.com
Printed in the USA
LVOW10s0051070514

384606LV00004B/18/P

9 780415 8706